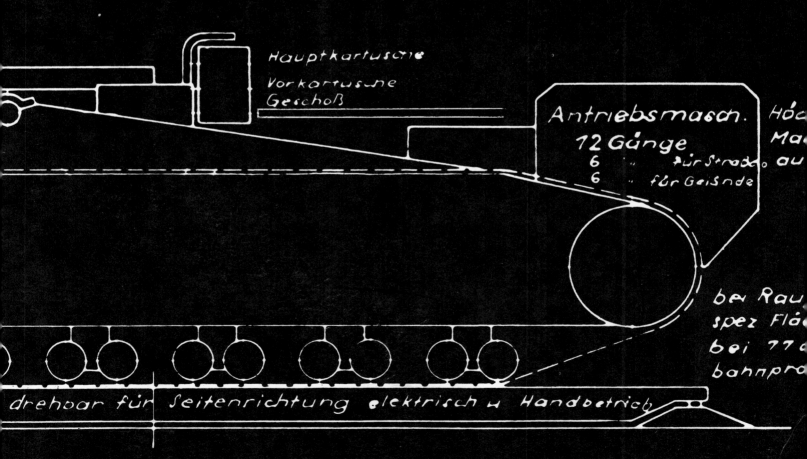

Zieleinrichtung Seipa - Epa
Munitionsförderung (Fahrstuhl 3 - etagig)

Hauptkartusche
Vorkartusche
Geschoß

Antriebsmasch.
12 Gänge
6 für Straße
6 für Gelände

drehbar für Seitenrichtung elektrisch u Handbetrieb

German & Allied
Secret Weapons
of World War II

Written by Ian V. Hogg and J. B. King
Illustrated by John Batchelor
Edited by Bernard Fitzsimons
Compiled by Ian Close

This edition © 1976
Phoebus Publishing Company
BPC Publishing Limited
169 Wardour Street, London W1A 2JX
This material first appeared in Purnell's History
of the World Wars Specials © 1974/75
Phoebus Publishing Company

Made and printed in Great Britain by
Waterlow (Dunstable) Limited

ISBN 0 7026 0012 1

Ian V. Hogg enlisted in the Royal Artillery during World
War II, and served in Europe and the Far East – including
Korea – before becoming an Assistant Instructor-in-
Gunnery at the Royal School of Artillery. He subsequently
qualified in electronics and spent some years testing
military electronic equipment. In 1966 he joined the staff
of the Royal Military College of Science, from which he
retired in 1972 with the rank of Master Gunner. He then
became a professional writer, and his publications
include The Guns: 1939–45, Barrage, German Secret
Weapons, and Artillery with John Batchelor.

J. B. King first wore uniform as a rifleman in a light
infantry regiment during World War II. He retired thirty
years later having attained staff rank and after experience in different branches of the Army. Like most soldiers
he set about retiring into the countryside but, also like
most soldiers, he found it too quiet and emerged to
become a freelance writer and consultant on weapons.

John Batchelor, after serving in the RAF, worked in the
technical publications departments of several British
aircraft firms, and went on to contribute on a freelance
basis to many technical magazines. Since then his work
for Purnell's Histories of the World Wars, and subsequently the Purnell's World Wars Specials, has estab-
lished him as one of the most outstanding artists in his
field. A total enthusiast, he takes every opportunity to fly,
sail, drive or shoot any military equipment he can find.

ABOUT THIS BOOK

During World War II, secret weapons were the cause of much agitation and anxiety to the warlords of both sides. For by their very nature, such weapons held out the promise of some decisive war-winning advantage that would, at a stroke, nullify any superiority in men and material held by the opposing side. In a war that was rapidly becoming more and more technological, a good weapon, well used and in reasonable numbers, could turn the tide of war.

With any new weapon, secrecy was of vital importance, because once its workings were known to the other side, it was not long before they built a better one, or devised new tactics to keep it in check. The development of radar provides a good example of this technological to-ing and fro-ing. During the Battle of the Atlantic the Allies developed an airborne radar set to detect German submarines on the surface at night. This gave the Allies an enormous advantage until the Germans built a device to detect the aircraft first from their radar emissions. The Allies then built a better radar set and went on to win the Battle of the Atlantic.

In this book the readable and authoritative text of Ian V. Hogg and J. B. King explores the complex and fascinating field of Allied and German secret weapons, while John Batchelor, in his own inimitable style, illustrates the ones that worked, as well as the ones that remained a frightening possibility.

CONTENTS

Whenever secret weapons of the Second World War are discussed, it is inevitable that the mind turns to German developments, a tacit recognition of the inventive capacity of German ordnance engineers. But there was also a surprising variety of secret weapons developed by the Allied nations, though much less has been written or said about them.

This can be attributed to a number of reasons. In the first place the Allied weapons were, in general, less spectacular than the more publicised German efforts. In the second place they were, for the most part, extensions of weapons which already existed, so that they did not make an impact by virtue of their unorthodoxy. And in the third place many of them remained secret for several years after the war, so that while there was a great deal of publicity in the immediate post-war years about German developments, the equivalent Allied weapons were never mentioned. Indeed it must be pointed out that many of the developments which the Allies initiated during the war are reflected in weapons current today, and for this reason some of the wartime secrets are still secret.

Another common misconception is that the Allies were unprepared for war, and that in consequence much of the wartime development consisted of brilliant inspirations thought up on the spur of the moment by civilian scientists and draftees because the regular weapon development system was too reactionary and cumbersome to cope with wartime demands. This facile assessment would, in fact, be more true of German development than it would of British or American, though admittedly a number of weapons were produced which appear to justify it.

One fairly famous British secret device was the proposal to flood the surface of the sea with gasolene or oil and then ignite it to form a flaming barrier in order to prevent landing craft or small boats from approaching the shore. This is usually pointed to as an example of the hurried improvisations of 1940 when the German Army was expected any day. But the truth of the matter is rather more prosaic. As early as April 1937 this system had actually been installed and tested on the Essex coast line, and in December 1937 the Director of Armament Development minuted that 'consideration is being given to the possible use of a film of burning petrol on the surface of the sea at defended beaches, in ports, and in congested anchorages.' Obviously the idea of setting the sea on fire was one which had been thoroughly investigated in peacetime, and when the events of 1940 made it pertinent, the old guard were ready with the answer, although they were the first to admit that it was far from being a perfect solution.

Different systems
The principal reason for the dearth of Allied secret weapons of the more spectacular kind lay in the weapons procurement systems. In Germany, any and every company or individual was at liberty to start developing a weapon idea; they would then approach one of the military services, obtain their interest, enlist political aid from some prominent Party Member, and get to work. They might never know that another company, or even several companies, were all working on the same idea, each surrounded by its own web of intrigue and secrecy and each struggling with the

THE SMOKE-SCREEN OF ALLIED SECRECY

more intractable problems as they arose. As a result, the end of the war revealed a multitude of parallel projects, often held up at some significant stage of development. Had all these parallel efforts been interconnected, the exchange of ideas might well have resulted in a workable weapon actually reaching the troops in time to have been of some use. Doubtless, it would also have resulted in some of the ideas being knocked on the head in their infancy in the interests of saving effort, money, time and precious war material.

On the Allied side, control was more rigid. If an inventor suggested an idea to one of the Services, he was immediately directed to a central reviewing authority – in Britain, the Ordnance Board, in the USA the Ordnance Committee. These bodies, composed of technical experts of all three services, were able to assess the inventor's idea, decide on its value and application, and then guide its development by placing the inventor in touch with the various technical development establishments which could help him. They could also turn an idea down flat, either because there was already, unknown to the inventor, a similar weapon under development; or they could reject the idea because it had been tried before and found not to work for some technical reason which the inventor hadn't yet reached – or because, as was often the case, the inventor simply didn't have the faintest idea what he was doing.

As an example of the latter case, we might consider the 'Croker Gun'. This was a device which burned an oil/air mixture to provide the explosion to fire a round steel ball which, in the words of the Ordnance Committee, was 'little better than an air gun'. The inventor appreciated that a spherical projectile was not the best ballistic shape, and in his specification he proposed to 'draw out the shot to a cylindrical shape during its passage through the bore' though he neglected to explain how this trick was to be done. The verdict of the Committee was forthright: 'This inventor seems to have a very hazy idea regarding the essentials of a gun; such a scheme can only be described as fantastic and not worthy of any further consideration. We have no objection to him taking out a patent on it should he so desire.' It may or may not be significant that the date of the Committee's report was 1 April 1938.

'Cockatrice' mobile flame-throwers set the sea alight. The flame barrage was one of the more spectacular of Britain's 'secret' anti-invasion devices

One thing uppermost in the minds of the Allied defence departments was the inadvisability of burdening the soldier – or sailor, or airman – with too many new weapons which didn't offer much improvement over what he already had. In August 1941 the British Director of Artillery, confronted with a proposal for a new weapon for the infantry, minuted to the Ordnance Board that 'It is becoming a matter of urgency to reduce the varieties of types of weapons and ammunition to those that are really essential to the main military tasks, if timely and adequate supplies of these essentials are to be achieved. Even were this weapon in a state of development suitable for production, I cannot see what important military task it would fulfil which is not already done by service weapons.'

But in spite of this organisation, there were ways in which a weapon idea could be presented so as to evade this control, though in many cases the result only strengthened the case for control. One such side door was via the various clandestine organisations which were set up in order to assist the Resistance groups in Occupied Europe. These organisations operated under an impenetrable shroud of secrecy and, in their early days, were highly reluctant to let any of the recognised weapon development agencies know that they even existed, let alone what they contemplated doing. In many cases they originated weapons for their own operations, obtained the necessary facilities for manufacture or even manufactured them in secret workshops within their organisation, and proceeded to issue them to their own forces.

Frequently, technical problems arose during their use, whereupon the recognised experts had to be approached to see if they could produce a solution; they were often horrified to see what was being used.

The primary thought of the Ordnance Board when confronted with a new weapon was 'Does it work?', and closely after that 'Is it safe to use?'. The Americans were slightly less concerned over safety. Indeed, it was once said that the British would invent a fuze which was safe and then spend the next ten years trying to make it work, while the Americans would invent a fuze which worked and then spend the next ten years trying to make it safe; this was said in jest, but often there was more than a grain of truth behind it.

A case in point was the 'Sticky Bomb', developed privately in 1940 as an anti-tank

grenade. It consisted of a glass ball filled with nitroglycerin, attached to a handle containing a five-second delay and safety pin. The ball was sheathed in coarse cloth covered in a powerful adhesive, and this surface was protected by being enclosed in two tin hemispheres clipped to the handle, which thus prevented the grenade sticking to everything it touched while being carried.

When ready to use it, the thrower pulled a pin which released the protecting covers, then pulled the safety pin and threw the grenade at a tank. As it left his hand the delay began burning, and after striking the tank and adhering to it, the nitroglycerin would detonate.

This device came before the Ordnance Board and was turned down as being grossly unsafe to handle; the flask was prone to break, the delay mechanism frequently misfired, and when all was said and done, nitroglycerin was no sort of liquid to carry around freely. It was then, by means not entirely clear to this day, accepted by MD1, an organisation which existed to provide weapons for the Secret Operations Executive. They took it primarily as a weapon to be used by French resistance fighters; as well as its anti-tank

capability, it was an excellent device for sabotaging such things as oil storage tanks and transformers. The Sticky Bomb, by this back door, then found its way into the British Army and Home Guard as an official grenade, and here its shortcomings were revealed, just as the Ordnance Board had foreseen. The complaints from the users reached such a volume that the Army took it to the Ordnance Board for their recommendations for improvement, and the Board were rather dismayed to find the device they had thrown out being returned to them. Their report reflected their opinion, one particularly telling phrase being 'The whole article is most objectionable', but they accepted the fact that it was into service and set about re-designing the grenade to make it safer and more reliable.

Reliable, efficient and useless
Later in the war MD1 produced another grenade, equipped with magnets in order to make it stick to the tank. It appears to have been based on a German design, but this time MD1 took it to the Ordnance Board first; trials soon showed that while it stuck firmly enough to the target, operated reliably and detonated efficiently, it still

had one small defect – it didn't do any lethal damage to the tank. The inventor took the hint and no more was heard of that weapon.

On the other hand, one has to be fair and say that in addition to their failures, MD1 produced some very useful weapons. One of the most useful, and the one with the farthest-reaching effects, was the spigot launcher. This was by no means a new idea, since the German Army had a *minenwerfer* operating on the principle in 1916. The idea is to dispense with the gun barrel, since this is an expensive and difficult item to manufacture, and use a steel rod instead. The projectile has a hollow tail which fits tightly around the rod – or 'spigot' – and inside this tail is a cartridge. The bomb is launched by firing the cartridge by some convenient method. The explosion then blows the bomb from the rod and into the air, the brief contact between tail and spigot being sufficient to give the bomb its correct direction.

This system of operation was more or less forgotten after 1918, but it was revived in the Thirties by a Lt Col Blacker, who set out to improve it and took out several patents. He offered various designs to the Army, all of which were refused for different

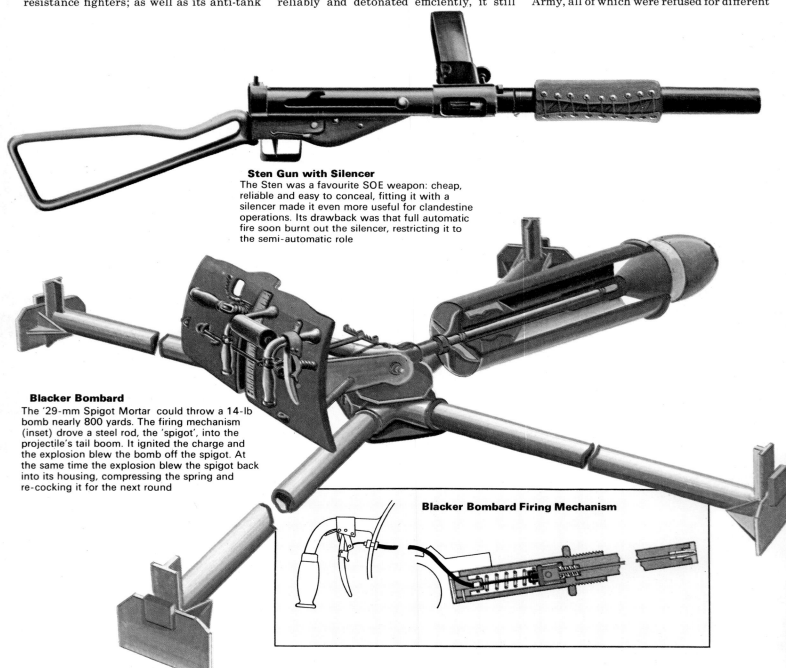

Sten Gun with Silencer
The Sten was a favourite SOE weapon: cheap, reliable and easy to conceal, fitting it with a silencer made it even more useful for clandestine operations. Its drawback was that full automatic fire soon burnt out the silencer, restricting it to the semi-automatic role

Blacker Bombard
The '29-mm Spigot Mortar could throw a 14-lb bomb nearly 800 yards. The firing mechanism (inset) drove a steel rod, the 'spigot', into the projectile's tail boom. It ignited the charge and the explosion blew the bomb off the spigot. At the same time the explosion blew the spigot back into its housing, compressing the spring and re-cocking it for the next round

Blacker Bombard Firing Mechanism

reasons – mainly because they could do nothing which could not already be done by the standard trench mortars. Then, in 1940, he hit on the idea of using a spigot device to fire an anti-tank grenade. At the same time he became involved in the activities of MD1, and through their agency he was able to put his idea forward and have it accepted. It became the 'Blacker Bombard' or, more officially, the 29-mm Spigot Mortar, and was widely issued to the Home Guard and to airfield defence units of the Royal Air Force Regiment.

Blacker then began developing a smaller version which he called the 'Baby Bombard', but before he could complete the work he left MD1 for a post which left him no opportunity to carry it through to its completion. The project was taken over by Major (later to be Major-General) M R Jefferis, and it eventually entered service as the 'Projector, Infantry, Anti-Tank' which, not unnaturally, got shortened to 'PIAT' by the soldiers. This soon became the standard infantry anti-tank weapon and remained so for several years.

A sticky bomb demonstration. Not the most sensible of weapons, it still managed to get into service

Sticky Bomb

'Look on it as a portable demolition charge which can be quickly and easily applied' said the 'S.T. Grenade's' manual. But a glass sphere filled with nitro-glycerine and covered in glue could be of more danger to its user than to any German tank

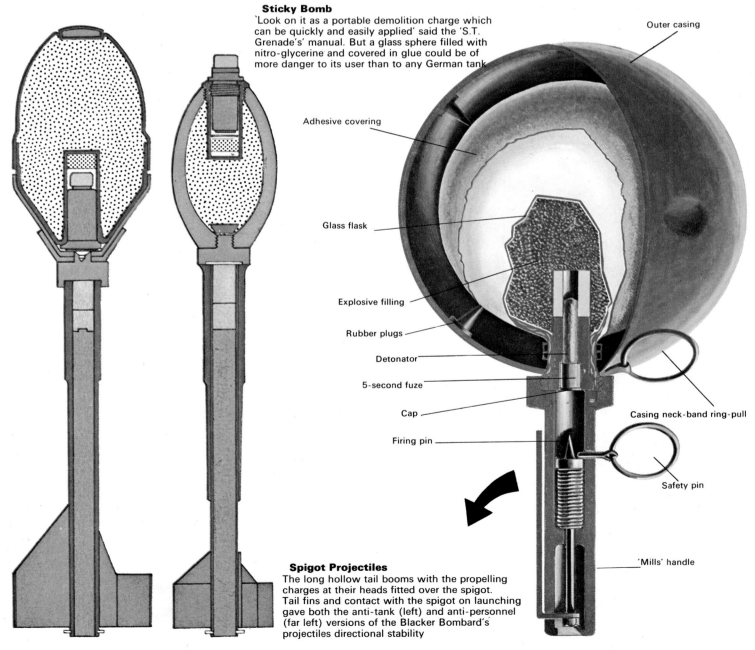

Outer casing

Adhesive covering

Glass flask

Explosive filling

Rubber plugs

Detonator

5-second fuze

Cap

Firing pin

Casing neck-band ring-pull

Safety pin

'Mills' handle

Spigot Projectiles

The long hollow tail booms with the propelling charges at their heads fitted over the spigot. Tail fins and contact with the spigot on launching gave both the anti-tank (left) and anti-personnel (far left) versions of the Blacker Bombard's projectiles directional stability

SECRECY AND THE BALANCE OF WAR

Every weapon, at the early part of its career, is secret to some degree; its existence may be known to the outside world, but its precise performance will be kept carefully concealed against the day when it is necessary to use it. On the other hand, many weapons involve some totally new concept, so that even a suggestion of their existence would be sufficient to alert an enemy to take preventive measures or even begin the development of a similar sort of weapon – which might turn out to be better.

The weapons produced in Germany before and during the Second World War fall into both these categories and their revelation in battle caused a brief period of superiority for the German forces before the Allied scientists managed either to develop something similar or to produce a countermeasure. Moreover, there were a vast number of weapons under development at the end of the war which, had the conflict continued, would have brought totally new concepts into play, giving the German forces an advantage which would have taken considerable effort to counter-balance.

During the Second World War every nation had secret weapons of one sort or another: the Americans developed the nuclear bomb; the British, microwave radar; the Russians, the 'Stalin Organ' multiple rocket. But the words 'Secret Weapons' almost invariably invoke the response 'German' because the Germans developed so many more than anyone else and covered such a vast array of technology in doing so. The phrase has root in a relatively unimportant speech made by Adolf Hitler shortly after the outbreak of war in which he promised the use of 'new and secret weapons' by which Germany would be victorious. Nobody took him particularly seriously, since it was the sort of propaganda phrase to be expected in the circumstances. But shortly afterwards the British Intelligence authorities received a mysterious letter by way of the British Consul in Oslo, Norway. It was anonymous, but contained details of a variety of peculiar weapons, long-range guns, rockets, aircraft and other things, which the writer claimed the Germans had under development at the outbreak of war.

The 'Oslo Letter'

The information was so far-fetched that for a long time it was dismissed as a hoax of some sort, designed to make Britain waste her time and energy in pursuing a number of useless ideas, but gradually one or two weapons appeared on the scene which seemed to bear out some of the contentions of the 'Oslo Letter'. Eventually, well into the war, it became obvious that whoever had written the letter (and its authorship,

Left: A V-1 flying bomb as seen from a Fleet Street rooftop, silhouetted against the London skyline just before impact

Popperfoto

if it is known, has never been publicly admitted) had a vast knowledge of what the German research stations were doing, and that bit by bit all the predictions were coming true. Indeed, the Head of RAF Intelligence later said that whenever things got slack in his department, they would get out the Oslo Letter and re-read it in order to have some idea of what might be coming along next.

But it was not until the war ended and interrogation teams went into Germany to examine the research stations and question the scientists that the full extent of Germany's weapon programme was realised, and the revelations were daunting.

The reason for the vast number of weapons under development, in addition to the ones which got into service, lies in the peculiar development structure within Germany. In brief, instead of having one major investigative body to which all armament questions were referred, and which acted as a filter for the wilder ideas and a forcing-house for the useful ones, every branch of the services appears to have had its own development team, and all these were working away without much thought about what anybody else might be doing on the same lines.

The passion for secrecy was so great that every agency kept its ideas to itself, and nobody ever had an over-all picture of what was going on. As a result there could be, and often were, three or four different establishments all trying to do the same thing, all making the same mistakes, and all competing for factory space, raw materials and scientists. For this the Allies could be thankful, for if some of the dead wood had been cut away, work on useless projects stopped and the energy directed onto the more feasible projects, many of them would have come into service in time to make things very difficult, if not to change the course of the war completely.

A complete listing of every single weapon development would be impossible in the space available. There were, for example, 86 different rocket projects in progress at the end of the war. Moreover, there could be no guarantee that the list is complete, for there are many cases where a suspicion of a project exists. A name is known, but nothing else, and no documents were ever found to verify the rumours. Doubtless many weapons were flirted with briefly during the war, then abandoned for other projects of which no record now exists. Therefore the descriptions which follow are those of the weapons which were most likely to succeed, or which used the most unusual principles, or which ought to be recorded as being the ancestors of weapons in wider use today. But even such a curtailed story will go some way to explaining why, even at this late date, there is so much of interest to be found in the study of the secret weapons of Germany.

11

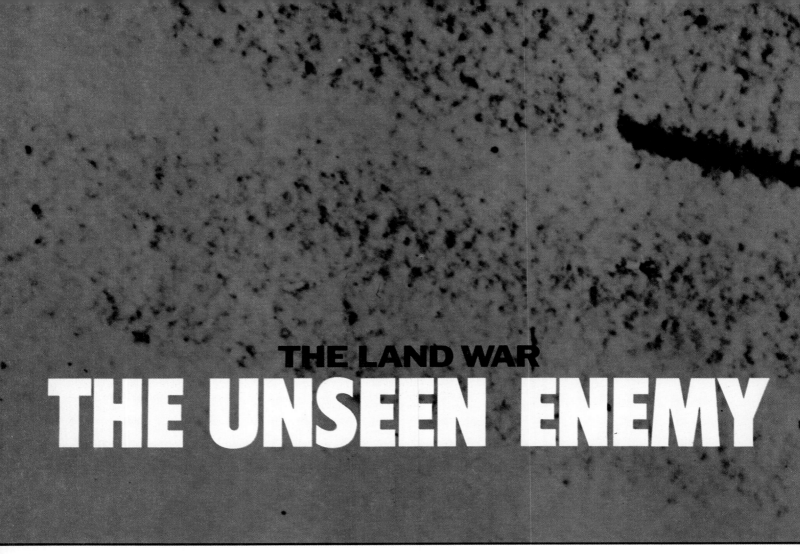

THE UNSEEN ENEMY

The incredible ingenuity of the Germans was no less impressive in the field of land-based weapons. The V-1 flying bomb and the V-2 rocket are the best known of these, but there were countless others, from giant howitzers to taper-bore guns — and a machine-gun that could fire around corners

Whichever way the German Army moved out of Germany, it was going to be confronted with concrete fortifications; the Maginot Line was a well-known example, and there were similar defences on almost every other frontier. In 1914 they had produced the 42-cm Krupp howitzer 'Big Bertha' to batter the Belgian forts at Liège, but in 1939 the pace of war was going to be much faster and it meant that weapons of greater mobility would be required. In this case it would need something more scientific to defeat concrete, rather than the simple brute force of the 42-cm shells of 1914.

The solution to any hard target is simply to bring to bear on it a harder projectile and concentrate as much energy into as small a space as possible. From this simple formula came the 'Röchling Shell' developed by the Röchling Steel company of the Ruhr. The question of the Maginot Line loomed large in the minds of the German Army in pre-war days, and they made enquiries in a number of directions in order to concentrate designers on this problem of defeating fortresses. The Röchling solution was the best one which came along, and was no more than a very long and thin shell with a hard point. Due to its length it was heavy, and due to being thin, it concentrated all its weight into a very small area at the tip and thus pierced layers of concrete as if they were cardboard. In order to stabilise such a long shell it was necessary to fit it with fins instead of spinning it in the normal artillery fashion, and these fins sprang out into the airstream after the shell left the gun.

The development of the Röchling shells was left behind by events; the German Army outflanked the Maginot Line and never needed these special projectiles. But when development was completed, in early 1942, a stockpile was built up of 21-cm shells ready for use should they be needed. Tests were fired against Fort Neufchatel near Liège which showed that the shell would penetrate through the concrete cover of the fort, pass through the underground chambers into the ground below for several more feet and there detonate. This performance was so impressive that Hitler expressly forbade them to be used without his permission, in case an enemy got hold of one and copied them for use against German defences. Since nobody particularly wanted to be the one to ask permission, the Röchling shells were more or less forgotten and the stockpile remained piled up until the end of the war.

A more conventional approach to fortifications was, of course, simply to build bigger guns firing heavier shells, but, as already said, they had to be more mobile than their First World War equivalents. Krupp's were approached in the early 1930s to give their opinions on guns which could demolish the Maginot Line, and, without formal approval, began working on designs for an 80-cm (31·5-in) gun which would fire a seven-ton shell. Due to the size of the weapon, it had to be a railway gun, and even then it had to be taken to pieces to move and then be re-assembled at the desired firing position. Krupp's promised this weapon for the spring of 1940 and on this understanding authority was given to proceed with the design. Unfortunately they had underestimated the difficulty of manufacturing such a monster and the campaign in France came and went without the assistance of the 80-cm gun. Eventually it was finished and test-fired in 1942 in front of Hitler, who approved of it, and it was then sent to Sevastopol to join the siege of the Russian fortress there. Krupp's had presented the gun to Hitler as their personal contribution to the war effort, and had called it *Schwere Gustav* in honour of one of the Krupp family, but the German artillerymen preferred to call it 'Dora'. It fired fifty or so massive shells into Sevastopol, causing immense damage, and then was taken off to besiege Leningrad, but the Russians had other ideas and pushed the German Army back from Leningrad before the gun could be made ready. After that it disappeared and was finally found wrecked, on its special travelling train, by a US Army unit in Bavaria at the end of the war.

Another weapon which appeared at Sevastopol was the self-propelled howitzer *Karl*,

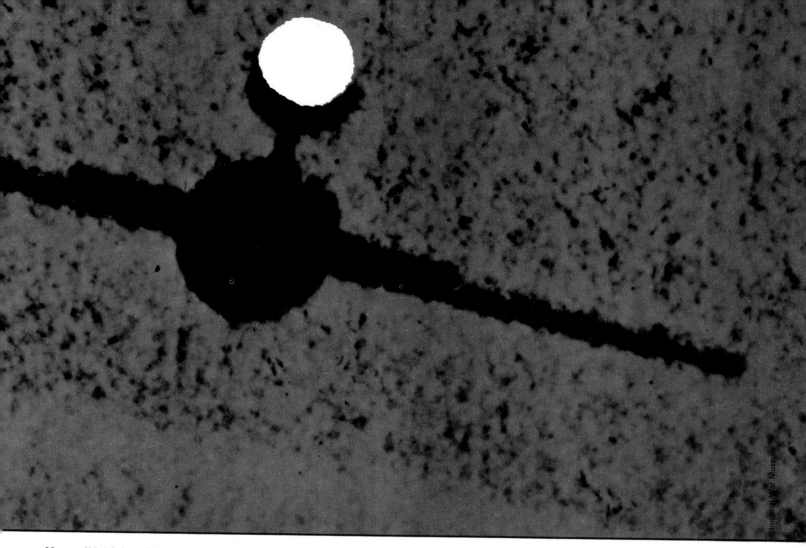

a 60-cm (23·6-in) calibre, short-barrelled weapon firing a one-and-a-half ton shell to about 7000 yard range. This had been demanded by the Army in 1935 in order to have a super-heavy concrete-smasher which could go where there were no railway tracks. Rheinmettal-Borsig were given the task of developing the weapon, and the first one was ready in 1939, followed by two more in 1940. Although cumbersome, they were highly effective, and the Army were of the opinion that a slight reduction in the shell would be acceptable if the weapon could be given a better range. In response to this, Rheinmettal developed a 54-cm (21·2-in) calibre barrel which could replace the 60-cm if necessary, and built three more equipments. These 54-cm models fired a 2770-lb shell to 11,500 yards.

To move the weapons, there were three different systems. For short moves, they could be driven under their own power, propelled by Mercedes-Benz V-12 diesel engines. For somewhat longer moves the gun barrel and breech and the gun mounting were lifted off the tracked chassis and carried by special trailers while the chassis was carried on a tank transporter. Finally, for very long distance trips, the whole weapon could be slung by special trusses between two railway wagons and hooked up to a train.

The *Karl* howitzers saw little use except at Brest-Litovsk when Germany invaded Russia, at Sevastopol and at Leningrad. Three were found after the war, two of which had been thoroughly wrecked. The third was in serviceable condition and was removed by the US Army to their Ordnance Museum in Aberdeen, Maryland.

While these weapons were effective, they could hardly be said to be cost-effective, as they absorbed a lot of men and time and could only be used in special situations. The ordinary guns of the Army were more easily operated and were far more flexible in their roles, but for one or two of them it was felt that something special might be useful in order to give them a long-range capability.

Rocket assisted shells

With all the experimentation on rocketry which was going on in Germany, it will come as no surprise to learn that the first idea put forward was to have a rocket-assisted shell. The first of these was issued for the 15-cm Heavy Field Howitzer 18 in 1941 and numbers were used in the Russian campaign. It was not entirely successful, but it gave a good deal of information which enabled better designs to be developed. The normal shell for the howitzer ranged to 14,500 yards. The rocket shell boosted this maximum range to 21,000 yards but the accuracy suffered in proportion. The shell itself carried its high explosive content in the nose and the rear half was filled with a solid-fuel rocket motor exhausting through a number of jets in the shell base. It was fired from the gun in the usual way, and the flash of the cartridge lit a delay unit. This burned through during flight and then lit the rocket motor just as the shell was reaching the highest part of its flight. The rocket gave an additional boost to improve the range, but if the shell happened to be slightly unsteady in flight at the moment the rocket fired, this unsteadiness would be magnified, forcing the shell off trajectory.

Above: A V-1 flying bomb, photographed through a cine camera synchronised with an RAF pilot's guns as he went in to attack it

Encouraged by the general success of this, the designers then turned to a heavier gun, the 28-cm railway gun Model 5. This was a long-range weapon, using special shells with ribs formed in the outside walls to engage with deep rifling grooves in the gun barrel; with the standard shell the gun could reach 38·6 miles. A rocket-assisted shell was designed in which the rocket motor was in the nose, firing through a blast pipe which passed through the high explosive compartment at the rear. The rocket motor was lit by a time-fuze fitted into the nose, and with full rocket assistance, this 550-lb shell went to 54 miles range. While this was satisfying to the designers, what was less satisfying was that the accuracy was such that the shell might land anywhere in a rectangle four miles by half a mile.

However, all was not lost. The Peenemünde Research Establishment, as well as providing information on rockets, had been equipped with the best wind-tunnels in existence, and they had been doing a lot of research into aerodynamic shapes and the effect of fin-stabilising missiles. They came to the conclusion that there was a future for a dart-like shell, stabilised by large fins, but that for best effect it had to be fired from a smooth-bored barrel. One of the spare barrels for a 28-cm railway gun was bored out to 31-cm calibre, and a 'Peenemünde Arrow Shell' was developed to suit. With this, plus a specially powerful propelling charge. the gun now ranged to a staggering 93·8 miles, with quite acceptable accuracy. By the time all the development work had been done, the war was in its closing stages, but one of the 31-cm barrels was mounted into a railway gun chassis and used to shell the US Army in the area of Bonn from a range estimated to be some 73 miles. It caused quite a commotion, since it was assumed to be some sort of aerial bomb or long-range missile when the shells began landing.

The Peenemünde Arrow Shell had advantages beyond simple long range. Due to the gun being smooth-bored and having a heavier cartridge, it gave the shell a much higher velocity, and this, of course, was desirable in anti-aircraft guns. For this reason much work went on into developing a 105-mm smooth-bored gun to fire the arrow shells against high-flying aircraft. A variety of designs were produced, giving velocities in the area of 3100 ft per second, but there was a good deal of trouble in developing a design which carried enough explosive to

make the effort worthwhile. Another difficulty lay in the fact that the shells demanded high-quality steel, which, by late 1944, was in short supply and could not be produced in the vast quantities needed for their manufacture.

The Germans had startled the world in 1918 by their use of the 'Paris Gun', a super long-range gun which shelled Paris at a range of some seventy miles. This so upset the French that they made sure in the Peace Treaty that such things were not likely to happen again by forbidding the Germans to build long-range artillery. In an attempt to get around this, research began into the use of rockets for long-range bombardment at the Artillery Research Station at Kummersdorf in the 1920s. A young enthusiast named Wernher von Braun obtained a post on the staff and soon became the guiding spirit in the development. All the rockets developed in this Army programme were known by the letter 'A', and the first, 'A-1' was designed at Kummersdorf

Röchling Shell

The '21-cm Röchling Granate 42 Be' was developed and issued for use with the standard 21-cm Howitzer Model 18. Weighing 425 lb, and with a length of 102 in, it had folding fins at the rear. Maximum range was 11,275 metres and it could penetrate upwards of four metres of reinforced concrete

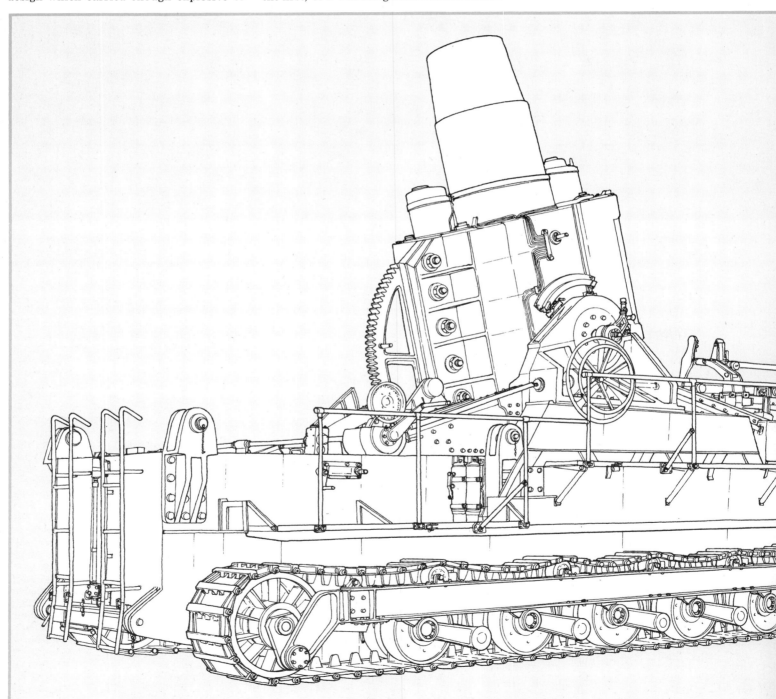

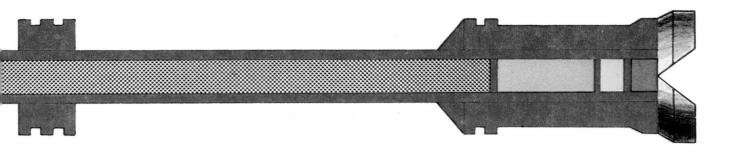

Rocket-assisted shell

Several designs of rocket-assisted shell were developed by the German scientists in order to improve the range of standard artillery guns. The solid-fuel rocket motor was ignited by a delay device after leaving the gun muzzle, and improved the range by about one-third, though at the expense of accuracy

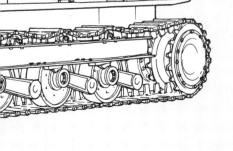

in the early 1930s, though it was neither built nor launched. In 1933 von Braun set to work on the 'A-2' design, and two of these were built and launched from a test site set up on the Baltic island of Borkum in 1934. These rockets were liquid-fuelled, and it was their successful flight which gave encouragement to the liquid-fuel idea, which until then had been regarded as a trifle optimistic. Another advantage which accrued from this successful flight was that the War Department began to take some interest in what was going on and allotted more funds to the rocket programme as well as allowing more staff.

But by now it was obvious that the Kummersdorf proving ground – which had been set up as an artillery testing station in the 1870s, when guns were a good deal less powerful than they were in the 1930s – was too small to hold the rocket research department, and they began hunting for somewhere they could build a full-sized research station, away from the eyes of the curious and with plenty of room to fire their inventions. A site was found on the island of Usedom on the Baltic coast, and at the very northern tip of this lonely area construction of the Peenemünde Research Station was begun. In 1937 the rocket research department moved in and within months they had the 'A-3' ready for test firing. This was the first design to use a control system, having a gyroscope connected to the control surfaces so as to keep the rocket in an upright attitude during flight. It didn't work as well as was hoped, and very few of the test flights of the A-3 were satisfactory, but it was a step on the road, and even failures taught something at that stage of the game.

However the A-3 was basically a test vehicle, not intended to be a serviceable missile; its function in life was to help to design A-4, which was to be the Army's long-range bombardment rocket. The designs for this went on paper even before the move to Peenemünde. A-4 was to carry a ton

60-cm SP 'Karl'

The *Karl Mörser* was produced in two versions, with 54-cm and 60-cm barrels. The 60-cm version here weighed 123 tons and fired a 3476-lb shell to 7325 yards, while the 54-cm fired a 2776-lb shell to 11,485 yards. They were rarely used

of high explosive, to range for at least 150 miles, be undetectable in flight, and travel at such a speed that there would be no possible means of countering it. To do all this demanded, firstly, a very powerful liquid-fuel motor which would run for some time without fault: then it required some form of control, and finally it demanded some very elegant engineering in fields which had never been explored before. Undaunted, the Peenemünde team set to work. In order to get the control situation sorted out, a fresh design called A-5 was built; this was only 16 ft long and was powered by a hydrogen peroxide motor. Several variations of this were built, some fired from the ground, some launched from aircraft using different control systems and techniques – each teaching some vital lesson which was incorporated into the gradually-evolving A-4 design.

In 1942, after all sorts of problems had been solved, the first complete A-4 was put together in the experimental workshops in Peenemünde, taken out to the testing ground and on 13 June 1942 it was fired. It rose a few feet from the launcher and then one of the fuel pumps broke down. The rocket dropped back, toppled over and exploded. The second model was prepared and on 16 August it was fired. This time it left the pad, soared into the sky, broke the sound barrier, and then, probably for the same reason as before, the motor cut out and the rocket fell into the Baltic. Finally, on 3 October the third test model was fired, with complete success, roaring across the sky to land almost 120 miles up the Pomeranian coast.

With a successful launching behind them, the design team were confident that they had the answer, and after a few more demonstrations to important functionaries, approval was given in 1943 for production to go ahead on high priority in order to bring the weapon into service and bombard England with it. Factories were taken over, sub-contractors appointed, and an enormous underground assembly factory was built in the heart of Germany. Accounts vary, but certainly well over 5000 A-4 rockets were built. Hitler, having seen one fired, immediately christened it his *Vergeltungswaffen* (vengeance weapon), and since the Air Force already had a bombardment rocket on the stocks which Hitler had called *Vergeltungswaffen 1*, this became 'V-2'; it has always been known as that in Britain,

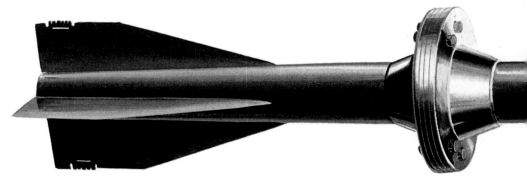

but in German Army circles it was never known as anything but 'A-4'.

On 8 September 1944 the first A-4 was fired against England, by which time there were something like 1800 rockets in stock. Altogether, 1115 were fired against England, and the results were exactly as the designers had forecast: the one-ton warhead devastated a wide area; it travelled so fast that there was no warning of its arrival; and there was no possible way of stopping it, even if you did know it was coming. All that the Allies could do was set up long-range radar to watch the entire German coast in the hope of detecting a rocket as it passed over, but even then, apart from alerting the air raid precautions there was nothing they could do about it.

What may surprise many people is to learn that more A-4 rockets were fired against the Belgian population in Antwerp than were fired against England. No less than 1341 were fired at Antwerp, since it was, at that time, one of the most useful ports for supplying the Allied invasion armies. In addition, 65 rockets were launched against Brussels, 98 against Liège, 15 against Paris, and 11 against the bridge at Remagen on the Rhine after it had fallen into American hands.

Having got the A-4 into production, the research team at Peenemünde turned to the development of better things. A-6 was the next idea, though this was little more than an A-4 which used a different type of fuel. Then came A-7, an A-5 with wings, which was intended as a trial model for a design called A-9. In between came A-8, a variation of A-6 which used a different design of motor and fuel.

A-9 was similar to A-4 but had one set of fins extending forward to form wings. It was built of the lightest possible material and used the sulphuric acid fuel system tested by A-6 in order to reach a range of 400 miles. The idea for this had been in the air for some time and in 1942 there was a considerable body of opinion that this was the design to go for instead of the A-4. But the A-4 was simpler to build and cheaper, and it also looked more likely to be put into service with minimum trouble, so while the A-4 went into production, the A-9 was put to one side, to be brought out later and reconsidered. A-10 was a super-powered A-4 which used a much more powerful rocket motor, but it was not accepted by the Army since they were quite happy with the

A-4 and didn't want to upset production just when it had started to run smoothly. The Peenemünde team then designed the A-9/A-10, which was the A-10 with an A-4 or A-9 mounted in its nose to give a two-stage effect. The A-10 would lift the lot off the ground and push it as far into the stratosphere as it could. Then the A-4 or A-9 (both were proposed at different times) would ignite, leaving the now-useless A-10 to fall to the ground, and roar off to reach a maximum range of 5600 kilometres, or 3478 miles. This, it was hoped, would bring the United States within bombardment range of Germany, but the project got no further than the drawing board before the war ended.

Competition from the 'Luftwaffe'

At the same time as the A-4 was being put into production, the *Luftwaffe* were developing a long-range bombardment rocket of their own, basing their activity on the assumption that anything which flew through the air was a *Luftwaffe* responsibility. For this reason, indeed, they fought hard against the adoption of the A-4, but they lost that particular battle when Hitler decided that there was room for both the A-4 and the *Luftwaffe* weapon, the FZG-76, which later became better known as the V-1. The FZG-76 was a wooden pilotless aircraft driven by a pulse-jet motor. The development was initially done at the Glider Research Centre at Darmstadt, but was transferred to Peenemünde in 1942 when it became necessary to test-fly the machines. The whole idea began in the 1920s with the development of the pulse-jet motor. This was taken up by the Argus aero-engine company in the 1930s and perfected by them, and by some channels which are not quite clear the Feiseler Aircraft company got interested and designed the

small aircraft body to go with the motor. This was known as the Feiseler Fi-103, and some time in late 1940 the Glider Research Station took the whole project over and began turning it into a pilotless missile. The motor was set on a pylon, above the airframe, while a warhead contained 1870 lb of high explosive and an impact fuze. Guidance was to be done by a pre-set mechanism carried within the missile, so that once set and fired there could be no possibility of any jamming device interfering with the planned flight.

Development moved to Peenemünde in June 1942 and carried on very smoothly, and the first experimental firings were carried out in December of that year. Mass production was put in hand in March 1944 and the first missile was fired operationally on 12 June 1944 with a stockpile of 12,000 missiles on hand. It has been estimated that almost 35,000 missiles were manufactured before production stopped in March 1945. Some 9251 were fired against England and 6550 against Antwerp, but they were less successful than A-4 because of their low speed. They averaged between 300 and 400 miles per hour and flew straight and level, a gift to the anti-aircraft gunners of Britain. Many were destroyed by RAF pilots who flew alongside them and, by edging their own wingtip beneath that of the missile, tipped it over, upset the gyro pilot and caused the missile to crash into the sea. Almost half of the missiles launched against England were destroyed before they reached the coast, the majority by gunfire.

While the Army were most impressed with A-4, they were less than impressed with the circus which had to accompany it: special trailers, special fuel trucks, special inspection platforms, firing trucks, testing trucks. While the rocket's launching pad was admittedly small and easily concealed,

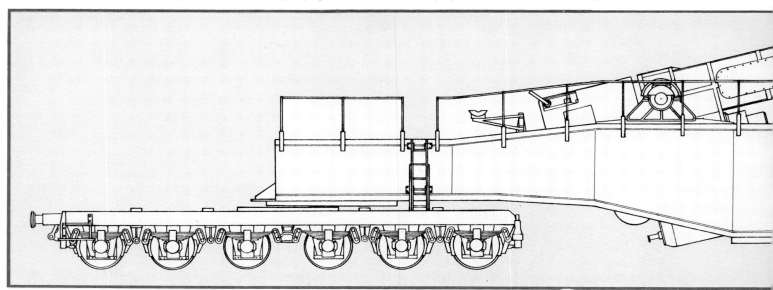

Peenemünde Arrow Shell
The 31-cm Peenemünde Arrow Shell for the smooth-bored version of the 28-cm K5 railway gun. Weighing 300 lb and 75 in long, it ranged to 93 miles

the same could not be said for all the apparatus which had to back it up. The V-1 was no better, since it needed special concrete launching ramps and a complicated procedure for setting the automatic pilot before launching. What was needed was something simple which could be driven into the firing position, fired, and that was that.

Rheinmettal-Borsig were given a contract in 1942 and produced a four-stage solid-fuel rocket called the 19-cm *Fernzielrakete 61/9*. This carried a 40-kilogram warhead to 220 kilometres, but it appears to have had one or two defects and it was replaced by an improved model known as *Rheinbote*. This used a three-stage solid-fuel rocket with extra boost motor for take-off and carried a warhead of 120 kilograms to 200 kilometres range. Unfortunately this made it somewhat bigger than the Army had bargained for. The *FZR 61/9* had been 11·4 metres long and was launched from a modified 88-mm anti-aircraft gun carriage. *Rheinbote* was 15 metres long, weighed over two tons, and needed a special erector-trailer to carry and launch it. Nevertheless, it was a far simpler proposition than the A-4 rocket and it could be fired off at a rate of two an hour. Late in 1944 it was approved for production, but only 220 were ever built, all of which were fired off against Allied installations in the Antwerp area early in 1945.

There is some evidence which suggests that Rheinmettal were busy with an improved version at the end of the war. An official German document printed in 1945, listing various rocket weapons, mentions a 56-cm *Fern-Rakete* as being developed by the company. This was 9·7 metres long, carried five rocket stages and was to have reached a range of 350 kilometres. So far as is known, this project never got out of the drawing office.

This list is also interesting because it mentions a 'V-3' rocket, which was said to be an improved version of the V-1, but with a multiple incendiary-bomb warhead instead of a high-explosive filling. This is the only time this weapon has ever been as much as suggested, and the term V-3 is generally applied to a much more outlandish weapon than any missile: V-3 was 'The High Pressure Pump' or 'Busy Lizzie' or 'The Millepede' – you could take your pick of names, but they all describe the same weapon, the multiple-chamber gun.

The multiple-chambered gun
Ever since it became fashionable to load a gun from the breech instead of the muzzle, inventors have been lusting after the multiple-chambered gun. The idea is very attractive: you have a gun with a very long barrel, with a normal shell and cartridge. Along the gun barrel however, extra chambers are arranged, each with an additional cartridge inside. When the gun is fired, the first cartridge pushes the shell up the bore in the normal way and, just as the expansion of gas from the cartridge reaches its limits, the shell passes the entrance to the next chamber, whereupon the cartridge inside is fired. This adds more gas to the propulsive force and gives the shell another boost. As

this is dying away, the shell passes the next chamber and the next cartridge is fired, and so on until you have the shell moving at the speed you want, whereupon it comes to the gun muzzle and departs. It all sounds very simple and attractive on paper, which is no doubt why so many people have tried to make it work – and failed.

The principal drawbacks can be very simply explained. In the first place, some flame from the first cartridge usually passes over the shell before it is firmly seated in the rifling, and this is enough to ignite the other cartridges, so that instead of pushing the shell up the bore their force is actually acting against the shell. In the second place, the ignition of a cartridge takes some definite time to achieve – let us say one-hundredth of a second from pulling the trigger to having the charge completely exploded. In that short time the shell will have travelled twenty or thirty feet, so that the amount of space to be filled by the gas will never be constant, and unless the gun is impossibly long the shell will have passed three or four chambers before the first one has fired. In the third place, if it is all working successfully, after two or three chambers have fired, the shell will be moving so fast that it will be going faster than the gas can be evolved behind it, so there is no further advantage to be gained.

In spite of these arguments, the idea still comes along every now and then, and it appeared in Germany in 1942, proposed by an engineer called Cönders who worked for the Röchling company. It seems likely that he had the idea of developing a gun which would give the Röchling anti-concrete

28-cm Rail Gun
The 28-cm *Kanone 5 (Eisenbahnlafette)* railway gun, familiarly known as 'Schlanke Emma' and to the Allied troops in Italy as 'Anzio Annie'. As well as normal shells, it was provided with rocket-assisted shells and later with a fin-stabilised Peenemünde Arrow Shell

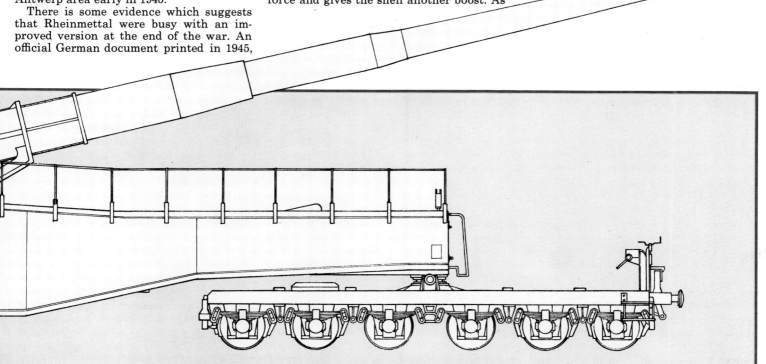

Maus

The German super-tank *Maus* was designed by Dr Porsche from 1942 onwards. This monster weighed 183 tons and carried a 12·8-cm gun and a 7·5-cm auxiliary gun. A 1375-horsepower engine drove through an electric transmission to give a top speed of 12 mph. The layout of the vehicle was unusual in having the engine compartment in the middle and the fighting compartment at the rear. Armour of up to 9-in thickness was fitted. The whole concept was out of date before it ever began, since every other nation had abandoned the idea of super-tanks due to their immense bulk, slow production, and vulnerability in the battle-field. Although construction of one or two specimens was under way when the war ended, no *Maus* tanks were ever completed, and even had they reached the field they would probably have disappointed their backers

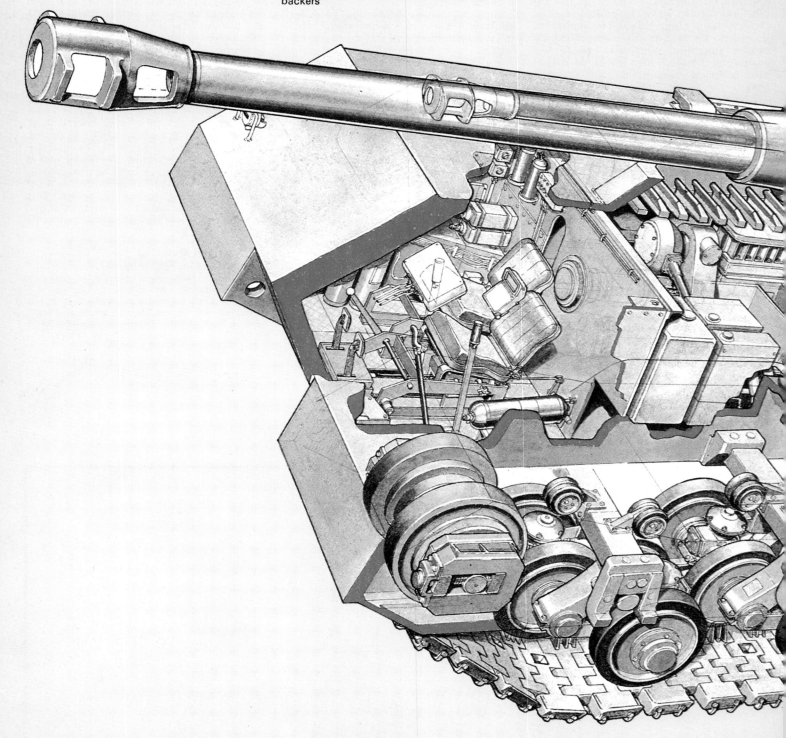

A weapon which surprised the Allies was this 38-cm Rocket Launcher. The blast from the rocket was turned around and vented through the ring of holes surrounding the muzzle

shell a really powerful thrust to be able to obtain long ranges and extra penetration. The gun as envisaged by Cönders was to have a 50-metre barrel with up to 28 side chambers, and would propel a fin-stabilised shell at 5000 ft per second to a range of 180 miles or more. He built a small model using 20-mm projectiles, and this worked reasonably well. The idea was shown to Albert Speer, and he in turn put the idea in front of Hitler who immediately approved it and furthermore insisted that it be carried through by Cönders without the Army Weapons Department having anything to do with it. This last proviso was probably because Cönders was afraid that if the conventionally-minded Weapons Office were shown the idea they would throw it out. He was right, they would have done, because they knew all about multiple-chamber guns and their problems. So, isolated from the mainstream of weapons development, Cönders went ahead. He produced a half-scale model and had it erected at Misdroy, a small island on the Baltic, for test firings. He designed a shell and had it put into production, and, under the direct orders of Hitler, the Todt organisation was set to work carving out the inside of a hill near Calais to take a fifty-barrel battery of these guns, aimed at London.

In October 1943 a full-sized 15-cm gun was built at the Artillery Proving Ground at Hillersleben, between Braunschweig and Magdeburg. Experiments soon showed that the shell was unstable in flight, but nevertheless it was hoped that this might be cured by attention to the flexible fins, and production of shell bodies carried on. The test weapon at Misdroy also ran into trouble, bursting its barrel at distressingly short intervals.

Early in 1943 the Chief of the Army Weapons Office, General Leeb, was making an inspection tour of various coast defences in the Calais area when he came across the enormous workings in which the fifty-barrel gun was to be installed. He was amazed – and far from pleased – when he found out what was going on. Leeb made enquiries and in March he attended a firing trial of the weapon. This was an absolute disaster, as the barrel burst, the shells were unstable, and everything which could go wrong went wrong. At General Leeb's suggestion some ballisticians were called in who found a fundamental error in the design of the shell, but by that time over twenty thousand bodies had been manufactured. The General further pointed out that if it were up to him he would cancel the whole project there and then, but since it was one of Hitler's favourite projects, nobody wanted to be the one to tell him it was useless, so it was a case of rallying round and making the thing work somehow.

The Reich Research Council were asked to help, and an expert in high-velocity ballistics was given the job of designing a stable shell, which he achieved fairly quickly with the aid of a supersonic wind tunnel. With some specimens of improved shells, a gun was set up again at Misdroy and fired; after 25 shots the barrel burst, and the rounds which had got away only managed to reach a range of 27 miles. This was very nearly the end. A conference of engineers was called in Berlin where the whole problem was debated at length, but it all came back to the argument 'Who's going to tell the Führer?' Again it was decided to play safe and try to make the

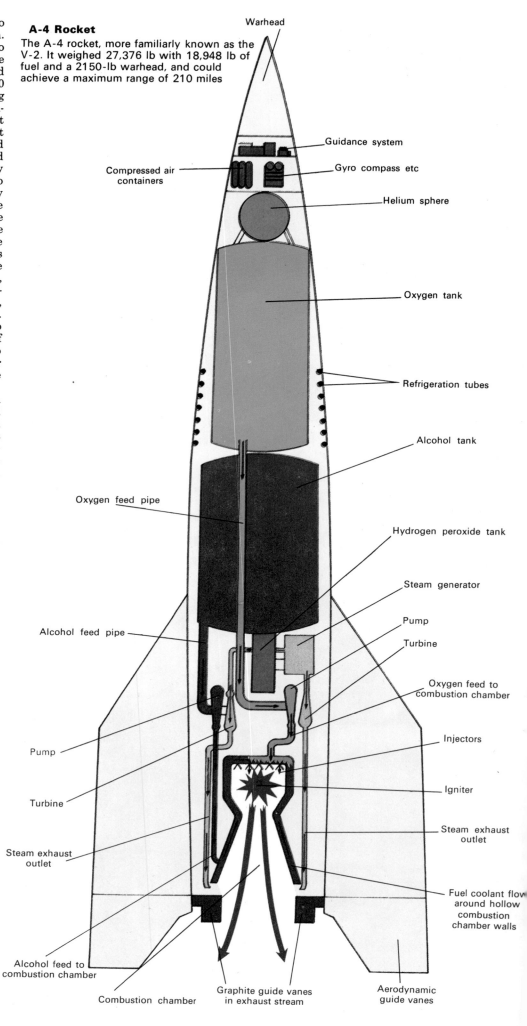

A-4 Rocket
The A-4 rocket, more familiarly known as the V-2. It weighed 27,376 lb with 18,948 lb of fuel and a 2150-lb warhead, and could achieve a maximum range of 210 miles

Warhead

Guidance system

Compressed air containers

Gyro compass etc

Helium sphere

Oxygen tank

Refrigeration tubes

Alcohol tank

Oxygen feed pipe

Hydrogen peroxide tank

Steam generator

Pump

Turbine

Alcohol feed pipe

Oxygen feed to combustion chamber

Pump

Injectors

Turbine

Igniter

Steam exhaust outlet

Steam exhaust outlet

Fuel coolant flow around hollow combustion chamber walls

Alcohol feed to combustion chamber

Combustion chamber

Graphite guide vanes in exhaust stream

Aerodynamic guide vanes

weapon work. And indeed now that some competent ballisticians and ordnance engineers were turned on to the project, things began to improve. Stable shells were produced, ranges of up to 55 miles were reached, and things began to look as if the gun might yet do all that its designer hoped.

But one thing the designer hadn't reckoned with was the Royal Air Force. In the course of scouring France for V-1 launching sites, they found the activity near Calais, assumed it to be connected with the V-1 in some way, and proceeded to bomb it. This set building back by at least six months, and the damage was so severe that half of the fifty-gun battery was closed down and work was concentrated on repairing the other, less damaged half. Then before the trials were completed, the Allies invaded Northern France, and in August 1944 the site of the monster gun was overrun by Allied troops. Trials still went on at Misdroy, however, though most of the personnel working on the weapon were by now convinced that they were wasting their time. Finally two shortened versions were put together and sent to the front in order to be tried in action. One was laid out in a railway truck and then fired against the US 3rd Army at a range of about 40 miles during the Ardennes offensive in December 1944, while the other was laid in concrete on a hillside at Hermeskeil to fire in the direction of Luxembourg. Neither appear to have had much effect and both were blown up when the offensive failed and the German troops retired.

The installation at Mimoyeques was blown up by the Allied troops in 1945; the gun at Hillersleben was discovered there, rusting away, by Allied technical investigators, while the one at Misdroy is believed to be there still, in pieces. Although the weapon was plagued with burst barrel problems throughout its development – which was probably due to flash-over from one chamber to another – there seems little doubt that if the Army Weapons Office had been brought into the project at an early stage (assuming they could have been persuaded to give the idea a chance) then it is quite possible that it could have been made into a serviceable weapon. Fifty 550-lb high explosive shells arriving in London every ten or fifteen minutes would have been a severe trial. On the other hand, one cannot help thinking that there must have been something more useful to the German war effort which all those scientists and engineers could have been doing instead of wasting time on 'Busy Lizzie'.

Not every far-fetched idea was accepted though. One which got turned down at an early stage was another electric gun, proposed by an engineer named Otto Muck. In May 1943 he produced a paper proposing 'an electric gun which can fire without flash or detonation 12 streamlined shells a minute at a range of over 250 kilometres with a velocity of 1640 metres per second. The shells are of 15-cm calibre and 200 kilograms in weight. They are especially adapted for continuous bombardment of immobile targets of great area. For this purpose the 100-metre barrel is set up out

Right: An A-4 (V-2) rocket shown ready for firing (centre) and just after blast-off (background) during Allied experiments with the weapon after the war. In the top corner is Wernher von Braun, the German rocket designer who became head of NASA, photographed in 1972

Popperfoto

Imperial War Museum

J. B. King

of sight in a steep shaft inclined at an angle below 55°. The power supply (100,000 kilowatts) and the installations for supplying coal and projectiles are arranged underground beneath a strong bomb-proof covering. Main Purpose: the destruction of greater London from St. Omer (in Artois at the edge of the Lille coalfields). The firing of 500,000 shells monthly (total weight 100,000 tons) requires 54,000 tons of coal for power. One single electric gun replaces the employment of 2000 bombers daily; the new highly effective means of fighting can therefore have a decisive military effect on all fronts'.

Muck was certainly enthusiastic about his weapon, and he backed up this opening argument with pages of impressive figures. Basically, what he proposed was no more than the old idea of the solenoid gun, improved slightly by the use of modern materials. He claimed to have been working on the idea since 1937 with the support of the Siemens company, and had performed a number of experiments with small-scale models which appeared to support his ideas. He sent his paper to a colleague in Berlin who passed it to *Reichminister* Speer, requesting that it be put before Hitler, but Speer passed it instead to the Army Weapons Office with the request that they give it a close examination. The Commission for Long Range Gunnery examined the proposal carefully. What they knew, and what Muck did not know, was the capability of such weapons as the V-1 and V-2, which were by then entering production. The result was that several rather sweeping statements made by Muck about the superiority of his system over anything else had to be discounted. Their final report took more than that into account; in part it read 'Muck starts from several mistaken ideas, and apart from this the development would involve problems which far exceed any of the technical demands made today. The expenditure which must be put aside for this development is absolutely colossal. But the proposal is of unusual interest and in more peaceful times would have to be thoroughly developed'. One is inclined to feel rather sorry for Herr Muck; after all, some wilder ideas than his got to the hardware stage.

Anti-tank guns

If the German development of Super-Cannon was a fairy-tale realm, how to stop a tank was a more practical problem. At the outbreak of war the usual anti-tank gun was a small piece of artillery firing a hard steel shell at high velocity so as to punch through the tank armour. But tanks were getting thicker, and as a result it became necessary to make the anti-tank guns bigger and bigger so that they could fire heavier charges to get more velocity. In the hopes of keeping the size down to something which could still be pushed about the battlefield by two or three men, the Germans began work on what was later described as the first German Secret Weapon ever to be revealed during the war – the taper-bore gun. This was yet another proposition which had first been suggested years before but which had never been made to work due largely to the engineering difficulties, and the fact that even if it could be made to work there didn't seem to be much use for it. The basic idea is to make the gun barrel of reducing calibre from breech to muzzle, and make the shell in such a fashion that it

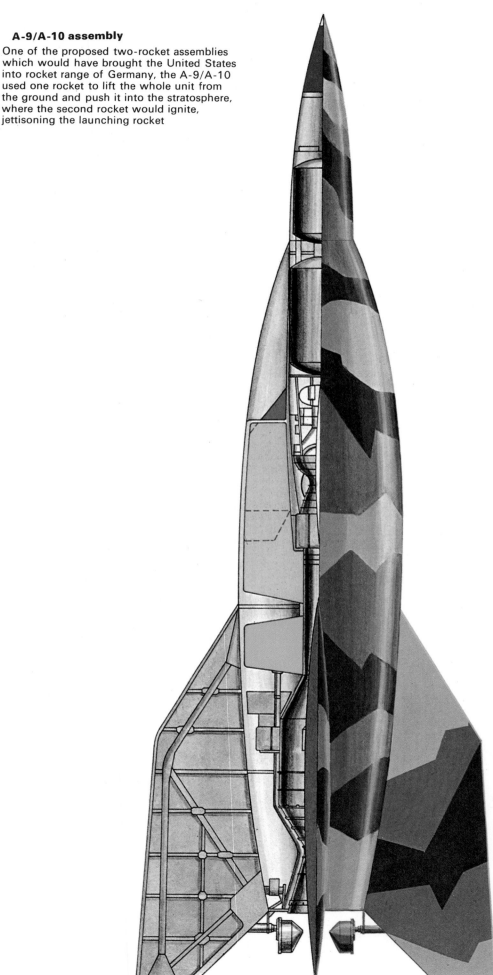

A-9/A-10 assembly
One of the proposed two-rocket assemblies which would have brought the United States into rocket range of Germany, the A-9/A-10 used one rocket to lift the whole unit from the ground and push it into the stratosphere, where the second rocket would ignite, jettisoning the launching rocket

gradually shrinks in size as it passes along the barrel. It follows from this that the area of the bottom of the shell, which is being pushed by the propelling gas from the cartridge, is gradually reducing. This means that the pressure per square inch of area must be increasing, and from this it follows that the velocity of the shell will also increase, giving the shell a much higher muzzle velocity than could be reached in a conventional barrel of the same calibre.

Much of the development work on this weapon was done in the 1920s and 1930s by a German engineer named Gerlich. In conjunction with a gunmaker called Halbe, he produced a number of 'Halger' sporting rifles which used tapered barrels producing very high velocity, and he attempted to interest various of the world's armies in these weapons as possible sniping rifles. He

was retained at various times by the US Army and the British War Department as a technical adviser, but the weapons were far too delicate and expensive for military use, although there is plenty of evidence to show that they were formidable and accurate big-game rifles. In the 1930s he returned to Germany. His subsequent activity there is not recorded, but shortly afterwards work began in applying his ideas to heavier weapons with a view to producing a light anti-tank gun.

The biggest problem lay not in making the gun barrel but in making the shot or shell so that it reduced in size evenly, without jamming or deforming as it did so. Moreover, at the high velocity which this weapon would reach, steel projectiles were of little use, since they would simply break up when they hit the target due to the immense

impact blow, instead of penetrating the armour. The design finally developed used a small central core of tungsten carbide (exceptionally hard material which would resist the impact and remain in a condition to penetrate), surrounded by a soft iron sheath formed into supporting skirts. The skirts were of the correct diameter to fit the bore at the breech, and as the shot passed down the barrel they were pressed backwards evenly, adapting themselves constantly to the reducing bore. These projectiles left the muzzle at over 4000 ft per second, far faster than any projectile had ever done previously, and its effect on an armoured target was astonishing.

The first weapon to go into action using this system was the 'Heavy Anti-tank Rifle 41', the barrel of which was 28-mm calibre at the breech and 21-mm calibre at the

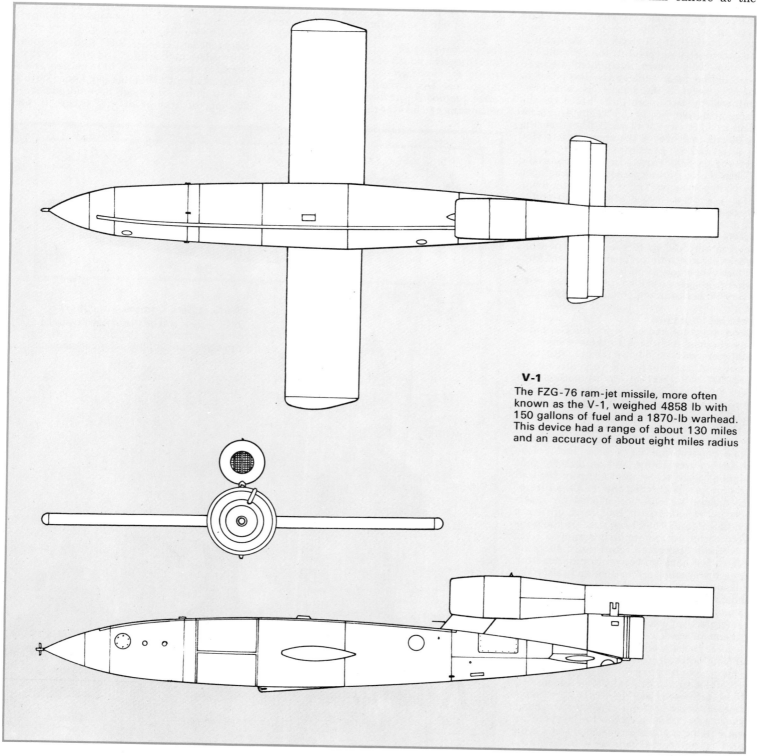

V-1
The FZG-76 ram-jet missile, more often known as the V-1, weighed 4858 lb with 150 gallons of fuel and a 1870-lb warhead. This device had a range of about 130 miles and an accuracy of about eight miles radius

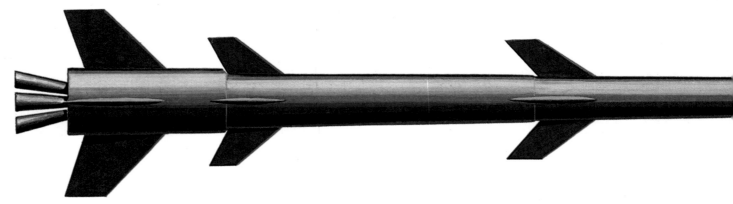

muzzle. Although the shot weighed only three ounces it could go through two inches of armour at 500 metres range, and if aimed at a vulnerable part of the tank it did quite a lot of damage by ricocheting around inside after penetrating. The gun was first seen in action in the North African campaign against the British 8th Army, and caused quite a surprise to the British. The principle was known, but nobody dreamed that it had been sufficiently developed to such a serviceable degree. It was later followed by two more guns based on the same principle, firstly the 'Light Anti-tank Gun 41' which was of 42-mm calibre tapering to 30-mm and fired a 12-ounce shot at 4150 ft a second to penetrate three inches of armour at 500 yards. In 1942 came the 7·5-cm *Panzerabwehrkanone 41* developed by Krupp, a heavy and powerful gun firing a 5¾-lb shot at 3900 ft a second to punch through six inches of armour at 1000 yards. This began as a 75-mm gun and tapered down to 55-mm by means of a tapered section screwed in to the muzzle of what was otherwise a normal parallel-bored gun. It was sent straight off to the Russian front where it proceeded to play havoc with every Soviet tank which came in sight.

Critical shortage

There was, unfortunately for the Germans, an economic drawback to these weapons – tungsten was largely imported into Germany and the supply was very limited. By mid-1942 the situation was so critical that the choice had to be made between using the available supplies of tungsten for making machine tools – vitally necessary in the aircraft industry and for building tanks – or using it for ammunition. According to some reports the facts were laid before Hitler for his ruling, and he ordered that supplies were to be used entirely for tool production. With this, the manufacture of the special ammunition needed for taperbore guns came to a halt, and once the available stocks had been used up the guns were withdrawn and mostly scrapped.

Without tungsten, anti-tank shooting had to fall back on conventional anti-tank guns firing steel projectiles and, after the introduction of the American 'Bazooka' shoulder-fired rocket, German copies and developments were based on the same principle. But, as might be expected, the amount of work which was being done on various rockets and missiles in the air-to-air and anti-aircraft field eventually led some people to think about using the same principles to attack tanks. One of the first to be proposed was *Pfeifenkopf*, a small winged rocket with an explosive warhead. It was to be radio-controlled by the operator, and carried a super-iconoscope – a simple form of television camera – in the nose

which transmitted a dim picture of the target back to a screen on the operator's control board. Due to the limitations of the iconoscope system, it demanded the maximum visual contrast between the target and its background in order that the operator could see what was going on, and this sort of condition is not easily achieved in battle. Tests were carried out at a small range near Stargard, south of Stettin, in late 1944, but the guidance system failed to live up to its promise. As a result, another version called *Steinbock* was designed, using infrared homing and leaving the operator nothing

to do but fire the missile. Like *Pfeifenkopf*, this weighed 55 lb and had a range of about 1000 metres, but it is doubtful that it ever managed to get built.

Ruhrstahl AG, who had developed the X-4 air-to-air missile, were also drawn to the anti-tank field, and they produced a smaller version of X-4, called 'X-7' or *Rötkappchen* (Little Red Riding Hood). Only thirty inches long, and weighing 22 lb, it had a range of over 1000 metres and a speed of about 250 miles per hour. With a hollow-charge warhead, it could penetrate 200 mm of armour at any range. It was

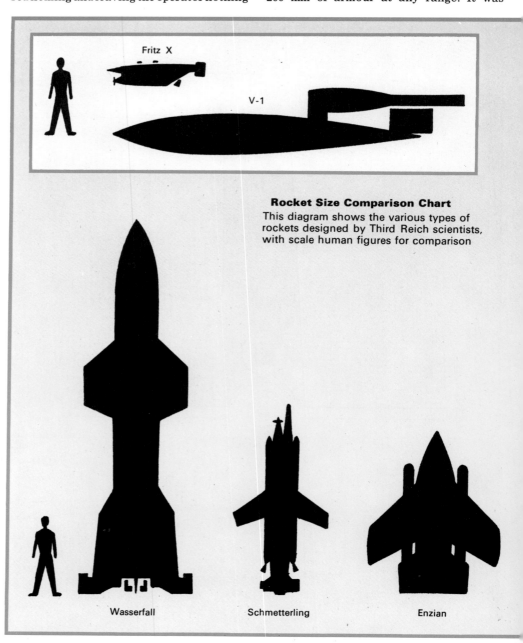

Fritz X

V-1

Rocket Size Comparison Chart

This diagram shows the various types of rockets designed by Third Reich scientists, with scale human figures for comparison

Wasserfall

Schmetterling

Enzian

Rheinbote

The Rheinmettal Rh 2·61/9 surface-to-surface missile was intended to carry 40 Kg of high explosive to a range of 160 kilometres. A four-stage rocket, it later became known as *Rheinbote* and could eventually reach to 220 Km

gyro-stabilised and wire-guided like the X-4, and was driven by a two-stage solid propellant motor. There is no record of the testing of this weapon, but several specimens were found after the war, none of them whole, and without doubt the X-7 must be given credit for being the ancestor of all the many wire-guided anti-tank missiles which have appeared in more recent years.

In early 1944 the increasing number of tanks appearing on the battlefield and their increasing thickness led the German army to re-assess their infantry anti-tank weapons. They had copied the American

Bazooka, and had also developed the hand-held *Panzerfaust*, but neither of these had very much range capability. On the other hand the only conventional gun which could do much damage to the current tanks was of 75-mm or 88-mm calibre, far too big to be handled by two men and concealed under a bush. In view of this a specification was issued calling for a light anti-tank weapon which would use less propellant than a recoilless gun, have a range of at least 800 metres, penetrate at least five inches of armour, and put all its shots into a one-metre square target at 500 metres

range. In response to this difficult demand, they got three remarkable weapons.

The most simple of the three was *Puppchen* (Dolly), which consisted of a lightweight 88-mm launching tube fitted to the carriage of the obsolete 28-mm taper-bore anti-tank gun. A simple breech block was fitted at the end of the tube, and into the barrel went an 88-mm rocket taken from the German 'Bazooka'. Thus, instead of shooting its blast out of the back of an open tube, the rocket force was now contained in a gun barrel, which boosted its speed and range. Instead of the 165 yards of the 'Bazooka', it now had a range of 750 yards, together with better accuracy.

The second weapon was known variously as 'Hammer' or *Panzertodt*, and this involved a new ballistic principle which was still being perfected when the war ended. It was a remarkable application of the rocket principle. The missile was an 88-mm warhead (the same one as used with *Puppchen*) attached to a long stem which swelled out to a pear shape and carried a set of 105-mm calibre fins. The barrel into which this was loaded was 105-mm calibre, which meant that a special steadying sleeve had to be fitted around the warhead. The propellant was simply wrapped around the stem

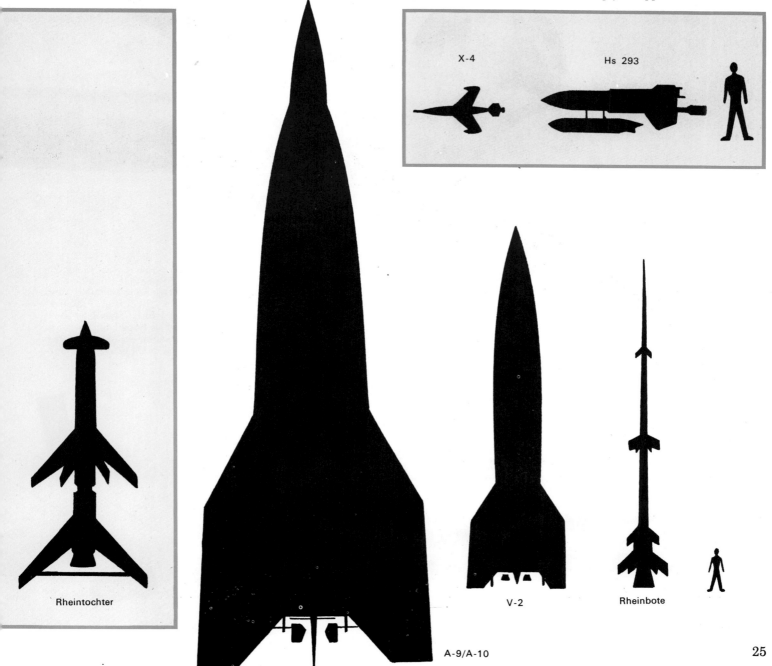

Rheintochter

X-4

Hs 293

V-2

Rheinbote

and the barrel was a simple open-ended tube. When the propellant was fired the gases escaped to the rear around the pear-shaped block. The space between the block and the launching tube acted as the venturi to give the necessary thrust to the missile. In other words, the launching tube formed part of the rocket, a system of manufacture which greatly simplified production. The accuracy was within the specification demanded, although the maximum range was only about 600 yards, and the weight of the entire equipment was about 90 lb. It was mounted on a machine-gun tripod and fitted with two small wheels to allow it to be pushed about. Although the design had been settled and approval given for manufacture, no production had begun before the war ended.

The only weapon to answer the specification and get into anything like volume production was the 80-mm *Panzerabwehrwerfer,* a smooth-bored breech-loading gun which again used an entirely new ballistic principle. In order to keep the weight of the weapon as low as possible, the barrel was made of very thin section steel. This of course meant that the pressure inside it had to be kept low. In order to manage this, the projectile was fin-stabilised and the barrel smooth-bored. The gun chamber, however, was made of the usual thick section, with a sliding wedge breech, so that it could withstand a much higher pressure than the barrel. The complete round of ammunition consisted of a field howitzer cartridge case carrying the propellant, closed at the front by a heavy steel plate pierced with a number of holes. The projectile was attached to this plate by a shear pin. When the cartridge was fired, a high pressure built up inside the cartridge case and chamber, but the gas could only leak out to the barrel through the holes in the steel plate, which was firmly anchored against the end of the gun barrel. Thus while the pressure in the breech was high, the pressure in the barrel was kept low. As the gases built up behind the projectile, strain was placed on the shear pin until the pressure was high enough to ensure the desired velocity, at which point the shear pin broke and the bomb was launched. Although the pressure in the barrel was no more than 3½ tons (a conventional gun would work at something in the region of 20 tons) the projectile had a velocity of 1700 feet per second and a maximum range of 750 metres. A considerable number of these guns were built and issued in late 1944 and early 1945, and they caused a great deal of interest among Allied scientists when they were found, but the principle has seen little use since.

The infantry of the German Army had other things to worry about besides tanks. One of the things which concerned them was the high proportion of head wounds due to snipers, and they asked the Weapons Office if somebody would produce a rifle which could be operated from inside a trench without the firer having to show himself over the top to take aim. At the same time,

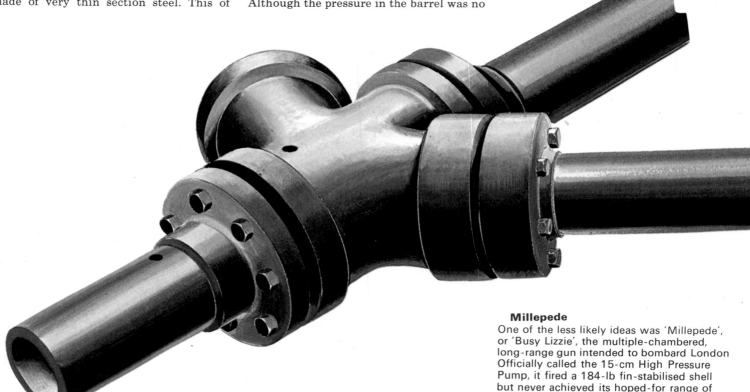

Millepede
One of the less likely ideas was 'Millepede', or 'Busy Lizzie', the multiple-chambered, long-range gun intended to bombard London Officially called the 15-cm High Pressure Pump, it fired a 184-lb fin-stabilised shell but never achieved its hoped-for range of 150 miles. The arrangement of chambers is shown right, with a detail of one of them above

Hammer
Gerät 'Hammer', an odd type of recoilless-gun-cum-rocket intended as an anti-tank weapon for infantry use. The shaping of the rear end of the projectile converted the gun barrel into part of a rocket venturi, an ingenious and effective design

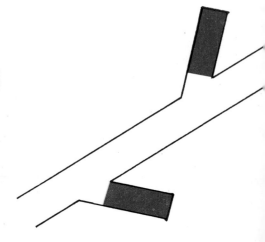

in 1941, tank crews were asking for some sort of weapon which would enable them to shoot from the tank at very close ranges, as the normal tank machine-guns could not deal with anyone closer than about twenty feet from the tank; once inside the 'dead zone' enemy infantry could attack with mines and grenades comparatively safely.

As it happened, one of the military testing stations had been faced with a problem in the testing of machine-guns. When testing machine-guns, particularly those intended for aircraft use, it is necessary to try them out in various positions, one of which involved shooting straight up into the air. This was somewhat hazardous for the testing station when the bullets came down again, and they had devised an attachment to go on the front of the machine-gun – simply a long curved tube which deflected the bullets into a sand pit. Taking this idea as a starting point, a curved barrel attachment was produced for the Machine Pistol 44 which deflected the bullets on a predictable course. Two models were made, firstly the *Sturm Gewehr Vorsatz Jager* (Assault rifle attachment for infantry) or 'SGV-J', which turned the bullets through 30 degrees, and secondly the 'SGV-P' (SGV for Panzer), which turned the bullets through 90 degrees. The SGV-J, which is often called the *Krummlauf* or *Gebogener Lauf* (bent barrel), was fitted with a prismatic sight which allowed the firer to stay hidden in a trench and fire over the top or, by altering the attachment, to fire around corners. The SGV-P was fitted into a ball mounting in the roof of the tank and had a periscopic sight as part of the mounting, and allowed the occupants of the tank to fire close in to the vehicle. Naturally enough, this deflection was not achieved without some loss of efficiency of the bullet, but it still had sufficient velocity and range to make it a suitable weapon for short range use. Some 10,000 of these attachments were ordered in late 1944, but relatively few of them ever got into service.

Target detection
A field in which German experimenters were particularly active was that of infrared target detection. A lot of this was due to a mistaken belief that the British Army were liberally equipped with infrared devices at the outbreak of war. Large numbers of infrared target seeking aids for fighter aircraft and missiles were projected, while in the ground field there were a number of night-driving aids consisting of infrared headlights and special vision units for drivers. One of the more useful equipments was 'Vampire', a combined lamp and tele-scope unit to be mounted onto the assault rifle 44. Although quite effective, it was extremely cumbersome and heavy, and it appears that even when they were issued to troops, they were rarely used. Another Army device which indicates how sensitive infrared detectors could be was *Donau*, a target locator for coast artillery. Built by Zeiss in large numbers, these were situated on the German coast and later on the coasts of various occupied countries and consisted of a central plotting room in communication with four detectors spread out over about ten miles of coast. Each detector station had a sensitive infrared detector mounted at the focus of a parabolic mirror, and these could detect ships at sea, from the heat of their funnels, at ranges of up to six or seven miles. The reports from the observing stations were plotted at the control room and the results passed to batteries of coast guns to allow them to open fire at night.

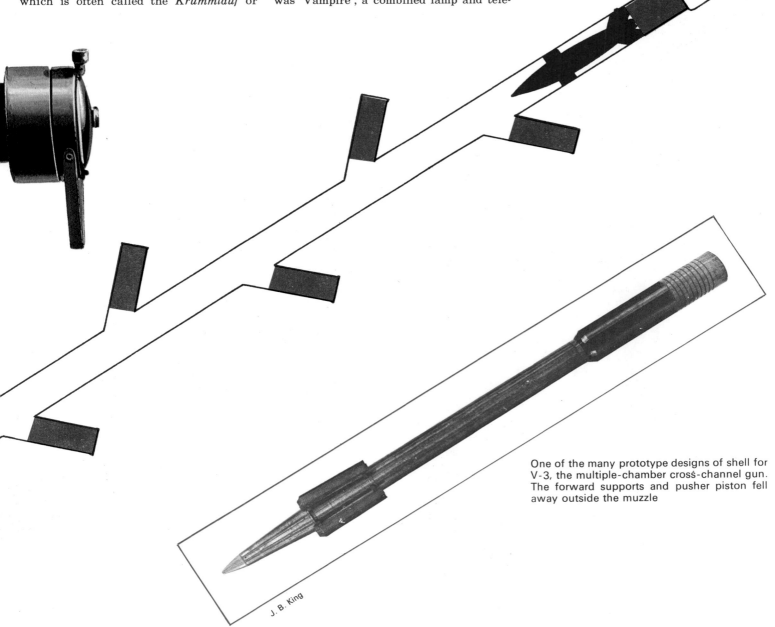

One of the many prototype designs of shell for V-3, the multiple-chamber cross-channel gun. The forward supports and pusher piston fell away outside the muzzle

J. B. King

Puppchen

Puppchen (Dolly) was an 88-mm anti-tank rocket launcher mounted on a light carriage in order to provide infantry with a lightweight anti-tank gun, since the conventional guns had become too cumbersome to be easily handled in combat

Taper-bore gun

One of the most effective of German secret weapons was the development of a tapering barrel for anti-tank guns, enabling the shot to achieve a much higher velocity than had previously been thought feasible. Only the shortage of tungsten for the special ammunition prevented this type of gun from becoming a decisive factor in anti-tank warfare

Above: The 75/55-mm Taper-bore PaK 600 photographed by John Batchelor at Aberdeen Proving Grounds in the United States.

PAW 600

Another ingenious design was this *Panzerabwehrwerfer* 600, using a new ballistic principle called 'high and low pressure'. The cartridge was fired in a reinforced chamber, and the gas leaked into the barrel at low pressure to propel a fin-stabilised projectile. This economised in propellant and allowed an extremely light and simple gun to be built quickly

These photographs show 'Puppchen', the 88-mm Rocket Launcher, being fired at a proving ground. Note the escape of gas at the breech. (Stills from a high-speed film)

John Batchelor

J. B. King

29

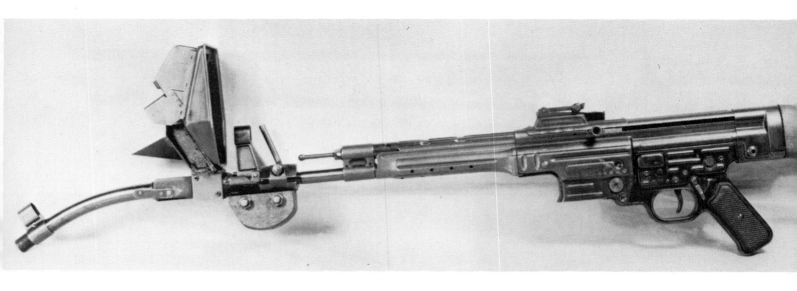

MP 44 with *Krummlauf*

The *Krummlauf* attachment, the gun which shot round corners. The curved attachment on the front of the Machine Pistol 44 caused the bullet to curve round so that the weapon could be fired from tanks and armoured vehicles to hit men clustered closely to the side, out of the zone of fire of normal weapons

German MP43

Although called a Machine Pistol, this was a bit of political camouflage to get the weapon into production behind Hitler's back. It was actually the first 'Assault Rifle', firing a shortened cartridge and capable of single shot or automatic fire

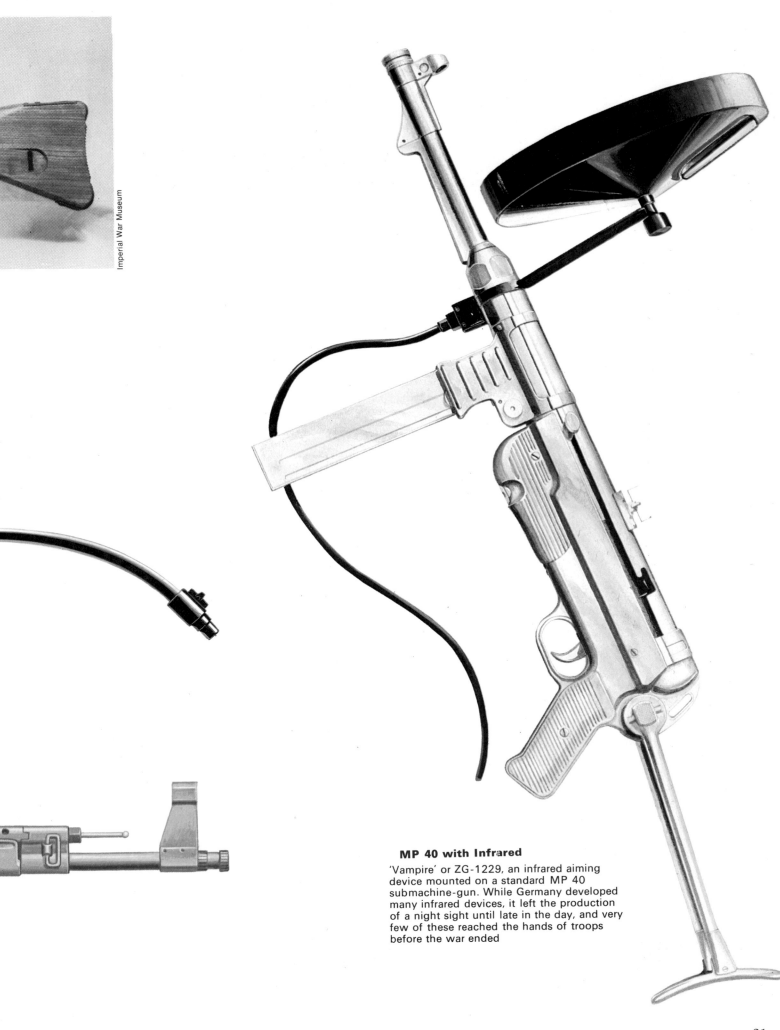

MP 40 with Infrared

'Vampire' or ZG-1229, an infrared aiming
device mounted on a standard MP 40
submachine-gun. While Germany developed
many infrared devices, it left the production
of a night sight until late in the day, and very
few of these reached the hands of troops
before the war ended

ANTI-TANK WARFARE
A POWERFUL BURST OF INVENTION

In 1939 the fighting of a normal ground war seemed to present few problems other than the simple one of production of sufficient equipment. The Allied armies had their stocks of field and anti-tank guns, tanks, small arms and the other necessities of war – all, it was thought, of designs representative of the best thoughts on the subject and incapable of improvement. Given a short war there was no reason why these designs should not see them through; this was the prevailing opinion in Germany as well. But soon enough it became obvious that the war wasn't going to be a short one, and it also became obvious that the war wasn't going to be run on the same lines as the First World War – clearly, some improvements in weapons would be needed.

Stop the panzers
One of the first fields in which the need for change arose was in the matter of stopping the German panzers. The standard British anti-tank weapons in 1939 were a tiny 2-pounder gun and a heavy anti-tank rifle of ·55 calibre. These had been developed in 1937/38 for the tanks in use at that time, and by 1940 it was apparent that even if they had managed to hold their own in France and Belgium, they were soon going to be outclassed by heavier tanks. Moreover, the German tanks had better guns on them than most of their contemporaries, and they could stand well away from small anti-tank guns and shoot them up with impunity. So the anti-tank field was the first one to see a burst of inventive activity.

One of the first German secret weapons to be unveiled in the war was their revolutionary taper-bore anti-tank gun, in which the shot was squeezed down to a small diameter during its passage through the gun barrel. This meant that the area of the bottom of the shot was reduced while the propelling gas remained constant, and thus the velocity was increased to a startling degree, leading to vastly better penetration of armour.

This idea was by no means a complete secret and had been toyed with in many quarters before the war. In Denmark, the Ultra Company of Otterup had gained something of a reputation in the experimental field, and the French Government had actually purchased 50 taper-bored barrels from them in 1938, for research and experimental purposes only. Britain too had

made a number of tests on the principle, but the Allied opinion in general was that while there was undoubtedly some scientific truth in the idea, and while it was all very clever and interesting, it would take years of development before it was ever brought to a state where it could be usefully employed as a weapon, and even then there was a considerable body of opinion that wondered what it might be used for. The capture of a German taper-bore gun in the Western Desert in 1941 surprised everybody; somebody had actually made it work and put the idea to use in a practical fashion.

As the German Army completed its occupation of Czechoslovakia in 1939, a number of Czechs decided it would be healthier to live elsewhere and took themselves off to other countries. Among this number were several weapons technicians who came to Britain and resumed work on their various specialities. One of these men was a Mr Janacek, who had been experimenting with his own ideas on taper-bore guns for some time, and in July 1940 he offered his revolutionary designs to the British Government. Instead of making the entire gun barrel with a tapered bore, he suggested screwing a tapered smooth-bore extension to the muzzle of the gun. By using a specially designed shot which could be collapsed as it went through the extension, he boosted the velocity and improved the armour penetration of a normal gun, without going to vast expense.

The idea was discussed for some time and eventually it was decided to put some experiments in hand at low priority. Nobody really expected it to work, but there might just be something in it. Then came the discovery of the German taper-bore gun, and overnight Janacek's idea suddenly became important. A contract was given to Janacek to develop an attachment and the necessary ammunition for the standard 2-pounder anti-tank gun. But turning his ideas into a practical weapon took time, and it was late in 1942 before the weapon – now called the 'Littlejohn Adapter' – was ready for issue.

Littlejohn Adapter
An attachment to a normal gun barrel which simulated the effect of a taper-bore gun. The projectile's skirts were squeezed by the adapter to give better muzzle velocity and armour penetration

By this time the 2-pounder had been cast aside in favour of a 6-pounder and this, in its turn, was about to be replaced by a 17-pounder, so that the original intention of using the adapter on anti-tank guns was no longer feasible. Instead, the adapters were issued to tanks and armoured cars, numbers of which were still in service with the 2-pounder gun. It proved to be quite as successful as Janacek had forecast, although the tank crews were less than pleased with the need to leap out and unscrew the adapter before they could fire ordinary ammunition through the gun or re-fit the adapter when they needed to fire armour-piercing shot. As a result of this, it became unofficial practice to leave the adapter off all the time and fire the special shot through the normal barrel. It seemed to work quite well, according to reports by men who used them, and it certainly saved the gunner the dangerous task of unscrewing the adapter in the middle of a battle.

A similar adapter was developed in Britain for the US 37-mm gun, also mounted in armoured cars, and plans were laid for producing versions of such weapons as the RAF 40-mm Class 'S' gun and the 6-pounder intermediate AA gun with the Littlejohn adapter. Trial models were actually made and fired, but by the time the designs had been perfected, some new developments had come along and the idea was shelved.

Squeezing the shot
The new developments stemmed, in a way, from the taper-bore work. In order to make a projectile for these guns, it was necessary to have a hard central core and fit it with flanges which could be squeezed down in the tapering process. Since the striking velocity of this type of shot was high, it was found necessary to make the core of tungsten carbide because steel cores could not survive impact without smashing to pieces instead of penetrating. Tungsten was shown to be good, and the next question was how to put it to use in ordinary guns. Making a shot of tungsten was impractical because of the expense of the material and its great weight compared to steel. After looking at one or two possible solutions, the designers of the Armaments Research Department looked more closely at an idea which had been toyed with in France before the war – the 'sabot' shot.

A French designer named Edgar Brandt had found that by taking a 75-mm shot, and fitting it with a sleeve to make it 105-mm calibre and then firing it from a 105-mm gun, he could achieve some notable advantages. If the sleeve was arranged so that it fell from the shell after leaving the gun muzzle, the 75-mm shell was being pushed by a 105-mm cartridge, and the range was considerably increased. Moreover, since the weight of the 75-mm shell and its sabot,

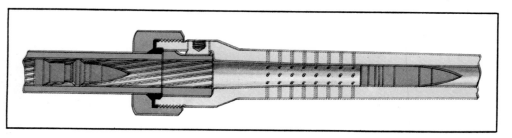

Discarding Sabot Shot

One of the most important Allied breakthroughs in the anti-tank field, the tungsten core of this shot was surrounded by a light sabot or jacket. The force of the propelling charge was applied to a wide base, but on leaving the gun barrel the sabot fell away, concentrating the shot's momentum in the armour-piercing core for higher velocity and better penetration at long range or sleeve, added up to less than the normal weight of a 105-mm shell, the sabot shell accelerated faster up the barrel and had a higher velocity.

The British designers took over this idea and began to apply it to an anti-tank shot. By making the shot of tungsten and then shrouding it in a light alloy sabot they were able to step up the velocity obtained from the 6-pounder anti-tank gun from 2600 ft a second to 3500, and the penetration of armour at 1000 yards jumped from 74 mm to 146 mm. They then applied their talents to the 17-pounder and improved the armour penetration from 109 mm to 231 mm at 1000 yards. The designs were put into production immediately – the 6-pounder sabot shot was available in time for use in the invasion in 1944, and the 17-pounder shot was issued in August of that year, in time to be usefully employed in the fighting in Normandy.

While the discarding sabot projectile was the greatest Allied success in the anti-tank field and the one which became the supreme tank destroyer, there was no shortage of other offerings in this sector of operations. Among the more conventional approaches were the American 76-mm and 90-mm anti-tank guns, conversions of anti-aircraft guns which would put their high velocity to work. The most interesting portions of the designs lay in the mountings. Instead of the conventional sort of gun carriage, these used carriages in which the shield formed part of the structure and was not simply an added afterthought. Moreover the barrels were swung around through 180° to lie along the top of the trail legs when travelling to reduce the overhang and make the weapon more manoeuvrable.

Somewhat less conventional was the Cam-Al gun, developed by an unlikely-sounding establishment in Britain called the Petroleum Warfare Department. This establishment had been founded to deal with such things as flame-throwers and incendiary bombs, but once these devices were organised time hung heavy on their hands and they began to look around for something to keep them occupied. In 1944, the infantry were beginning to get worried about the way that anti-tank guns were going: the 2-pounder had weighed 1750 lb, the 6-pounder went up to 2500 lb, and the 17-pounder turned the scale at 4600 lb. Just to make the future seem more gloomy the weapons experts were working on the 32-pounder gun which threatened to weigh about seven tons.

Diminishing returns

All this increase in weight had made the anti-tank gun into something which needed heavy tractors and prepared positions, and it had cancelled out the old advantage of being able to push it around rapidly and hide it behind a bush. What the infantry wanted was a return to this sort of weapon. Fortunately the hollow charge projectile, using a shaped charge of explosive to blast a hole in armour, had come along in time to allow lightweight weapons to have some effect on tanks, and the PWD now began designing a light cannon using a hollow charge shell.

The Cam-Al gun took its odd name from the two facts that it was developed in Cambridge and made largely of aluminium. It was fairly conventional in appearance, though the recoil system apparently relied largely on two springs and the breech mechanism resembled nothing which had

ever come from a professional gun designer's drawing board. But the novelties of the Cam-Al gun were entirely internal: it was a smooth-bore gun, firing an elongated projectile. On the face of it, this was a contradiction in terms. Smooth-bore guns in years gone by had always fired round shot, since they had no way of stabilising a long projectile to prevent it turning end-over-end as it flew through the air.

But the designers of the Cam-Al gun came up with a fresh approach to stabilising the shell – their projectile was simply a cylinder with blunt ends. The front end was heavy, while the rear end was largely a hollow sleeve, and as this flew through the air it stabilised itself by air drag. The theory of it is rather involved but it can be visualised simply by imagining the blunt end of the shell pushing the air aside, this air then sweeping back over the rear end of the shell with sufficient force to hold the tail end steady. Another explanation was that the heavy head and light tail operated like a spear to keep the head flying foremost. Whichever explanation one cares to accept, the fact remained that the Cam-Al shell flew straight and hit what it was aimed at most of the time.

Unfortunately it was not in a fit state to go for trials by the time the war ended, and although work was carried on intermittently for a year or two in order to settle some of the more abstruse problems which it posed, the gun never got anywhere near service. Nevertheless the drag-stabilisation system

has lived on, notably in a variety of weapons developed by the Carl Gustav factory in Sweden, though it is unlikely that the Cam-Al gun had any effect on this development.

Recoilless guns

One of the reasons that the Cam-Al gun never got past the drawing-board and prototype stage was the emergence of another type of lightweight gun which seemed to hold out unlimited promise – the recoilless gun. This class of weapon made its first appearance in the war in German hands, during the invasion of Crete in 1941, and as a result of the impression made there exploratory work began in both Britain and the USA. In Britain the whole development was in the hands of one man, Sir Denis Burney, a notable engineer who had actually begun investigation of recoilless guns shortly before the German weapons were revealed. His first attempt was a recoilless four-bore duck gun, a weapon not normally recommended to be fired from the shoulder. Once converted by Sir Denis, however, it became quite possible to fire from the shoulder without ill effect, and with such a simple but startling demonstration, Sir Denis managed to interest sufficient people to make his proposals acceptable to the War Office.

The principle of operation of the recoilless gun is relatively easy to understand. Instead of firmly closing the breech end of the gun and making the explosion propel the shell forward and thus by reaction make the gun recoil, an aperture of some sort is left in the breech through which a portion of the gas generated by the explosion can escape in a controlled fashion. Since this gas has mass and velocity, it can be arranged so that the amount which escapes multiplied by the speed at which it escapes matches the mass times velocity of the shell leaving the barrel in the normal way. If both forces are equal, then the gun itself will remain perfectly still and will not recoil.

The German designers allowed the gas to escape by making the base of the cartridge case of plastic and piercing the breech-block with a Laval nozzle, similar to the venturi of a rocket. This system had its advantages and disadvantages, but Sir Denis chose to adopt a different system. In his design the cartridge case body was pierced with holes and lined with thin metal shim. The gun chamber was also pierced with holes which led to an outer chamber provided with rearward-facing jet nozzles. When the round was loaded and fired, the pressure started the shell moving up the

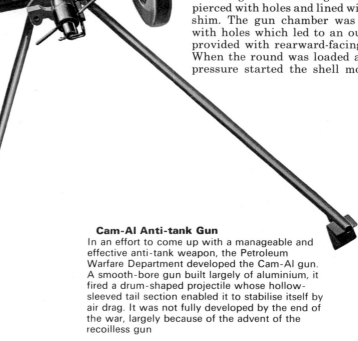

Cam-Al Anti-tank Gun
In an effort to come up with a manageable and effective anti-tank weapon, the Petroleum Warfare Department developed the Cam-Al gun. A smooth-bore gun built largely of aluminium, it fired a drum-shaped projectile whose hollow-sleeved tail section enabled it to stabilise itself by air drag. It was not fully developed by the end of the war, largely because of the advent of the recoilless gun

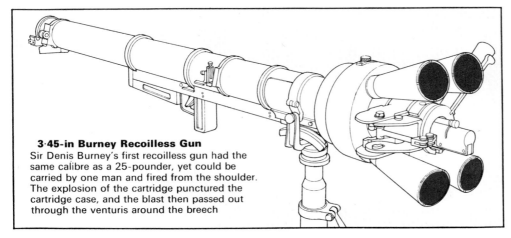

3·45-in Burney Recoilless Gun
Sir Denis Burney's first recoilless gun had the same calibre as a 25-pounder, yet could be carried by one man and fired from the shoulder. The explosion of the cartridge punctured the cartridge case, and the blast then passed out through the venturis around the breech

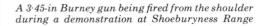

A 3·45-in Burney gun being fired from the shoulder during a demonstration at Shoeburyness Range

attracted attention from various people who were busy worrying about the question of attacking the massive concrete fortifications which were being rapidly erected along the French coast by the German Army. Sir Denis now decided to add one more gun to his range specifically for the attack of the Atlantic Wall, a 7·2-in firing a 139-lb wallbuster shell. In September 1943 a trial of the 7·2-in shell against a five-foot thick reinforced concrete wall gave spectacular results: the reinforcing rods of the wall were completely severed and chunks of concrete blown 60 yards away to the rear.

Copying the Germans

Meanwhile there was even more activity going on in the United States. The Artillery Section of the Research and Development Service concluded that the quickest way to success would be simply to take the German design as it stood and adapt it to their own ideas, rather than waste time doing any research into some other system. As a result they went to work to design a 105-mm Howitzer T9 to fire the standard 105-mm howitzer ammunition already on issue for the M1 field howitzer, merely designing a new cartridge case with a plastic blow-out base. Their aim was to produce a weapon having a muzzle velocity of 1100 ft per second and capable of firing to a range of 6000 yards.

By early 1944 the prototype had been produced and was test fired, the designers were delighted to find that it achieved 1140 ft per second and 7500 yards range. However there were a number of small technical troubles. The cartridge case allowed gas to leak past it, thus permitting more gas to escape to the rear than was designed, and the plastic disc blew out with such force that it blew fragments of plastic half an inch deep into plywood screens 40 ft behind the gun. There was also considerable erosion of the breech due to the gas wash, and it looked as if there was going to be some long delay in getting the weapon into a serviceable state.

However, somebody else had also been looking at recoilless guns. The Infantry Section of the R and D Service had moved in a different direction, basing their work on the Burney gun design. They had adopted the perforated cartridge case, although using more and smaller perforations, and had also added the refinement of preengraving the driving band of the shell so as to cut down the stress set up as the band was forced into the rifling. This allowed at least one variable factor to be cut out of the reckoning, and by November 1943 they had produced and fired a 57-mm recoilless rifle with considerable success, sending a 2·75-lb hollow charge shell to almost 5000 yards. Elated by this success they then went on to develop a 75-mm version which could fire the standard 75-mm gun shells, suitably modified by pre-engraving the driving bands. This was successfully fired in the spring of 1944, giving a maximum range of 7000 yards.

These three weapons were now placed before the Infantry Board so that they could come to some decision regarding their possible use. The 105-mm T9 was ruled out since it obviously needed more development, but the 57-mm T15 and the 75-mm T21 were both accepted as being viable weapons. Orders were given for the production of

bore and at the same time burst the thin metal liner, allowing the explosion gas to pass through the holes in the cartridge case and gun chamber, into the outer chamber, and then through the nozzles to the rear. Although this design demanded some careful engineering of the chamber and jets, the ammunition was much easier to make, since the cartridge cases could be turned out on conventional machinery and simply have holes bored in them. It also simplified the question of firing the charge, since the case, having a solid base, could use the standard percussion primers used by most artillery cases and the breech and firing mechanism could also be of conventional design. The German design, with its plastic case base, eventually led to some very involved engineering in order to get satisfactory charge ignition.

Sir Denis now set about designing three guns along these lines, a 3·45-in, a 3·7-in, and a 95-mm. The 3·45-in could be fired from the shoulder, although a tripod mounting was preferred by most people, while the 3·7-in was mounted on a light two-wheel carriage (though it was to be carried in a jeep for long distance movement) and the 95-mm, a much heavier weapon, was on a modified form of normal gun mounting. There were definite reasons behind producing each weapon: the 3·45-in was visualised as a lightweight method of bringing heavy fire power to bear in places where normal guns could not be moved – the jungles of Burma were commonly quoted in this context. The 3·7-in was to be a light anti-tank gun, and the 95-mm was to be provided with variable charges and be a lightweight field gun, possibly for adoption by airborne forces.

With work in hand on these designs, the next move was to produce ammunition for

them. The German weapons had used exactly the same ammunition as the conventional field guns of the same calibre, and Sir Denis was inclined to think that they had missed a good opportunity. The recoilless gun had certain ballistic characteristics which led him to think that it might be possible to improve on the conventional shell type so as to produce a more effective shell by taking advantage of these special features.

Broadly speaking the advantages were that the shell was less violently accelerated by the firing of a recoilless charge and was thus less highly stressed. The conventional shell had to be very thick in its walls in order to withstand this stress, leading to its having little room inside for explosive; a 'payload' of 10% of the weight was considered very good for a conventional shell. The Burney shell used a very thin wall, placed the fuze at the base so that the shell walls did not have to support it during acceleration, and then stuffed the shell with as much explosive as could be got in. In this way the payload was increased to 21% of the weight, which gave the weapons a power out of all proportion to their size.

Burney's next move was to try and put the explosive to work in a more useful fashion. By using plastic explosive and enclosing the charge in a thin mesh bag, the effect at the target was considerably enhanced. When fired against a hard target, such as a reinforced concrete wall, the outer body of the shell collapsed on impact while the bag of plastic smeared itself against the concrete like a poultice. The base fuze then detonated, and the force of the explosive was directed into the target instead of being dissipated on the outer surface. This gave such startling results against concrete that the Burney shell was christened the 'Wallbuster' shell, and it

2000 57-mm and 1000 75-mm weapons, together with the necessary ammunition, and by early 1945 they were on their way to combat units. Most of them were sent to the Pacific Theatre, where their light weight and powerful punch seemed to be most in demand, but the 75-mm was used in Europe by the 17th US Airborne Division at Essen during the closing days of the war. In the Far East they had their first outing on Okinawa on 9 June 1945 in the hands of the 383 Infantry Regiment, who put them to extremely good use, though they were somewhat hampered by the fact that the ammunition supply was extemely meagre, no more than 275 rounds per gun.

As a result of the success of these weapons, plans were put forward for the development of two more, a 155-mm Howitzer T4 and a 105-mm Gun T19. The howitzer was to use a blow-out base type of cartridge, while the gun was to use the perforated case. The gun was eventually built and fired but there is no record of whether the howitzer ever attained such status. In the event, no more was heard of the idea but the 105-mm gun formed the basis of the post-war 105-mm and 106-mm recoilless anti-tank guns.

A 7·2-in Burney in action, demonstrating the basic drawback of RCLs: it doesn't pay to stand behind them

7·2-in Burney Recoilless Gun
This gun was designed to attack the concrete fortifications of the Atlantic Wall. Test results using 139-lb wallbuster shells were spectacularly successful, but simpler solutions were found, and in the end only two prototypes of the weapon were built

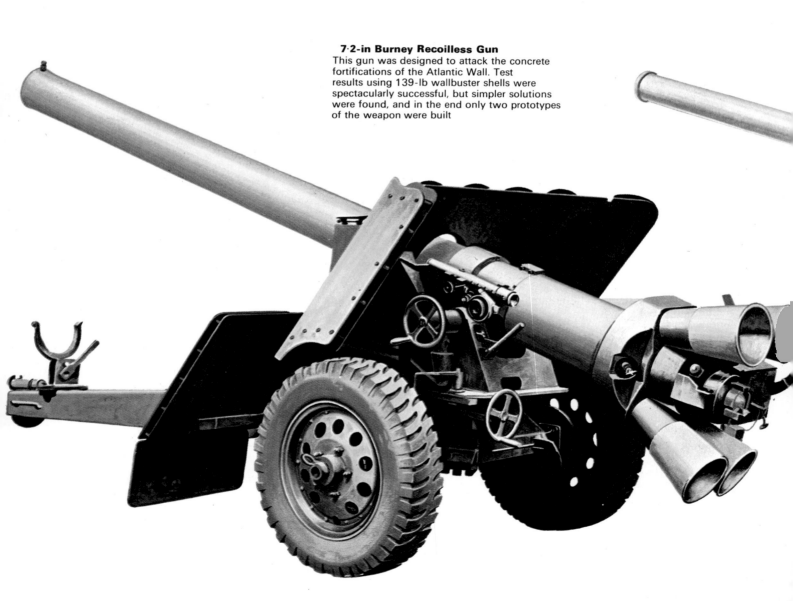

One other American recoilless development deserves attention: the Chemical Warfare Service used a 4·2-in muzzle-loading mortar as an infantry support weapon. Originally, this had been intended to fire gas bombs, but since the war never needed them the CWS developed a high explosive bomb and became a sort of private artillery force for the infantry. The prime feature of the mortar, of course, is that it always fires at angles greater than 45° so as to pitch its bomb high in the air and drop it behind cover. It follows from this that the mortar cannot possibly be used as a direct-fire weapon, and attacking pill-boxes or shooting at tanks is quite impossible.

The CWS thought about this for a while and then decided to try and see if there wasn't some way around this restriction, and they enlisted the aid of the National Research and Development Council. The NRDC were, at the time, involved in rockets of one sort and another, and after some thought on the matter proposed a rocket solution to the problem. The result was the 4·2-in Recoilless Mortar, a standard mortar tube with the breech cap replaced by a jet pipe. This was mounted on two standard mortar tripod units so that the barrel was horizontal.

Rocket-fired mortar

The problem now became one of how to fire the projectile, since in normal use it was dropped into the muzzle of the mortar, fell down the barrel by gravity, and struck a fixed firing pin in the breech piece. The fixed firing pin was retained, being placed on a steel 'spider' in the centre of the jet nozzle, but gravity was no longer of any assistance. The NRDC people produced a small 'driver rocket' which they attached to the nose of the shell; the shell was then entered in the muzzle of the horizontal mortar in the usual way, and the loader, standing clear, pulled a firing pin from the rocket. This ignited the rocket which drove the shell along the mortar barrel with enough force to strike the cartridge against the firing pin, whereupon the propelling charge ignited and the shell was blown back from the muzzle, giving the mortar an anti-tank or anti-bunker capability. The weapon was demonstrated successfully, but so far as is known none of them was ever issued for service, since the development came close to the end of the war. Moreover, a horizontal, rocket-loaded, recoilless mortar was a bit much to swallow.

Back in Britain the Burney guns slowly took shape. The 7·2-in got as far as two prototypes but was then abandoned, since something more simple had been found sufficient to deal with the promised fortifications in France. The smaller weapons, while effective in trials, took a long time to get some of the technical problems ironed out, and the war in Europe was over before any of them could be placed in production. It is believed that a handful of the 3·45-in were shipped to Burma, but none of them were used in action due to the sudden collapse of the conflict in the Far East. The 3·45-in and 3·7-in were retained for a few years after the war in order to familiarise people with recoilless guns and give the infantry some experience in using them, but they were eventually scrapped and it was some years before an improved recoilless gun appeared in British service.

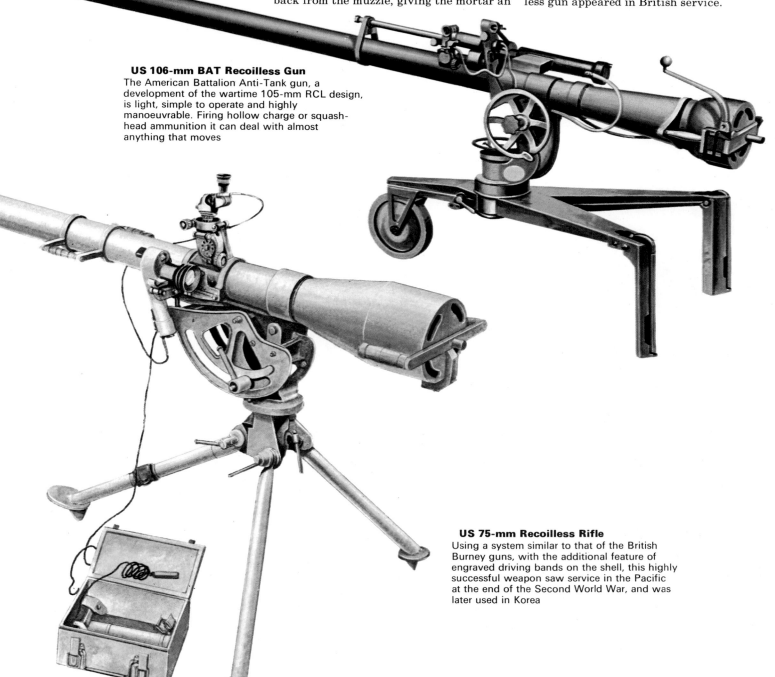

US 106-mm BAT Recoilless Gun
The American Battalion Anti-Tank gun, a development of the wartime 105-mm RCL design, is light, simple to operate and highly manoeuvrable. Firing hollow charge or squash-head ammunition it can deal with almost anything that moves

US 75-mm Recoilless Rifle
Using a system similar to that of the British Burney guns, with the additional feature of engraved driving bands on the shell, this highly successful weapon saw service in the Pacific at the end of the Second World War, and was later used in Korea

BREAKING OPEN A FORTRESS

By the middle of 1943 everybody sensed that the big task ahead was going to be the invasion of Europe. The Germans realised it and were busily pouring concrete and erecting steel obstacles and planting mines all over the places they considered likely spots for a seaborne assault. The British and Americans realised it, looked at what the Germans were doing, and went away to try and think up some ways to defeat all these obstacles. Much of what was done was, in fact, somewhat pointless, since well-meaning inventors and designers were looking at the formidable defences erected on the Pas de Calais area while the Allied commanders had already made up their minds that to attack such a tough nut would be fatal and were planning to go in over the less well-defended beaches of Normandy. Obviously, this decision couldn't be announced to all and sundry, so a number of projects went on which had no chance of ever being used. Nevertheless, they sometimes had greater effect than their inventors ever intended, in a roundabout fashion. Take, for example, the Great Panjandrum.

Catherine wheel crusher

The Great Panjandrum is probably the best-known of all the British secret weapons, largely because it didn't work and thus its secret cover was soon abandoned. Moreover it has frequently been held up as an example of wasted effort and misplaced enthusiasm, though one wonders if the critics would have been so hard on it had it worked a little more reliably. Panjandrum was an enormous demolition machine, the brainchild of the Admiralty Miscellaneous Weapon Development Department, and it was little more than an enormous pair of wheels carrying between them a two-ton charge of high explosive. Around the circumference of the wheels were a number of rockets.

The theory of the machine was flawless: Panjandrum would be carried on a landing craft to the selected beach, the ramp lowered and the rockets ignited. Their thrust on the wheel rims would revolve the wheels and thus Panjandrum would trundle off the landing craft, through the surf, and

Great Panjandrum
Two gigantic Catherine wheels carrying two tons of high explosive seemed an extremely potent way of smashing through the concrete fortifications of the 'Atlantic Wall'. But like an enormous firework, the 'Pandjandrum' was completely uncontrollable

up the beach until it came up against a wall or fortification of some sort. Upon striking this, the wheels would collapse, dumping the charge at the foot of the obstacle where it would detonate, to the considerable discomfort of the obstacle.

That was the theory – what happened in practice was rather chastening. Built in conditions of great secrecy, it was taken to a Devon beach in September 1943 for its trials. The first trial augured well and the monster roared off the landing craft and trundled up the beach almost exactly as intended. The only flaw was a slight change of direction when two rockets misfired. It seemed that the drag of the sand on the enormous wheels was more than had been anticipated, and instead of charging the full width of the beach, it ground to a halt halfway.

The obvious answer to that seemed to be more power, so more rockets were fitted and the trial repeated. There was still insufficient power to get all the way up the beach and the contraption showed a tendency to be unstable in patches of soft sand. A three-wheel version was built, the third wheel to give stability, but this model over-

turned as soon as it was launched and showered the area with burning rockets, and the design reverted to two wheels.

Next came a system of steering the monster by steel cables paid out from two winches, which showed little success. Various modifications were then tried, but the whole affair came to an end with a grand demonstration before a high-ranking audience in January 1944. The Panjandrum left its launching craft and, gathering speed, roared through the surf and onto the beach. Then it ran amok, charged the audience, turned on its heel and headed back to sea, falling on its side and shedding the rockets on its upper wheel while the rockets beneath erupted and exploded, thoroughly wrecking the whole device.

That was the end of the Great Panjandrum, and, as I have just pointed out, it has frequently been pointed to as a typically British waste of time. This may be so, but it has since been suggested, by people in a position to know the truth, that the whole thing may have been kept going as a deliberate deception move. The eventual landing areas of the invasion had no obstacles worthy of Panjandrum's gigantic charge. The trials on the West Country beaches had little or no security, and holiday-makers and bystanders frequently watched the trials. Had news of the device and its intended function leaked to Germany it would have confirmed the German belief that the prospective target for the invasion was the heavily defended Pas de Calais area.

Another potential concrete-smashing device was called 'Conkernut'. This was a heavy bomb filled with 137 lb of plastic explosive and propelled by a cluster of rockets. It was to be fired from an aircraft in order to breach concrete beach defences in positions where it would have been difficult to get guns to bear. A preliminary trial of the device showed, though, that a single rocket could not produce a breach large enough to allow a tank to pass through, and that the difficulties of aiming from a fast flying aircraft, together with the inaccuracy of the rocket, made it unlikely that a number of consecutive Conkernuts could have been fired at the same target in order to make a

Left: The concrete defences of Hitler's 'Fortress Europe'. But the Petard mortar (right) could reduce it to charred rubble

wider breach. An alternative method of launching, and one which looked as if it might be more accurate, was the suggestion that Conkernut could be fired from a specially equipped landing craft. This was considered possible, but by that time it seemed unlikely that there were going to be enough landing craft to carry the invasion force, let alone mount all the various oddball weapons which people were proposing, so Conkernut was abandoned.

The 'Flying Dustbin'

Early in 1943 Col Blacker had produced another spigot mortar design, which he called the 'Petard'. This he proposed mounting on a tank, so that it could be fired by a protected crew, and it launched a 40-lb finned bomb which proved to be extremely effective against concrete obstacles. The ungainly bomb, which showed no pretensions to streamlining or other refinement, soon gained the nickname of the 'Flying Dustbin', but after passing trials in August 1943 it was approved for immediate production. The Petard was assembled to a Churchill tank and the complete equipment was then known, somewhat oddly, as an 'Armoured Vehicle, Royal Engineers' or AVRE.

In mid-1943 a special armoured division, the 79th, was formed with the task of developing armoured vehicles which would be capable of defeating any obstacle likely to be met with on the French beaches, and the AVRE was allotted to this formation. In addition a wide variety of other specialised tanks was developed: tanks with flails for detonating buried mines, tanks

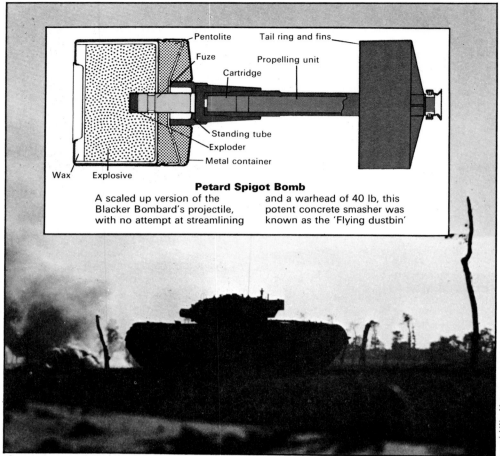

Petard Spigot Bomb

A scaled up version of the Blacker Bombard's projectile, with no attempt at streamlining and a warhead of 40 lb, this potent concrete smasher was known as the 'Flying dustbin'

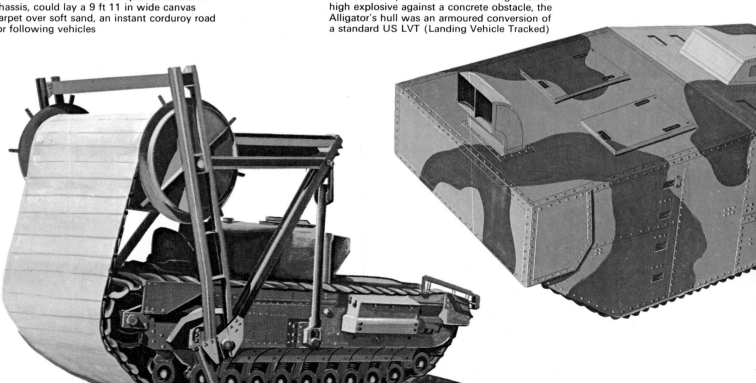

Petard-armed Churchill AVRE brings its specialist concrete-smashing ability into action at Le Havre

THROUGH I

Churchill fitted with 'Bobbin'

Bobbin mounted on the ubiquitous Churchill chassis, could lay a 9 ft 11 in wide canvas carpet over soft sand, an instant corduroy road for following vehicles

Alligator

Designed to swim out of the sea under remote control and lay a 'mattress' containing 1 ton of high explosive against a concrete obstacle, the Alligator's hull was an armoured conversion of a standard US LVT (Landing Vehicle Tracked)

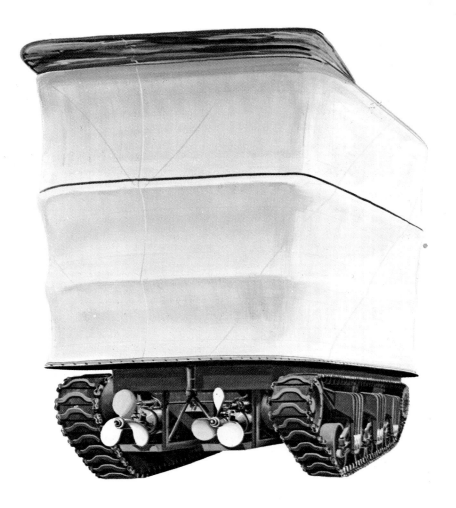

with ramps over which other tanks could drive in order to overcome walls, tanks with flame-throwers, tanks with bridges, tanks with enormous bundles of chestnut paling which could be dropped into ditches, even tanks with huge rolls of flexible roadway which they could unroll as they drove forward to provide firm roads for the vehicles following them. Whatever the obstacle to be met, the 79th were convinced they had a tank which would beat it.

As well as this specialist force, tanks of the normal armoured divisions were converted in order to be able to swim across the water from landing craft to beach; these were the 'DD' (for Duplex Drive) tanks. Standard Sherman tanks had a screw propulsion unit fitted at the rear (hence the Duplex Drive term) and a waterproof screen around the hull which could be raised so as to increase the bouyancy. Once ashore the screen was blown off by small explosive charges, the screw unit thrown out of gear, and the tank reverted to a land-crawler.

The effectiveness of this collection of purpose-built armour is well seen by comparing the course of the initial landings on the British and American beaches in Normandy. Although numbers of the 'funnies' – as the 79th Division's special vehicles were collectively known – were offered to the US Army, they were refused. As a result, while British troops had a relatively simple task to move across the beaches which had been effectively cleared by the special armour, the US troops were stuck on their beach for several hours before gaining more than a toe-hold.

AND OVER IT

Sherman DD (Duplex Drive)
Spearheading the assault on the invasion beaches, Sherman tanks were made amphibious by the fitting of twin propellers and a collapsible buoyancy screen raised by compressed air. The DD could make up to 4.3 knots in calm water

Churchill AVRE with Fascine
The 'Armoured Vehicle Royal Engineers' could carry a combat demolition team under fire and could be fitted with an array of devices from bridges to ditch-filling fascines. Its Petard mortar could breach a sea-wall

It was the success and simplicity – and the armour protection – of the AVRE and its Petard which led to Sir Denis Burney's 7·2-in recoilless gun being abandoned. It was obviously safer to attack the defences in an armoured vehicle than to attempt to trundle a light gun ashore and then man it in the face of German machine-gun fire. Seeing the logic of this, Sir Denis proposed mounting the 7·2-in guns in twin turrets on special landing craft, using blast deflectors to prevent the back-blast of the recoilless guns from damaging the vessel. Although the idea was examined and pronounced sound, once more the question of the availability of landing craft prevented it being used.

One device for which landing craft were provided was 'Hedgerow', which as its name suggests, stemmed from 'Hedgehog'. One of the problems of the Normandy beaches was the millions of anti-personnel and anti-tank mines buried under them, and late in 1942 the Chief of Combined Operations suggested that it might be possible to mount the Hedgehog anti-submarine bomb thrower in a landing craft and fire the bomb pattern onto a beach so that the concussion of the bombs set off any land mines in the area and cleared a path for a landing party. To achieve this it was necessary to detonate

the bomb just above the surface of the beach so that the blast laid a pressure wave on the ground and actuated the pressure-sensitive switches in the mines.

The simplest method of doing this turned out to be the most effective. A 20-in tube was screwed into the fuze hole in the nose of the Hedgehog bomb, and into its tip went a standard mortar bomb fuze. When this struck the ground the impulse passed down the tube and detonated the bomb at just the right height to spread the blast over a wide area, effectively detonating any mines beneath.

The genuine article

In order to prove that Hedgerow worked, it was vital to prove it against genuine German mines; it would have meant very little to have tested it against British or American mines which had different fuzing arrangements and required different pressure distribution to fire them. To make the test it was necessary to ship hundreds of German Tellermines from North Africa. The Army there were busy clearing up German minefields, and they were rather surprised to be ordered to carefully defuze the mines, overhaul them and ship them back to England, rather than simply follow the usual plan of piling them up in a big heap

'Hedgerow', a development of 'Hedgehog'. Pairs of bombs with extended mortar fuzes were fired at intervals to clear a path through beach defences

and blowing them up. The returned mines were carefully fuzed and laid, in accordance with the latest captured German Army manuals and instructions on depth and spacing, on the beaches and mudflats in the estuary of the River Parrett, in the Bristol Channel, after which they were attacked by Hedgerow-fitted landing craft.

The subsequent career of Hedgerow was somewhat chequered. Five landing craft were sent to North Africa to take part in the Salerno landings, but due to an administrative error – and the fact that the new weapon was so secret that nobody in North Africa knew what it was – the Hedgerow installations were removed from the craft. Two were later reassembled, but when tested, the recoil force was so violent that one craft split open and sank. The other, though damaged, was repaired and strengthened, and managed to take part in the Salerno assault where it achieved some useful results. More craft were then prepared for the invasion of Normandy, but again the fates were against them. Many sank on the voyage across the Channel, but those which actually arrived at their appointed locations made resounding contributions to the attacking force's ability to get across the beaches without being blown up.

With all the activity in rocket development which was going on in Britain at this time, it wasn't long before somebody began to consider using some form of rocket projectile for the attack of the Atlantic Wall. In August 1943 a Mr Frobisher of the Projectile Development Establishment produced a report entitled 'Rocket Projectiles for the Attack of Concrete Walls and Pillboxes', and as a result of this a meeting was convened to discuss ways of using rockets against land targets. By this time the invasion preparations were well under way, and forward-thinking elements of the Army were beginning to look at the question of defeating the Japanese 'bunker' in the Far East. This notorious obstacle was a strongpoint of logs or coral rock, always in the way and always just too tough to be damaged by anything the front line infantry carried with them. Mortars were no use, since the bunkers were provided with liberal top cover and rifle and machine-gun fire made no impression on the thick sides. The field of fire of the occupants was always carefully arranged so that it was difficult, if not impossible, to get up close and use grenades, explosive charges or flame-throwers. The only solution was to use artillery, but it was rarely possible to bring artillery through the jungle and get it close enough for a direct shot. What was needed was something capable of being carried by a couple of men through the worst jungle conditions, small, inconspicuous, and yet with an almighty punch. The recoilless guns of Sir Denis Burney promised one answer, but they were

a long way off, and the rocket was now examined to see if it could provide a solution.

The answer came in the shape of 'Lilo', which, in point of fact, appears to owe a great deal to the anti-submarine Rocket Spear. Lilo was a 60-lb semi-armour-piercing head, pointed so as to smash through obstacles and containing a 13½-lb high-explosive charge and a base fuze. It was propelled through the air by a standard 3-in anti-aircraft type of rocket motor. The whole weapon weighed 80 lb and was launched from a very simple stand. In order to improve the accuracy over its short range – rarely more than 100 yards – the launching stand had spiral rails which engaged the rocket fins and spun it at 800 rpm. For situations where piercing ability was not needed a 21-lb warhead was produced. This gave a higher velocity and a somewhat longer range than the heavy piercing head. Both weapons were duly put into production and supplies shipped to the Far East in 1945.

While that particular device was too late for the Normandy landings, others were produced in good time, and to trace the rise of these it is necessary to go back to 1939. At the outbreak of war there was a strong opinion that the war would soon settle down to a pattern of trench warfare similar to that which had prevailed during the First World War. Following from this it was expected that gas would play a significant

part. In 1918 the most effective way of delivering gas on the enemy was a simple form of mortar called the Livens Projector, which fired a cylindrical drum weighing about 60 lb and containing 30 lb of gas to a range of about 1800 yards. It was the most devastating gas warfare weapon ever used, but it had its drawbacks. The principal one was that it was a one-shot weapon, and to get the necessary volume of gas onto the target it was necessary to emplace hundreds – even thousands – of projectors before the start of an operation. Something with the same effect but with less labour was a desirable property, and in November 1939 the Chemical Warfare Staff approached the rocket researchers with a request for a suitable rocket to fling a 30-lb, 5-in diameter chemical-filled warhead to 4000 yards.

Built-in obsolescence
By November 1940 this weapon was completed. It used a 5-in diameter rocket motor which had several sticks of propellant arranged radially instead of the single long stick of the 3-in and 2-in rockets. This allowed the motor to be much shorter and, into the bargain, produced an extremely powerful and accurate rocket. Sufficient numbers were produced to satisfy the demands of the Chemical Warfare department, but, of course, they were never used and were scrapped as soon as the war ended.

Through the grapevine the Admiralty came to know about the 5-in rocket, and in 1942, when casting about for a suitable weapon for bombarding beaches, called it out of retirement. A new warhead was produced, much the same as the Chemical version but packed with high explosive, together with a most potent incendiary warhead as an alternative, and the original Chemical Warfare six-rocket launching rack was also adopted. Special landing craft were now equipped with dozens of these racks, arranged in ranks on the deck. Christened 'Stickleback', it carried 1080 5-in rockets which could be automatically fired in 'ripples' of six rockets at a time. This system was vitally necessary as firing all 1080 rockets in one massive salvo would have been spectacular but the enormous blast might well have sunk the ship. As it was, initial firings caused the deck plates to reach enormous temperatures – over 800°F was recorded – and it was not until some genius suggested flooding the ship's deck with a constant stream of seawater that success was achieved without endangering the vessel.

Later, 'Stickleback Mark Two' was developed, which allowed 72 rockets to be fired in each ripple, a technique which allowed the entire ship-load to be launched in a matter of seconds to swamp the target with explosive and flame. Stickleback managed to acquire a variety of names. It began life as 'Grasshopper', then became 'Stickleback' and then, for no very good reason, became 'Sea Mattress'. From this latter name came 'Land Mattress'.

The success of Sea Mattress as a bombardment weapon – some authorities have said that it was the most fearsome shore bombardment device ever handled by any navy – led to suggestions that something similar might be a useful land bombardment weapon for the Army. As it stood, the 5-in rocket as used by the Navy had insufficient range for land bombardment use, only 3500 yards being possible. But the 5-in warhead, carrying seven pounds of high explosive, was too

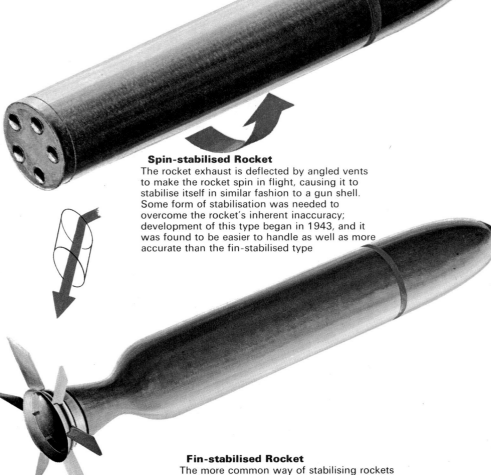

Spin-stabilised Rocket
The rocket exhaust is deflected by angled vents to make the rocket spin in flight, causing it to stabilise itself in similar fashion to a gun shell. Some form of stabilisation was needed to overcome the rocket's inherent inaccuracy; development of this type began in 1943, and it was found to be easier to handle as well as more accurate than the fin-stabilised type

Fin-stabilised Rocket
The more common way of stabilising rockets (originally known as 'unrotated projectiles') was to equip them with stabilising fins, either fixed or made to unfold on leaving the launcher

good to give up without a struggle, and soon came the inspiration to join the Naval 5-in warhead to the Anti-aircraft 3-in motor, thus producing a bombardment weapon which could reach out to the formidable range of 8000 yards.

A thirty-'barrel' launcher on a two-wheeled trailer was devised, and in July 1944 the first models were fired in a series of demonstrations on Salisbury Plain. It was the first time the field artillery had been offered a rocket weapon since the Hale War Rocket of the nineteenth century, and the reception was rather mixed. The general opinion seemed to be that it looked like being a useful 'area' weapon, but that accuracy was poor in comparison with the conventional gun. Hence it was unlikely ever to replace the gun. It would have to be considered very carefully – thank you for the demonstration, don't call us, we'll call you was the reaction.

While the deliberation was going on, so was the war, and in October 1944 the Canadian Army found themselves called upon to assault the German-held island of Walcheren, off the Dutch coast. Walcheren was stuffed with defensive guns and a garrison which didn't look as if it would be inclined to let the Canadians have the island without a struggle, and in weighing up possible methods of attack, the Canadian gunners thought of the Land Mattress. They managed to obtain half a dozen launchers and a stock of rockets. There were, unfortunately, not enough impact fuzes available to fit the shells, but the Canadians managed to locate a stock of very primitive fuzes which had originally been produced for the 5-in chemical rockets. These were completely devoid of any form of safety device once they had been loaded and prepared for firing. As a contemporary report put it: 'It only needs one gunner to slip and fall against a fuze while loading and the result will be swift and fatal . . .'. As a result the British authorities refused to approve these fuzes for service in high explosive shells but the Canadians were less concerned with official approval than they were with capturing Walcheren and took the fuzes to war.

On 1 November 1944 the first Land Mattress engagement took place, the launchers pumping 1150 rockets on to six different German gun positions. The results were spectacular, the German positions were completely wrecked, and the Land Mattress was henceforth assured of its place in the war. An improved fuze was soon produced, a 16-barrel launcher designed, and the rocket batteries were in continuous action in northwest Europe until the end of the war.

Landing craft fitted with banks of rocket launchers proved fearsome bombardment weapons. The empty projectors (right) held 1000 5-in rockets, which were fired in ripples (below), aft rockets first

Imperial War Museum

In the early days of Anglo-American cooperation, much of the British results of their solid-fuel rocket investigations was passed across to the United States, and this mass of information helped US rocket development to get under way relatively rapidly. One of the most useful products was a 4·5-in land bombardment rocket using spring-out fins to stabilise it in flight. This was fired from a tubular launcher, but the fin design gave some problems and very quickly the Americans produced an alternative method of stabilisation which was far more successful.

Instead of allowing the rocket thrust to blast through a single venturi at the rear, the base of the rocket was closed with a plate carrying a number of small venturi outlets, each slightly angled towards the side. As a result the thrust not only propelled the rocket forward, it also spun the rocket to stabilise it. This carried one other benefit: it allowed normal artillery shell

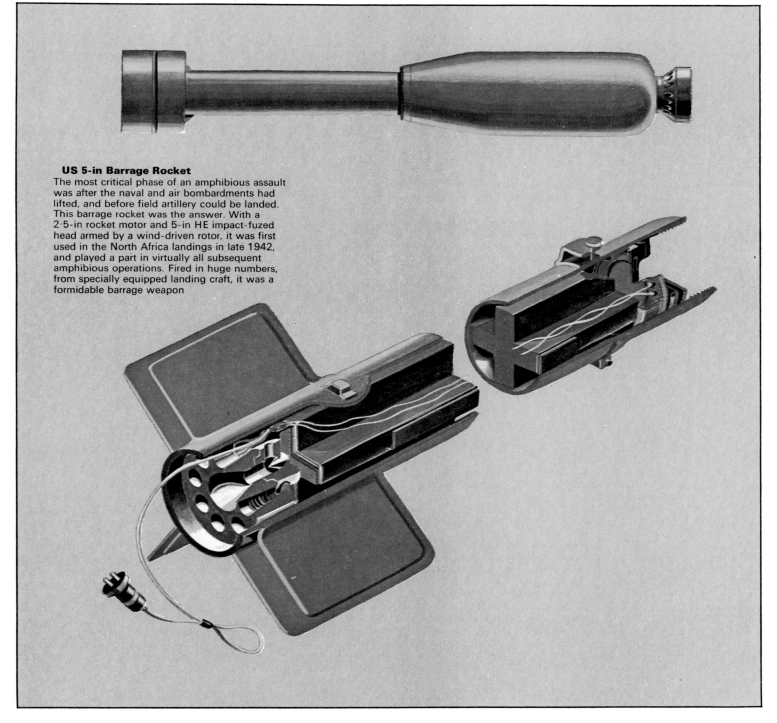

US 5-in Barrage Rocket

The most critical phase of an amphibious assault was after the naval and air bombardments had lifted, and before field artillery could be landed. This barrage rocket was the answer. With a 2·5-in rocket motor and 5-in HE impact-fuzed head armed by a wind-driven rotor, it was first used in the North Africa landings in late 1942, and played a part in virtually all subsequent amphibious operations. Fired in huge numbers, from specially equipped landing craft, it was a formidable barrage weapon

'Stalin's Organ'. Batteries of Katyusha rockets mounted on US Studebaker trucks smash into the heart of Berlin during the final Russian advance

Novosti Press Agency

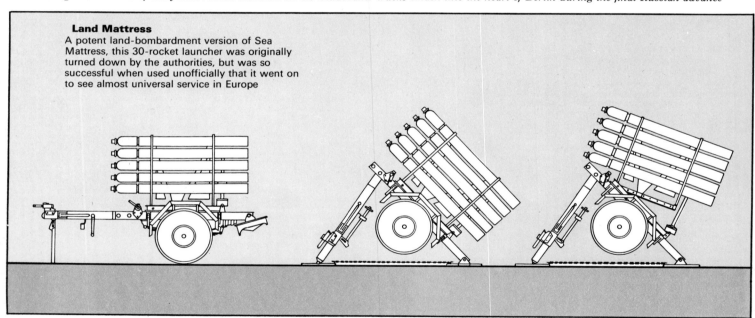

Land Mattress
A potent land-bombardment version of Sea Mattress, this 30-rocket launcher was originally turned down by the authorities, but was so successful when used unofficially that it went on to see almost universal service in Europe

fuzes, which armed on spin, to be used, and saved the designers the problem of having to develop a completely new type of fuze for the rocket. The 4·5-in rocket was issued to artillery batteries and extensively used in both Europe and the Far East theatres with considerable success.

Another land bombardment rocket of great potency was the 7·2-in, a fin-stabilised model which was very similar to the British Land Mattress in having a slender rocket motor pushing an over-sized warhead. Batteries of these were assembled on truck chassis and were used to good effect by, among others, the US Marines on Okinawa.

Probably the greatest contribution of the United States to the war lay in the application of the gasolene engine to every possible problem. The development of self-propelled gun and rocket carriages was enormous, though very few of them ever saw service since they were often superseded by an im-

proved model before they ever got to the production stage. Numerous self-propelled equipments were used to good effect in the war and can hardly be classed as secret weapons, but some of the ones which didn't make it displayed a refreshing strain of eccentricity often absent in other fields.

Some of the early self-propelled gun ideas were little more than the nearest handy gun flung on top of the first available chassis, and it would be straining the imagination to see them as effective weapons of war. But some of the models which were being proposed towards the latter end of the war had every promise of being effective. One notable design was a 10-in mortar in a ball turret on a tank chassis, intended to get close to concrete emplacements and bombard them with enormous bombs, much on the same lines as the British Petard.

An interesting feature of this was the design of a 'follow-through' bomb. For some

time a number of experimenters had been looking at the hollow charge and wondering if something else might be made of it. The normal hollow charge weapon simply bored a hole through concrete or armour plate and relied on the blast of the shaped explosive charge to do some sort of damage behind the target. It occurred to somebody that since the hollow charge had bored this neat hole, it might be possible to use the hole to allow entrance to a second missile which could pass into the target and detonate inside. As a result of this thinking, the 10-in 'Grenade, Shaped Charge, Follow-through' came into being. This was a 10-in calibre bomb that carried a shaped charge warhead, behind which was a small-calibre high explosive shell on guide rails. The shaped charge blew the hole, and the momentum of the bomb threw the shell through the hole to burst inside the emplacement. However, the war ended before it could be perfected.

Sherman with Rocket Launcher
US Sherman tank fitted with 'Calliope', electrically-fired rocket battery capable of single or barrage fire. An extremely useful bombardment weapon which illustrates how widespread was the application of rockets during the war

Follow-through Projectile
The US '10-in Grenade, Shaped Charge, Follow-through' used a hollow charge head to blast through concrete or armour, allowing a second, high explosive shell mounted on guide rails to shoot through the breach and explode inside. It was not fully developed when the war ended

Hollow head

Shaped charge

Follow-through projectile

Guide-rails

Launch cartridge

Spigot tube

Tail drum

Allied heavy tank development: Too heavy to be practical; too late to see service

Black Prince Infantry Tank
An improved version of the Churchill Chassis armed with the powerful 17-pounder, only six prototypes had been completed by VE-Day and development halted
Weight: 50 tons *Engine:* 350 hp *Armour:* 152 mm *Speed:* 11 mph *Armament:* 1×17-pdr; 2 mg

US Super Heavy Tank T28
This massively armoured and heavily armed US tank destroyer was an attempt to emulate German design practise, but was far too unwieldy to have been successful in offensive combat
Weight: 75 tons *Engine:* 350 hp *Armour:* 205 mm *Speed:* 10 mph *Armament:* 1×105-mm; 3 mg

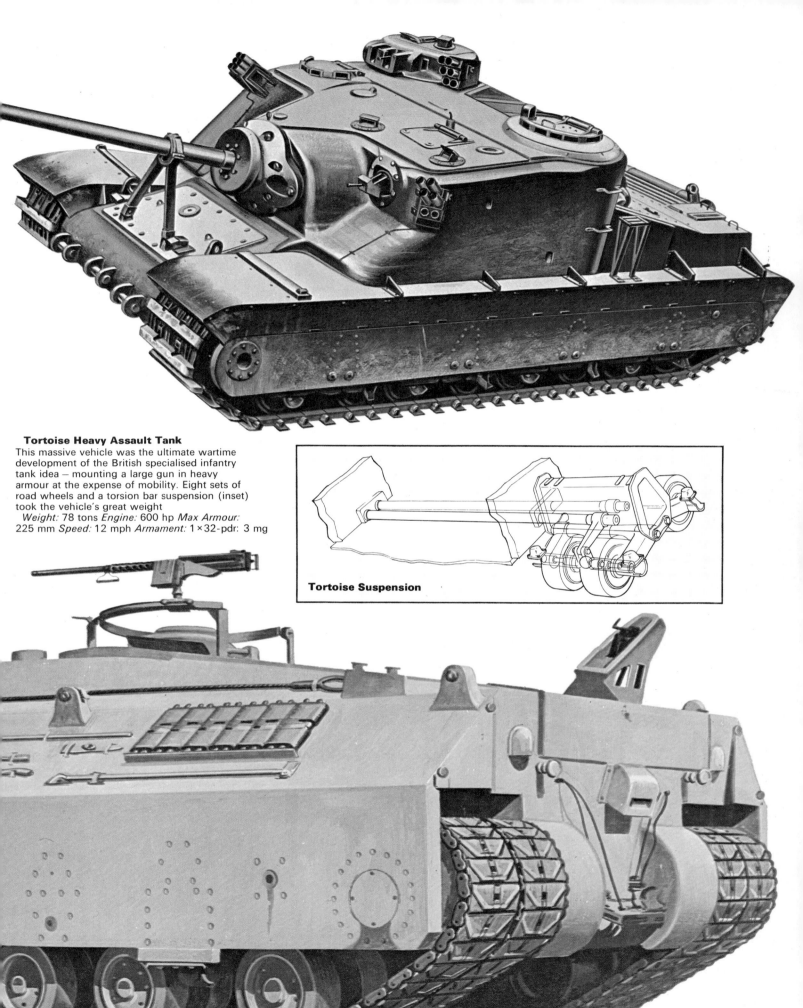

Tortoise Heavy Assault Tank

This massive vehicle was the ultimate wartime development of the British specialised infantry tank idea — mounting a large gun in heavy armour at the expense of mobility. Eight sets of road wheels and a torsion bar suspension (inset) took the vehicle's great weight

Weight: 78 tons *Engine:* 600 hp *Max Armour:* 225 mm *Speed:* 12 mph *Armament:* 1×32-pdr: 3 mg

Tortoise Suspension

As survivors abandon ship under machine-gun fire,
a U-Boat settles by the stern and sinks.

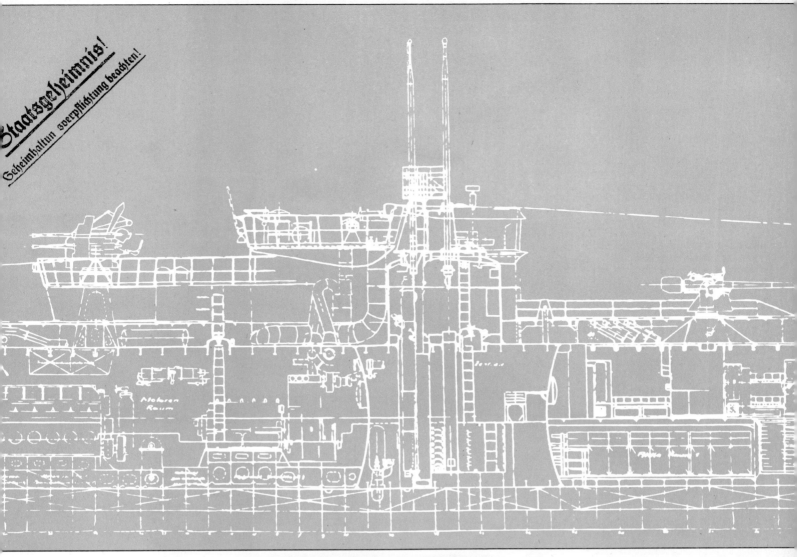

Staatsgeheimnis!
Geheimhaltun zverpflichtung beachten!

THE SEA WAR

BLUE-PRINT FOR THE WILD BLUE YONDER

By the time of the Second World War, the submarine, Germany's principal weapon in the sea war, was hardly a secret weapon. Nevertheless, many of the devices used to boost the U-Boats' powers were, and but for the same old story of political interference and general shortages of men and materials, they might have significantly altered the course of the war

It was the war at sea which first revealed some of the results of German pre-war research. Probably the first surprise for Britain was the liberal use of magnetic mines, but since the Royal Navy had been experimenting with these off and on since the First World War they could hardly be called revolutionary, although the steps needed to counter them involved some hard and fast work. The action against the *Graf Spee* off the River Plate also revealed that the German Navy were in possession of radar. Their radar was not as sophisticated as the British equipment of the time, perhaps, but

it was radar nevertheless, and showed that the British could not afford to sit on their hands in the assumption that the radar they had at the beginning of the war would see them through.

Hiding the U-Boats

But Germany's greatest sea warfare threat came from the submarine, and it was in this field that much of its naval research was directed. Great strides were made in the development of the hydrogen-peroxide motor and the well-known *Schnorkel* which allowed a U-Boat to remain submerged for

much longer periods than had ever been possible before, and this led to much greater difficulties in detecting them. But this development was only just coming into service as the war ended, and for the U-Boats actually in service, the greatest problem was defying detection by the various devices which the British and American naval and air forces were using. One device which came into use was *Bold* or *Pillenwerfer*, a perforated canister containing a chemical mixture. When released into the water from a torpedo-tube, the chemicals reacted to produce a gas, which in turn produced a thick cloud of fine

51

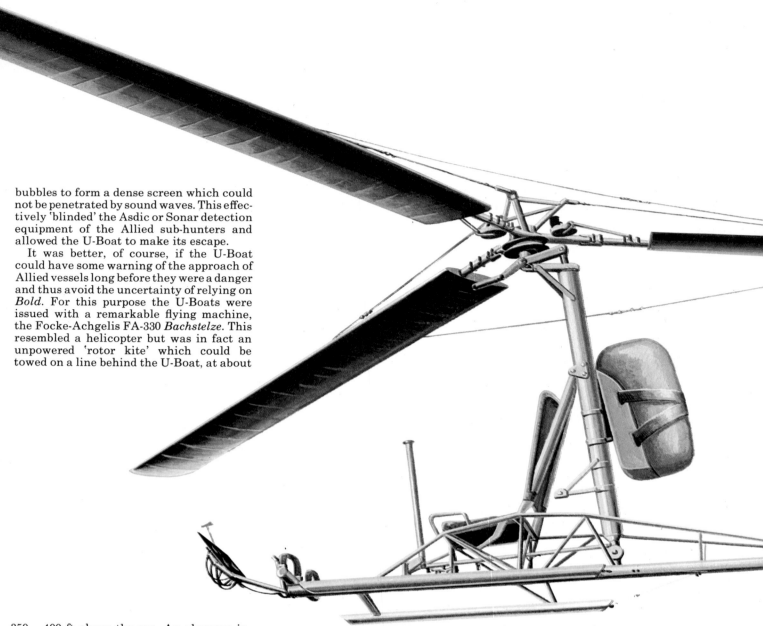

bubbles to form a dense screen which could not be penetrated by sound waves. This effectively 'blinded' the Asdic or Sonar detection equipment of the Allied sub-hunters and allowed the U-Boat to make its escape.

It was better, of course, if the U-Boat could have some warning of the approach of Allied vessels long before they were a danger and thus avoid the uncertainty of relying on *Bold*. For this purpose the U-Boats were issued with a remarkable flying machine, the Focke-Achgelis FA-330 *Bachstelze*. This resembled a helicopter but was in fact an unpowered 'rotor kite' which could be towed on a line behind the U-Boat, at about

350 – 400 ft above the sea. An observer in the kite had a much wider view of the area than was available to the occupants of the U-Boat conning tower, and he could see the approach of ships long before the ships could detect either him or the U-Boat. Whenever the U-Boat surfaced for battery charging or cruising by day, the kite was manned and flown, and was highly successful in giving early warning of the approach of Allied warships and also as a means of detecting convoys or other likely targets. Once something was seen, the kite could be rapidly winched down, dismantled and stowed away, and the submarine could then submerge and take whatever action was necessary. Should an aircraft appear and leave little time for winching, the pilot of the kite could pull an emergency lever which jettisoned the rotor blades and then actuated a parachute; by undoing his seat belt, he then allowed the useless fuselage to fall away while he floated down by parachute. About 200 of these kites were built and used very effectively and remained a secret from the Allies until almost the end of the war, though it appears that they were used less after mid-1944 due to Allied air superiority.

A rather more ambitious extension of this idea was to carry a small aircraft in the submarine which could be stowed away in pieces, rapidly put together when needed and used for reconnaissance. Such a plane

Schnorkel

The *Schnorkel* was under development in Holland when the Germans invaded in 1940. They seized upon it avidly and developed it into a serviceable device. It was simply an air-duct and diesel exhaust closed by a ball-valve which allowed the U-Boat to remain under the surface while still taking in air

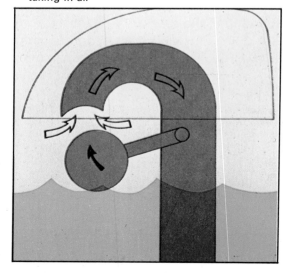

Bachstelze
The Focke-Achgelis rotor kite, towed behind a U-Boat to give the commander a reconnaissance and warning service. While successful in early days, it had to be abandoned due to the difficulty of retrieving it when Allied air activity increased

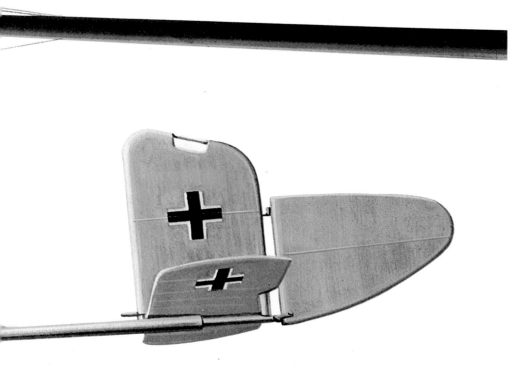

Arado Ar 231
The Ar 231, a lightweight floatplane, was carried by U-Boats as a reconnaissance machine. While effective, it hampered the operation of the U-Boat and was replaced by the *Bachstelze* kite

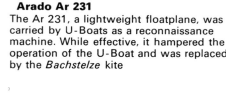

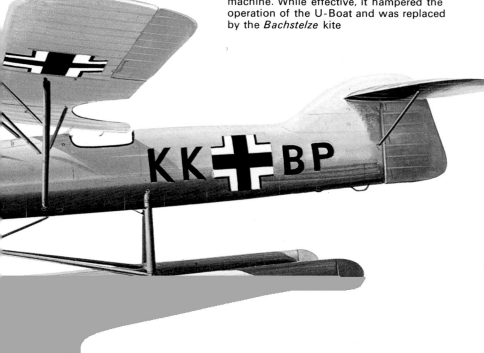

was built; the Arado Ar 231, equipped with floats, which could be stripped down to fit inside a six-foot canister on the U-Boat's after-deck. It had a top speed of just over 100 mph and a reconnaissance range of almost 300 miles, but when some were built and supplied to U-Boats for practical trials it was found that the business of getting the plane onto the deck, stripping it down and stowing it was only feasible when the sea was perfectly calm. With anything more than a slight chop, the job was virtually impossible, and U-Boat commanders were reluctant to hang around on the surface while their crews wrestled with a collapsible aeroplane. The Arado was replaced by the Bachstelze kite, which was almost as effective.

Another offensive-defensive device was the *Wasseresel* (Water Donkey) which was a dummy U-Boat conning tower stuffed with high explosive. This, it was proposed, would be towed along the surface by the submerged U-Boat in order to fool Allied warships into thinking it was the genuine U-Boat. Whereupon it was hoped they would sail full steam ahead in an attempt to ram, and blow themselves up. There is no record of this plan ever succeeding, probably because it appears that it was rarely – if ever – used. U-Boat commanders were very reluctant to go into action carrying a ton or so of high explosive strapped to their decks, and when they were being hunted, they didn't like being held back by the *Wasseresel* being towed at the end of a long line. Unofficial reports seem to show that most of the few which were issued were 'accidentally lost at sea' shortly after leaving harbour.

Improved torpedoes
The principal weapon of the U-Boat was the torpedo, but the torpedo in its simple form has a number of disadvantages. One was its lack of speed. A long-range torpedo might take four or five minutes to reach a target, whereas a gun shell would do the same trip in four or five seconds. This meant that the target could move, zig-zag or dodge before the torpedo got to it; a second drawback proved to be that once the torpedo was launched from the submarine, no correction was possible in order to make it hit the target.

Another defect was that the exhaust from the torpedo engine left a trail of bubbles in the water, and this, combined with the slow speed, gave even more advantage to the target. To try and overcome some of these disadvantages, a variety of torpedo projects were developed in Germany, some of which succeeded and some of which did not. One of the most fundamental was the development by Junkers of a highly efficient engine which would propel a torpedo at 40 knots, cutting the travel time down by half and thus giving the target less chance of manoeuvring out of danger. The Junkers Jumo KM 8 engine was a brilliant technical achievement: consuming its own exhaust gases so as not to leave a telltale trail in the water, it was a 4½ litre V-8 which developed 425 horsepower. This may sound incredible, but it must be remembered that submarine torpedoes were up to thirty feet in length and weighed about two tons, and they needed a highly efficient engine in order to produce workable speeds. However, the development of the motor took a long time, and due to various problems with priorities for material and difficulties in setting up production lines, it never got into production before the war ended.

The other method of trying to overcome

some of the drawbacks was to design a torpedo which would, after launching, actually hunt for its target, using some form of detector. The most obvious effects from the target which lent themselves to detection were the magnetic field of the ship and the noise it made, either by its engines or by the beat of the propellers in the water. The magnetic field was first explored by fitting magnetic-detecting fuzes which would detonate the torpedo even if it ran alongside or underneath the target, but the steps taken by the Allied navies to proof their ships against magnetic mines also proofed them against magnetic torpedoes, so that idea had to be abandoned. But it was impossible to get rid of the noise, and by the middle of the war most U-Boats were equipped with the *Falke* torpedo fitted with the *Zaunkönig* acoustic homing device. This picked up the noise of the ship and steered the torpedo towards it. The *Falke* torpedo was developed by the Torpedo Research Institute at Gotenhafen and was remarkably successful until the Royal Navy realised what sort of a weapon they had to deal with. Very rapidly they produced an incredibly simple antidote – they purchased all the 'Kangol' petrol-driven hammers they could find, fitted them into floats, and towed them behind the ships.

The hammer, beating away in its float, set up much stronger sound waves than did the ship's engine or propeller, and the torpedoes homed themselves on the noisemaking float. The German Navy responded with *Zaunkönig II*, an improved version which, it was hoped, would be able to sort out the noise of the hammer from the noise of the ship and home on the correct target, but a few adjustments to the noise-maker produced such a medley of tones and rhythms that the selective circuits of the new model were completely defeated and the torpedo still homed on the float.

In order to improve the chances of hitting, particularly in convoy attacks, torpedoes with random steering devices were introduced. These would leave the submarine on a set course but after a short time would begin to zig-zag in a random fashion. It was hoped that by this means a torpedo fired straight into the middle of a convoy, without aiming at a particular ship, would eventually zig-zag in such a fashion as to come up against a target. Another steerable device allowed the angle of turn to be pre-set, so that the submarine did not need to be actually headed at a target to launch the torpedo. It could be launched at an angle and would then turn and settle on a direct course.

Probably the development on these lines which appeared to have the greatest chance of success was the *Schnee-Orgel*, an array of ten torpedo-tubes fitted into late model U-Boats and aligned so that the torpedoes, when fired in a salvo, would spread out to cover a 10° arc and thus, again, would be almost certain to hit something in a convoy no matter how hasty the aim. Fortunately for the Allied convoys, very few of these arrays were built before the war ended.

However, the most promising of the German secret weapons at sea was the Type XXI U-Boat. Designed in 1945, it introduced many revolutionary ideas, and incorporated many new developments, including the *Schnorkel*, a streamlined hull, vastly increased battery capacity and rapid reloading for the torpedo-tubes. Technical difficulties meant that the first of them, *U-2511*, did not put to sea operationally until a week before the German surrender, but she was able to evade with ease the British hunter-killer groups she encountered, and made a totally undetected dummy run on a British cruiser before surfacing to surrender. Had production difficulties been overcome, the Type XXI might have made a significant impact; even so, it profoundly influenced all post-war submarine design.

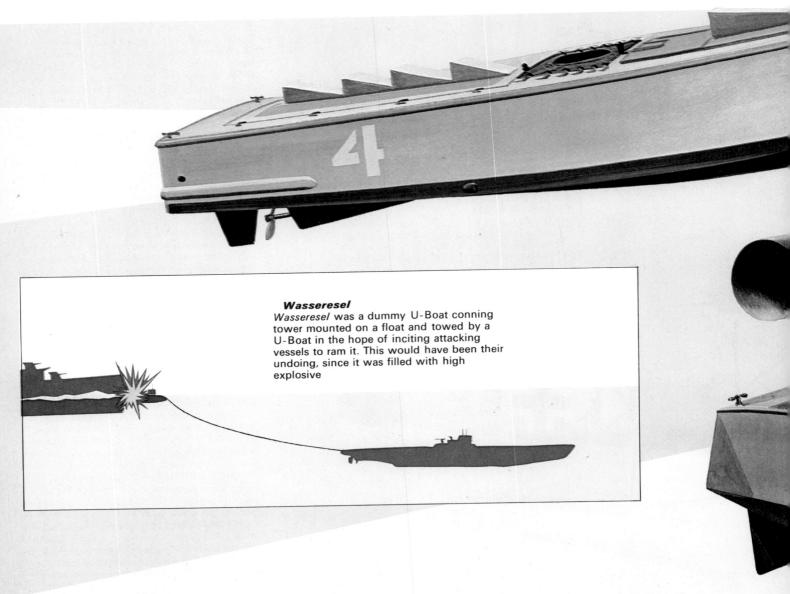

Wasseresel
Wasseresel was a dummy U-Boat conning tower mounted on a float and towed by a U-Boat in the hope of inciting attacking vessels to ram it. This would have been their undoing, since it was filled with high explosive

SINKING A MOORED WARSHIP

Turning now from the high seas, a tactic which attracted a good deal of favour in the German Navy was the possibility of dashing into Allied harbours with fast boats and there either torpedoing or otherwise wrecking as much of the moored shipping as possible. One of the first ideas in this line was *Linse*, a remote-controlled E-Boat capable of 35 knots and carrying a 400-kilogram demolition charge of high explosive in the stern. The theory was that this could be launched from a parent ship out at sea and guided into a harbour, brought up against a moored warship and then detonated by remote control. Some trials were done, but the principal objection seemed to be that even at 35 knots it was still highly likely to be blown up before it ever got to its target, either by shore defence guns or by the guns on the ships in harbour.

More speed was the answer to this, and 'Tornado' was designed. This was little more than a deck holding together two ex-seaplane floats, with the pulse-jet motor of a V-1 missile on top to push it through the water. A 700-kilogram demolition charge was carried in the nose, and the device (it could hardly be called a boat) could be remote controlled as the *Linse*, or it could be driven by a pilot who when close to the target locked the controls and dived overboard in the hope of being picked up later by a rescue boat. This was somewhat faster than Linse, and it also carried a much more powerful charge, but there were difficulties about getting a supply of V-1 motors. Since all the available production was booked for V-1 missiles and since the V-1 programme was by then under way, diversion of the motors to some other project was forbidden.

In no way daunted, the developers went away and, just before the war ended, came back with *Schlitten* (Sledge), which was a hydroplane propelled by a Ford V-8 engine. This could get up to 65 knots, carried the same 700 kilogram warhead as Tornado, and could either be remote controlled or piloted. It must be admitted that it looks as if the designers had got it right this time, but the end of the war prevented the boat from being tried out.

Piloted torpedoes

A more practical method of dealing with enemy ships at anchor was the midget submarine or piloted torpedo – the terms tend to be used interchangeably in German documents. There is a lot more interest in this field than is generally supposed. There were one or two occasions when Royal Navy midget submarines were used during the war, but it is less well known that the Germans, Italians and Japanese all had midget submarines of one sort or another either in service or in the design stage before the war broke out. The first German project

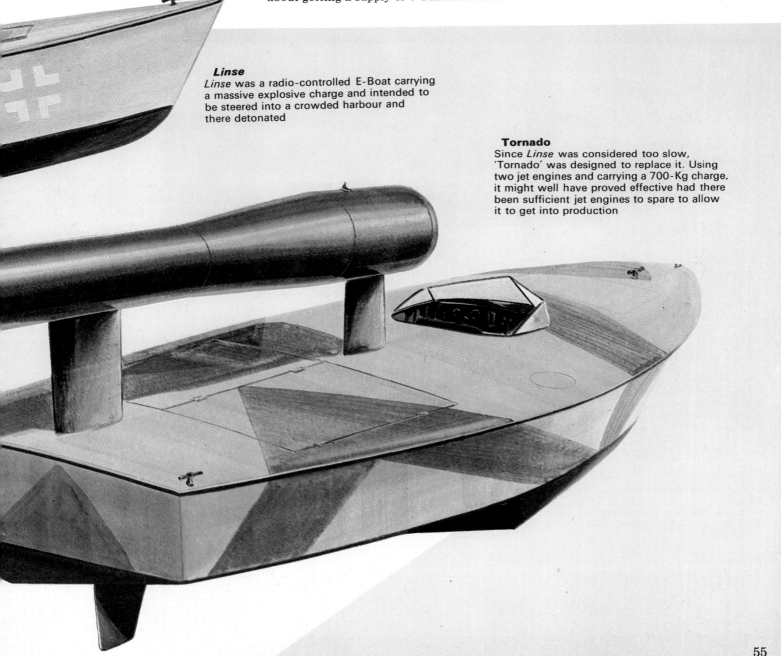

Linse
Linse was a radio-controlled E-Boat carrying a massive explosive charge and intended to be steered into a crowded harbour and there detonated

Tornado
Since *Linse* was considered too slow, 'Tornado' was designed to replace it. Using two jet engines and carrying a 700-Kg charge, it might well have proved effective had there been sufficient jet engines to spare to allow it to get into production

of this type was *Hecht* (Pike), little more than a piloted torpedo with a detachable head. Over fifty of these were built, but they were mainly used as experimental and training vehicles. It was powered by an electric motor driven by batteries, which had neither power nor endurance sufficient for operational work. As a result, an improved model powered by a petrol engine was produced under the name of *Neger*. This also changed the design by placing the engine and pilot in one tubular hull, such that the pilot had his head and shoulders above the waterline, while a 'proper' torpedo was slung beneath and could have its motor started and be launched by the pilot at will.

While *Neger* was satisfactory from the mechanical point of view, it had a drawback in that the pilot had to breathe pure oxygen,

and this tended to restrict its activities since there was a time limit on oxygen breathing. So *Neger* was modified to use a recycling air supply, and became known as *Molch*. Several of these models seem to have been used in late 1944 and early 1945 against Allied shipping in the approaches to Antwerp, but they were not generally successful. *Molch* was shortly superseded by an improved design called *Marder* which was much the same as *Molch* but could be completely submerged for short periods, allowing the pilot to make the major portion of his run awash and then submerge to close in on his target. In order to allow this, the propulsion system reverted to electric motors, but they were rather more powerful than those fitted to the original Hecht series of vessels.

With a certain amount of experience with

these small piloted torpedoes behind them, the designers now became more ambitious and decided to produce a midget submarine, one which totally enclosed the crew rather than having them riding on top. The first model to be produced was called *Hai* (Shark); it was a slender fish-like body which carried one man and was propelled by a petrol engine to give an underwater speed of over 20 knots, a most remarkable performance. It was capable of staying submerged for up to sixty hours stationary, and could travel submerged at top speed for two hours. While it was hardly a practical vessel – it carried no armament, for example, nor was there room for any – as a test-bed it was highly advantageous, and it was remarkably successful for a first try.

With this experience to guide them, the

Hecht (top)

The first German midget submarine to be produced was *Hecht*, a one-man torpedo with a detachable warhead. While it was of little operational use, it taught a lot of lessons which were incorporated in later designs

Molch (above)

An improved model of piloted torpedo was *Molch*, which allowed the pilot to remain submerged for greater periods. Numbers were used operationally

Seehund (right)

The last of the German midgets was *Seehund*, a two-man vessel carrying two torpedoes. This was used effectively in the North Sea during the latter months of the war

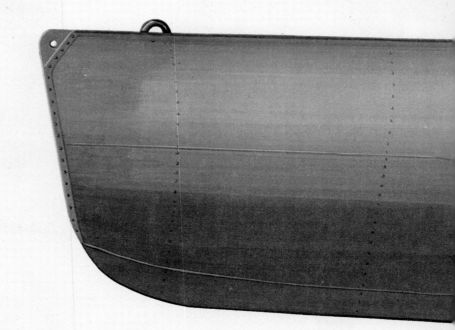

next model was a more warlike device. Called *Biber* (Beaver), it was 19 ft long, displaced three tons and carried two standard torpedoes slung alongside the hull. Originally a one-man affair, the later models allowed a two-man crew to be carried, and a number of these craft were used with success in the Scheldt estuary and also against Russian coastal shipping off Murmansk.

Finally came *Seehund*, a 15-tonner which carried two torpedoes and had a two-man crew. This could move at 8 knots on the surface or 6 knots submerged, and with auxiliary fuel tanks attached to the outside (which could be jettisoned when empty) it had a range of 500 miles. Development of the *Seehund* was completed in 1944 and in January 1945 they went into action, first in the Scheldt estuary and then, according to German sources, against shipping in the Thames Estuary and off Margate. Unfortunately, because of the dislocation in German reports due to the end of the war no definite details of any success they may have had off the English coast has ever been forthcoming, though it is known that they were responsible for the sinking of one or two vessels in the Scheldt.

Shaping the future

After the war, teams of Allied technical investigators descended on Germany and the occupied countries to examine every German weapon factory, research station, development facility and military technical department. They found so much that it was six years before they had finished assessing their results, and over fifteen thousand reports were issued, some of which are still classified documents. Many of the German secret weapons of yesterday are the American, British and Russian secret weapons of today. To give but one example, the most potent and secret part of any nation's armoury today lies in the nerve gas and bacteriological warfare area, and all the basic research on the nerve gases was due to German developments during the war. Without the efforts of Peenemünde there would be no intercontinental ballistic missiles and man would still be wondering whether or not the moon was really made of green cheese. So whether or not the German Secret Weapons had any decisive effect on the war for Germany, they have certainly had a decisive effect on the lives of every one of us since.

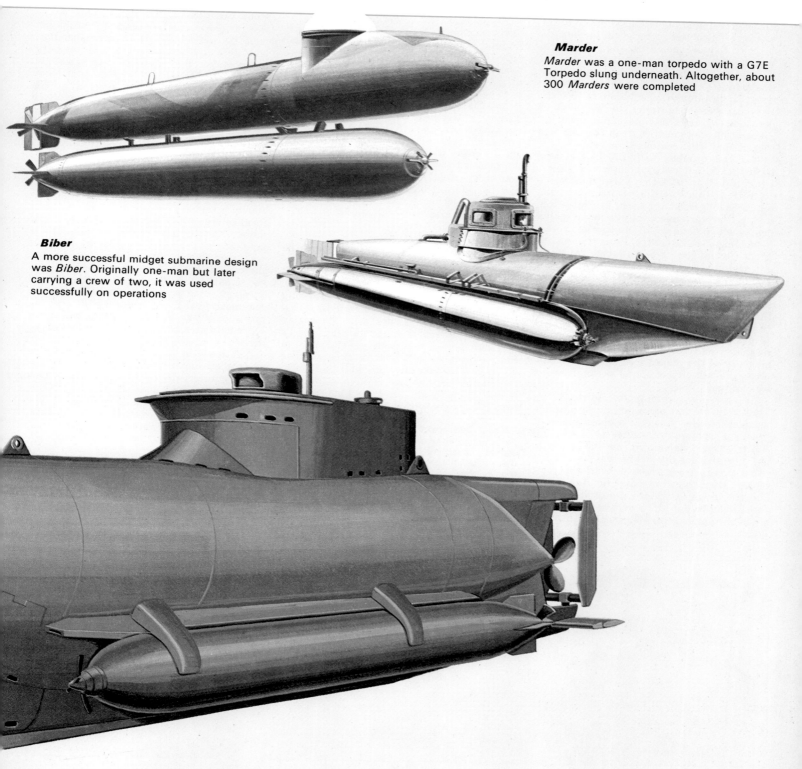

Marder

Marder was a one-man torpedo with a G7E Torpedo slung underneath. Altogether, about 300 *Marders* were completed

Biber

A more successful midget submarine design was *Biber*. Originally one-man but later carrying a crew of two, it was used successfully on operations

FIRST FIND IT SECOND SINK IT

At the time MD1 were developing the spigot mortar designs, the U-Boat was approaching the level of Number One Menace to the Allies, a status it was to retain for most of the war. Experience during the First World War had dictated the adoption of convoys as soon as the war began, and while there was a constant attrition of Allied shipping from the first day, by the middle of 1940 the U-Boats were beginning to make their presence felt more and more, and soon the greatest development effort of the war was turned against this difficult target.

The first problem with the U-Boat was to find it; the second problem was to sink it when found. In 1917 the Allied Submarine Detection Investigation Committee had laboured long and hard on the first question, and, as the war ended, they came up with a device which detected the submerged vessel by means of sound waves. From the initials of the Committee – albeit a rather transparent attempt at security – the weapon was known as Asdic in British service. The system was basically to emit a pulse of sound – a 'ping' – which travelled through the water and bounced from the submarine to be detected once more by the searching ship. The amount of time taken for the 'ping' to pass from transmitter to receiver was a measure of the distance of the submarine, since the velocity of sound through water was known.

At least, it was sometimes known. But as time went on and more and more practice was gained with Asdic, it became apparent that the velocity of sound in water did funny things, depending on the warmth, salinity and density of the water – among other things. Nevertheless, Asdic was a lot better than nothing, and in the early Thirties it was fitted into almost all ships of the Royal Navy. More and more practice made the sailors confident that with Asdic

they could detect the U-Boats a reasonable percentage of the time.

The United States worked on a similar device which they elected to call SONAR (SOund NAvigation and Ranging), and by 1939 this and Asdic were the only systems available for the detection of underwater targets. It was unfortunate that experience soon showed that neither of them was quite as good as their protagonists had hoped. But scientists were turned loose on it and eventually managed to improve the quality and performance of the intruments. Even so, a skilful U-Boat commander, once he appreciated the problems facing the Asdic operator, could make things difficult for him by taking advantage of water density layers and other natural features which distorted or obscured the sound waves.

Prospecting for U-Boats

Other systems of detection now began to be explored; one such was the Magnetic Airborne Detector – now more correctly called the Magnetic Anomaly Detector (MAD). Geologists had used magnetic detecting equipment in pre-war days when prospecting for minerals, making use of sensitive instruments to detect changes in the earth's magnetic field. The presence of such a large lump of iron as a U-Boat in an otherwise metal-free environment should, in theory, be detectable by its influence on the magnetic field, and in 1940 a major step forward came with the invention of a

Asdic Operation

Asdic consisted of a transmitter/receiver which sent out sound impulses and picked up an echo if these struck an object. The time between transmission and the return of the signal would give the range of the target. Asdic had its drawbacks: the receiver picked up echoes from fish and tidal disturbances, and depth-charges obliterated the contact

'saturable-core magnetometer' by Victor Vacquier of the Gulf Research & Development Company in the USA. This device was far more sensitive than any which had gone before, and Vacquier intended it to be a new and sophisticated tool for metal prospectors. But shortly after this the American National Development and Research Council began looking at the submarine detection problem. They realised that one of the very few phenomena not distorted by the passage from air to water was magnetism, and they took Vacquier's device and began to develop it as a submarine detector. By the end of 1941 they had achieved detections on submarines up to 400 ft below an aircraft carrying the device.

The MAD had one great advantage over Asdic: it was passive, ie, it did not emit any form of signal which the submarine could detect. On the other hand, the amount of magnetic disturbance provided by a U-Boat was incredibly small, which meant that the instrument had to be extremely sensitive – so sensitive, in fact, that the detection apparatus had to be aligned with the earth's magnetic field to an accuracy of some six minutes of arc, a figure which called for extremely precise flying by the pilots of the aircraft carrying the detectors.

Another system of detection was passive and relied entirely on the U-Boats themselves giving away their own position. This was the High Frequency Direction Finder, known from its initials as 'Huff-Duff'. The U-Boats were in the habit of surfacing daily in order to radio progress reports and locations to their headquarters in Germany and as a by-product of the electronics research being poured into radar, the Huff-Duff direction finder was born. Fixed land-based stations could detect the faint U-Boat transmissions and obtain a fix on the senders; receivers fitted into seagoing

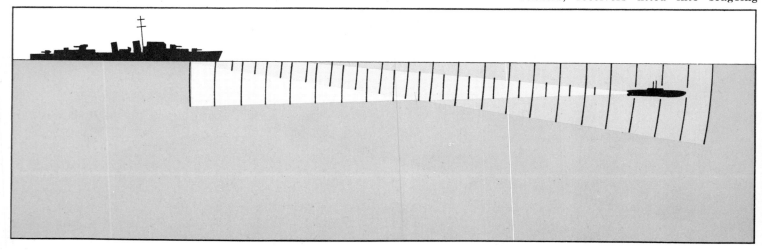

Depth-charges were the usual answer to submarines before 'Hedgehog' was introduced

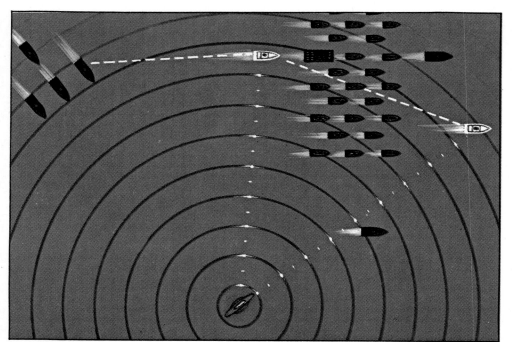

Huff-Duff, or High Frequency Direction Finding, located U-Boats by tracking their radio signals. Two escort ships fitted with Huff-Duff could get a cross-bearing on the U-Boat and relay the position of the target to the 'Hunter Killer' groups which could then get within Asdic range and destroy it

vessels could also be used in conjunction with the land stations to give even more accurate locations. With a search area thus outlined, corvettes and frigates could be sent there to begin searching by Asdic methods instead of wasting their efforts in empty waters.

Eventually, although it is believed that the German Navy never actually knew of Huff-Duff, they must have realised there was the possibility of such detection, and they developed and issued *Kurier*, a high-speed 'squirt' transmitter for basic data. The U-Boat radio operator would set on the dials of *Kurier* such information as latitude, longitude, identification data and a selection of prearranged phrases. Then on pressing a button the operator could transmit all the selected information at very high speed in the form of a short 'squirt' of pulses. The whole message was sent in seconds, thus cutting down the time during which the transmitter was open to detection.

But by that time it didn't matter so much, since radar was in use. The story of radar has been told so often that there is no need to go over it again here, but airborne radar of various types became one of the prime detection devices, although it never entirely replaced the other systems.

Once the U-Boat was detected, the next problem was to attack it and attack it successfully. At the outbreak of war there was only one method in use in any Navy: the depth-charge. This was simply a large steel drum carrying about 300 lb of high explosive, fitted with a fuze which was sensitive to the water pressure at a pre-determined depth. Having detected a submarine by Asdic, the attacker then attempted to position himself overhead and pitch a depth-charge – or a number of depth-charges – over the side as he sailed across. The charges were deliberately designed to sink slowly so that the ship which dropped them had a chance to get away before they went off. Then, having reached the correct depth, the water pressure snapped over a spring diaphragm, driving a firing pin into a detonator and setting off the contents. The subsequent underwater explosion was

sufficient to rupture the plates of any submarine within a hundred yards or so.

But the ocean is a big place and a hundred yards is a small distance and, for a number of reasons, the depth-charge wasn't as efficient as was hoped. First of all the submarine commander had his own ideas on the subject, and as the attacker steamed towards him, he could make an avoiding turn and a burst of speed which would take him out of the danger area. Then again, there was an element of chance about the depth-setting of the charges: the fuzes were not infinitely variable, and the setting had to be one of a small number of variants, based on Asdic readings, experience and hope. And if it was the wrong setting, again the

submarine could escape. Then too, at the critical moment the attacker always lost contact with the submarine; due to various technical reasons the Asdic indication vanished as the attacker moved close and sailed above the U-Boat, and in this dead time the target could often dodge away and be irretrievably lost. At the best of times it could take a few minutes for the attackers to pick up the target again after an attacking run.

The Royal Navy had appreciated all this in pre-war days, and their Underwater Weapons Establishment had been looking for a solution; indeed they had found one, the only trouble being that they couldn't make it work. The solution lay in developing some method of throwing the depth-charge ahead of the ship while the target was still in Asdic contact. Some designs had been drawn up, but the insuperable problem appeared to be the technical one of making a gun of some sort which would throw such a massive weight for a reasonable distance without the force of the recoil wrecking the ship as the weapon fired.

It was at this point that MD1 came into the picture; one of the fundamental points of their spigot mortar designs was that when the bomb left the spigot, the explosion also blew the spigot backwards, recocking it for the next round. Moreover, the firing of the bomb was done by having the spigot run forward under spring pressure to strike the cartridge. Thus the explosion not only forced the bomb off, it also had to halt, and then reverse, the spigot. All this helped to absorb recoil, making it possible, in the case of the PIAT, to fire a heavy and powerful bomb from a manageable shoulder weapon.

An Admiralty research unit heard of the work on the spigot mortars and realised that this offered a method of launching a heavy anti-submarine charge while keeping the recoil force low so that the deck of the ship could withstand it. The problem was passed to MD1 and Jefferis soon produced a design of electrically fired mortar. The

Hedgehog battery on an escort ship. Throwing contact-fuzed bombs in a pre-set pattern (top) designed to straddle the U-Boat gave maximum coverage, and reduced interference with Asdic contact

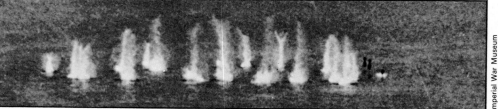

Imperial War Museum

Imperial War Museum

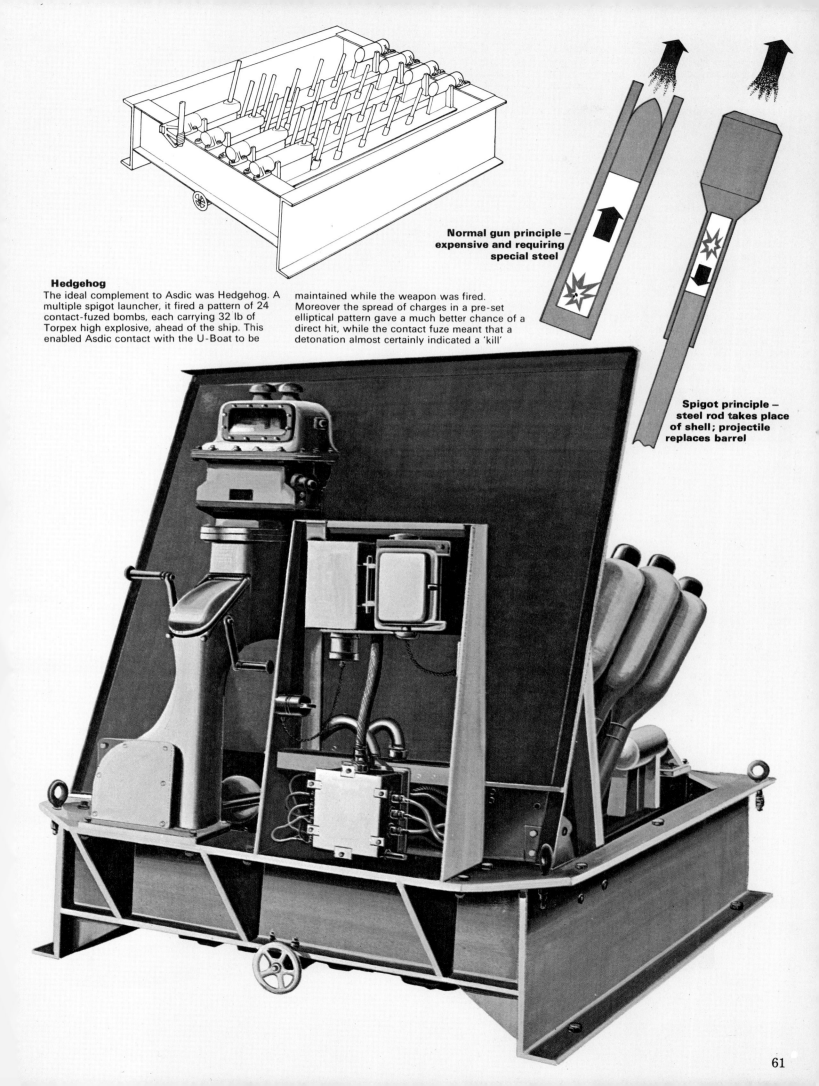

Hedgehog

The ideal complement to Asdic was Hedgehog. A multiple spigot launcher, it fired a pattern of 24 contact-fuzed bombs, each carrying 32 lb of Torpex high explosive, ahead of the ship. This enabled Asdic contact with the U-Boat to be maintained while the weapon was fired. Moreover the spread of charges in a pre-set elliptical pattern gave a much better chance of a direct hit, while the contact fuze meant that a detonation almost certainly indicated a 'kill'

Normal gun principle –
expensive and requiring
special steel

Spigot principle –
steel rod takes place
of shell; projectile
replaces barrel

pre-war investigation had also pointed to the fact that the best chance of killing a submarine would be by firing a group of charges. Tests, however, soon showed that the simultaneous firing would lead to such a strain on the ship's deck as to collapse it, and a timing device was introduced into the firing circuit to fire the spigots in pairs at short intervals.

The next problem was to determine the best method of distributing the charges, and trials on dry land against a tape outline of a typical U-Boat enabled the launching spigots to be aligned so as to drop the charges in a circle, the diameter of which was less than the U-Boat's length. The lethal areas of the charges were so close that the width of a submarine was greater than the space between them, ensuring that there was no way that a U-Boat could escape being struck by a bomb provided the group was correctly aimed.

This was vital to the success of the device, since the system was no longer to rely on depth-sensitive fuzes. It was because the depth-charge was depth-controlled that it had to be so enormous, in order to take effect over a large volume of water. But the charges to be fired by the spigot mortar were much smaller, carrying 30 lb of explosive instead of 300 lb, and since such a relatively small charge had to be in actual contact with the submarine in order to damage it, the new bombs were fuzed to operate only on contact with a target.

Eventually the device was ready, but needed a name. After a variety of suggestions had been canvassed, it was called 'Hedgehog', derived from the spiky appearance of the spigots when the weapon was unloaded. All that was now needed was to 'sell' it to the Royal Navy and have it officially adopted, which was a good deal more difficult than might be imagined. By this time the U-Boat menace had attracted a number of inventors and there were several potential anti-submarine weapons on offer, seemingly with little to choose between them on paper. In fact, none was as good as Hedgehog; one competing design was found to fire its depth-bombs at so low a velocity that the launching ship overtook them in flight and became the target of its own missiles – though fortunately this was discovered in early experiments and not by actually committing this form of water-borne suicide.

Distinguished audience

As luck would have it, Winston Churchill was scheduled to visit the MD1 test ground to witness the trials of another weapon, so by dint of persuasion he was inveigled to a 'spontaneous' demonstration of Hedgehog. It performed admirably (experience shows that weapons frequently become temperamental when asked to display their ability in front of distinguished audiences), Churchill approved, and Hedgehog went into service forthwith.

One slight drawback to Hedgehog was the electrical firing apparatus. This, officialdom felt, might well become deranged by wet conditions in stormy seas – such as existed in the North Atlantic for a considerable part of the year – and it was decided to design a fresh version using percussion firing gear. This was called 'Porcupine', but failed to come up to expectations. One pilot equipment was built and tested, but its operation was erratic and unsatisfactory, and the project was dropped.

While Hedgehog was highly successful, there was still the thought that a bigger bang at the target end might be more effective in the event of a near miss, and so 'Amuck' was developed. This consisted of a Mark II depth-charge holding 180 lb of explosive surrounded by 12 2-in rocket motors. Launched from a simple support of angle iron and steel, Amuck could fling the depth-charge to a 500-yard range. Should less range be required, pairs of rockets could be removed so as to reduce the thrust – a simple but effective control. Although first designed as an ahead-throwing device, it was soon realised that by making the launcher with a rotatable base, the charge could be pitched in any direction, thus

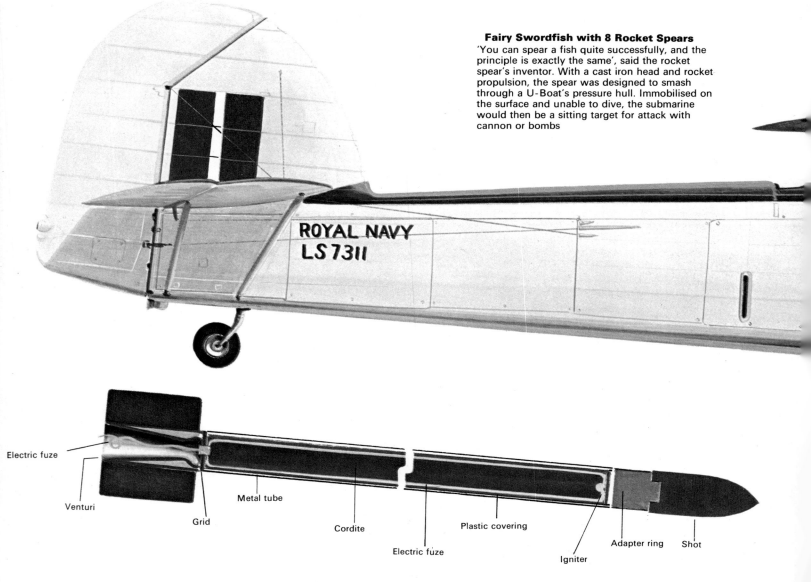

Fairy Swordfish with 8 Rocket Spears
'You can spear a fish quite successfully, and the principle is exactly the same', said the rocket spear's inventor. With a cast iron head and rocket propulsion, the spear was designed to smash through a U-Boat's pressure hull. Immobilised on the surface and unable to dive, the submarine would then be a sitting target for attack with cannon or bombs

Electric fuze

Venturi

Grid

Metal tube

Cordite

Electric fuze

Plastic covering

Igniter

Adapter ring

Shot

Fairey Swordfish launches a rocket spear salvo. Only eight weeks elapsed between the weapon being introduced, aircraft fitted, crews trained, and its use and first submarine kill in Mid-Atlantic

giving the submarine hunter the capability to cover the largest area of sea all around it.

The application of rockets took great strides during the war, as will be explained elsewhere, while in the anti-submarine field the rocket produced two more weapons which were of considerable value. The first was the 'rocket spear', a simple solid-propellant 3-in motor with a 25-lb armour-piercing solid head on the front. Primitive as it sounds, it was perfectly satisfactory, since the requirement was very simple. All that was needed was to punch a hole in the hull of the submarine to prevent it submerging; once trapped on the surface it could be dealt with in a variety of conventional ways.

Officially known as the 'Rocket, Aircraft, 3-inch Mark 1', the spear was issued to the Royal Navy Air Service, and in May 1943 scored a success on its first combat application. A Swordfish aircraft, flown from the escort carrier *Archer* by Sub-Lt Horrocks RN, caught *U752* on the surface. Of a salvo of eight rockets fired, one pierced the submarine's hull, after which a Wildcat aircraft accompanying the Swordfish moved in and machine-gunned the sitting target. The crew of the U-Boat promptly opened the scuttling valves and abandoned ship.

The other rocket application was rather more unusual. Aircraft fitted with MAD equipment were entering service, but the

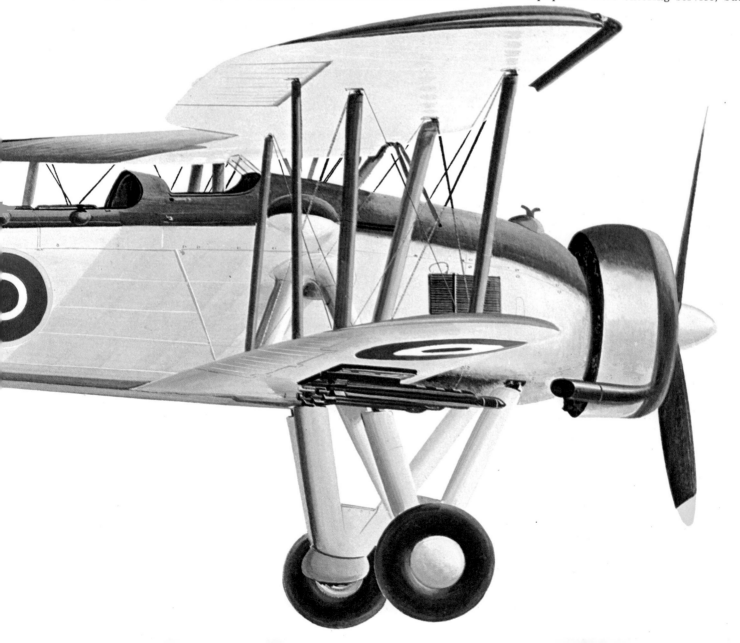

problem lay in how to get them to do something effective when they found a target. The magnetic detector indicated when the aircraft was immediately above the target, too late to drop any conventional form of bomb or depth-charge which would take the usual form of trajectory and land well ahead of the aircraft's position. Rockets or machine-guns could not be used for similar reasons. After considering this problem for a while the California Institute of Technology came up with the answer, a 35-lb 'Retro-Bomb', a normal high-explosive bomb fitted with an impact fuze and with a small rocket motor on the nose. The charge of this motor was carefully calculated to give the bomb a speed equivalent to that of the aircraft carrying it, and the time of burning was also carefully regulated. The result was that when the MAD aircraft detected a submarine, the operator pressed a button which fired the rocket of the retro-bomb. This launched the bomb backwards from the aircraft, with a velocity and length of burn calculated to keep the bomb vertically above the submarine by cancelling out the forward velocity of the aircraft. When the rocket burned out, the bomb then fell vertically on to the target. In order to reduce the chances of missing, the firing circuits automatically fired three salvos of rockets, timed and racked so as to disperse in the air and fall in three 100-ft rows, each ninety feet apart, a pattern which completely covered the length of the average submarine with a bomb density almost guaranteed to hit.

Aircraft fitted with MAD detectors were not used in all sea areas, since for a variety of technical reasons connected with the detection systems only certain geographical localities were suitable. One of the almost-perfect localities, as fortune would have it, was the Straits of Gibraltar, and a force of Catalina aircraft, familiarly known as MAD-Cats, flew patrols there in 1944 which effectively sealed the passage into the Mediterranean against U-Boats.

American technology contributed two

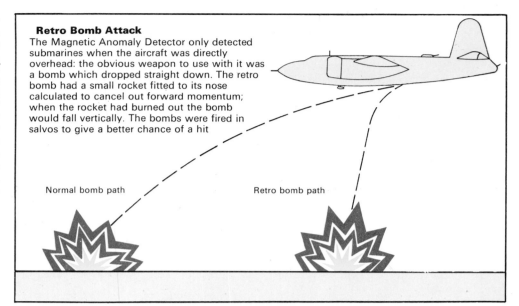

Retro Bomb Attack
The Magnetic Anomaly Detector only detected submarines when the aircraft was directly overhead: the obvious weapon to use with it was a bomb which dropped straight down. The retro bomb had a small rocket fitted to its nose calculated to cancel out forward momentum; when the rocket had burned out the bomb would fall vertically. The bombs were fired in salvos to give a better chance of a hit

Normal bomb path   Retro bomb path

other extremely useful and sophisticated weapons to the undersea fight. In the field of detection came the 'sonobuoy', a cylindrical canister containing sonic detection apparatus. Only 45 in long and four inches in diameter, numbers could be carried by a patrol aircraft and dropped into the sea in a carefully worked-out pattern. Descending by parachute, the buoys switched themselves on and, if any submarine noises were detected, transmitted the signals to the search aircraft. In order that such a useful weapon should not fall into enemy hands, a bung in the bottom of the buoy dissolved slowly and after four hours of searching the buoy sank to the sea bed.

With a suitable pattern of sonobuoys transmitting signals a submarine could be fixed to a relatively small area, and when this had been done the aircraft came in to attack with the second American invention,

the Mark 24 Mine. Called a 'mine' for the sake of security, this was actually a torpedo fitted with an acoustic homing head. When dropped into the water within three-quarters of a mile of the target, 'Fido' or 'Wandering Annie' as it came to be known could pick up the noise of the submarine engines and propeller and home on it with fatal results. In case the initial launch was slightly inaccurate a search routine was built in; if no noise made itself apparent, then Fido would begin circling in the water until such time as it did pick up the 'scent', whereupon it would home.

While such sophisticated devices were effective, there were never enough of them to go round, and, moreover, there was

Mosquito FB XVIII Sea Strike
Fitting a Mosquito with a 6-pounder gun promised to provide an extremely potent weapon. However, official policy swung towards rockets as a simpler proposition and only twelve aircraft were fitted with the gun

always the point that for something as relatively fragile as a submarine, a simple weapon could be just as effective as a complicated one. With this in mind the Royal Air Force had, in 1938, asked for a 40-mm automatic gun to be developed which could be fired from aircraft. As well as for anti-submarine work, it was hoped to use the gun as a weapon against other aircraft; one design, the 'S' gun, was developed by Vickers-Armstrong, while a second design, the 'BH' gun, was developed by Rolls-Royce. The 'S' gun went into RAF service and was largely used in the Middle East campaigns, while the 'BH' guns went to the Royal Navy and were used principally in light coastal craft, though a number went aloft.

Big guns for Mosquitos

However, the 40-mm shot was less effective than had been hoped, and in 1943 came the proposal to take the Army 6-pounder 57-mm anti-tank gun and fit it into an aircraft. As it happened, a highly effective automatic loading device had been developed by the Molins Company in connection with the proposed use of this gun in armoured cars and by the Navy as a deck gun to replace their 'BH' guns. The gun and autoloader were shoehorned into the bomb-bay of a Mosquito aircraft; this was successful at its first trial, as a result of which 12 Mosquitos were fitted with the '6-pounder Class M' gun, as it then became known.

By the time the Class M gun was installed

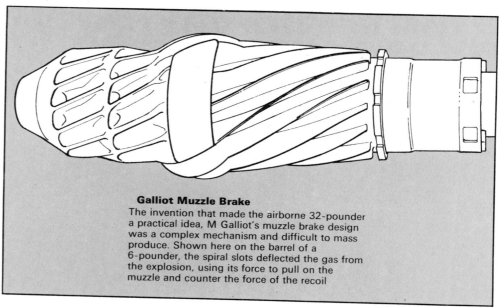

Galliot Muzzle Brake
The invention that made the airborne 32-pounder a practical idea, M Galliot's muzzle brake design was a complex mechanism and difficult to mass produce. Shown here on the barrel of a 6-pounder, the spiral slots deflected the gas from the explosion, using its force to pull on the muzzle and counter the force of the recoil

in the twelve aircraft, official policy had swung towards rockets as being a simpler proposition, and they were the only aircraft to be so fitted. The gun-carriers were issued in October 1943 to 248 Squadron RAF, stationed at Predannack, Cornwall, and on 7 November had their first success. A Mosquito flown by F/Lt Bonnet of the Royal Canadian Air Force came upon *U123* near Lorient and went in to the attack with his 6-pounder. The submarine turned back to base after the attack, and post-war investigation revealed that it had suffered seven holes in the pressure hull, a petty officer killed and two seamen wounded.

It might be expected that, having used the same calibre as the military anti-tank guns in 2-pounder and 6-pounder sizes, the RAF would have asked some leading questions about the next Army anti-tank gun, the 17-pounder. But there is no trace of any such suggestion being made. Instead, the RAF jumped straight across to the biggest calibre the Army have ever used in a con-

ventional anti-tank gun, the 3·7-in 32-pounder. This gun, which never saw service, can best be visualised as the barrel of the 3·7-in anti-aircraft gun mounted onto a two-wheeled field gun type of mounting. It fired a 32-lb armour-piercing shot at 2880 ft per second, and would undoubtedly have been one of the most potent anti-tank guns of the war had it arrived in time; as it was, the war was over before it was ready, and work on it was abandoned. Early in its career, however, while it was still little more than a mock-up, the RAF armaments design department had begun making calculations. With a new version of the Molins auto-loader, it was predicated as an air-to-air weapon, as well as an air-to-surface one, but the prime problem seemed to be keeping the aircraft in one piece when it was fired. The solution was to cut down the recoil force by fitting a highly complex muzzle brake, a product designed by a man called Galliot. Galliot had escaped from France in 1940 and was working in Britain as a

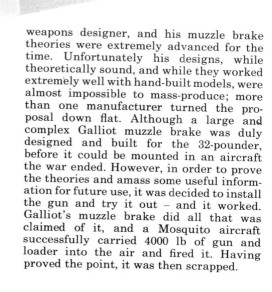

weapons designer, and his muzzle brake theories were extremely advanced for the time. Unfortunately his designs, while theoretically sound, and while they worked extremely well with hand-built models, were almost impossible to mass-produce; more than one manufacturer turned the proposal down flat. Although a large and complex Galliot muzzle brake was duly designed and built for the 32-pounder, before it could be mounted in an aircraft the war ended. However, in order to prove the theories and amass some useful information for future use, it was decided to install the gun and try it out – and it worked. Galliot's muzzle brake did all that was claimed of it, and a Mosquito aircraft successfully carried 4000 lb of gun and loader into the air and fired it. Having proved the point, it was then scrapped.

THE BOMBER OFFENSIVE
GETTING THROUGH TO THE TARGET

Bombing, both tactical and strategic, was a most important part of the Allied war effort. Radar, of course, played a vital part in this, and against the background of a continuous battle of wavelengths, bombs of all types and sizes were produced.

One of the most common misconceptions generally held about the Allied bombing offensive is that the Allied air forces were quite happy with small bombs until sometime in the middle of the war when they realised that heavier bombs were going to be needed, whereupon they went into a crash designing action. Like many other common beliefs, this isn't entirely true. The Royal Air Force were well alert to the need for heavy bombs and were busy with the designs of bombs up to two tons in weight well before the war broke out.

The principal trouble lay in the contemporary aircraft. In the pre-war days, it would seem, the aircraft designers set out firstly to make an aeroplane which flew at the speed and height required, and afterwards set about hanging a bombload on it. It was not until the experience of war showed the fallacy of this method that they reversed their priorities and began designing bombloads and then putting a suitable aeroplane around the outside of them. Once this system took over, it was possible to fit the enormous bombs in and actually carry them. While the Flying Fortress and some of its contemporaries could carry impressive weights of bombs, their construction made it necessary for the bombs to be small ones, and it was not until the advent of the British Lancaster, with its 33-ft long unobstructed bomb-bay, that really big bombs could be carried.

However, not all bombs have to be big ones, and some of the most effective bombs, and the ones of which little is known, were quite small. They were also highly specialised in their application, as, for example, the British 8-lb 'F' bomb. The letter 'F' seems to have had no special significance, since many of the British bombs were in a lettered series, but it is coincidence that this bomb was officially demanded for 'fouling' airfields. In other words, they were to be scattered by dozens across German military airfields in order to prevent aircraft from taking off or landing and involve the airfield staff in a massive clean-up operation before the field could be serviceable. These small bombs were fitted with an 'anti-disturbance and delay' fuze so that after landing on the ground they would lie there and detonate at random intervals up to six or seven hours after landing. This, of course, constituted a considerable hazard and it was necessary to

A 'Grand Slam' is hoisted from an RAF bomb dump. Such a colossal bomb (22,000 lb) could drill deep into the ground setting off 'earthquake' tremors to destroy the most massive of structures

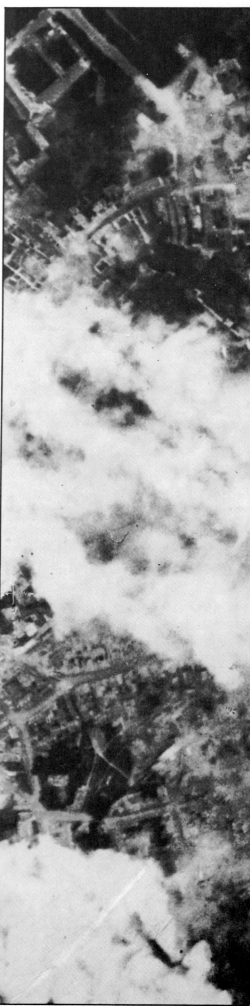

Window was lengths of tinfoil corresponding to German radar wavelengths which, when dropped, produced a vast number of echoes

Mandrel: pairs of circling aircraft radiating signals with jamming devices formed a barrier which German radar could not penetrate

The radar war:
Jamming
and counter-jamming

Piperack was an enormous jamming transmitter carried in a lead aircraft, behind which Allied bomber streams could shelter in a radar-proof cone

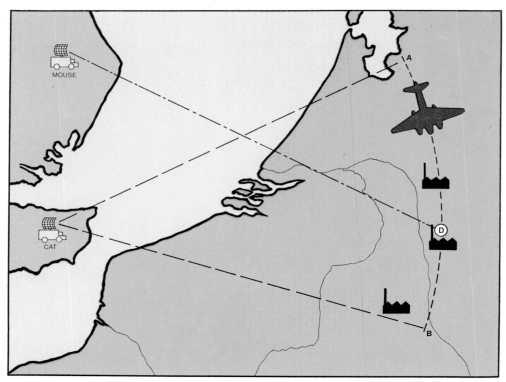

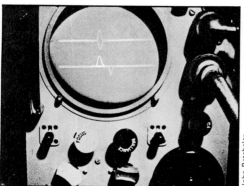

Oboe: Signals were transmitted from 'Cat' and 'Mouse', and returned by the aircraft, thus fixing its distance from the Cat. When it reached a pre-calculated distance from the Mouse it was over the target D. Oboe's range of 270 miles encompassed the Ruhr. *Above:* Oboe's twin 'blip' screen and navigator's position. A pair of transmitters controlled one aircraft, limiting its use to Pathfinder Mosquitos

nomy. Several raids had been directed against this target, but it was a difficult article to hit and it had survived most of the war unscathed. A single Earthquake bomb dropped several yards away was sufficient to bring several arches of the viaduct crashing down, closing that particular line for the remainder of the war.

Six-ton smash

An earlier design of Wallis's, the 12,000-lb 'Tallboy', had similar characteristics and was widely used for interdiction bombing prior to the Allied invasion and for attacking rocket launching sites. One spectacular result was the attack by the Royal Air Force of a railway tunnel in France, through which trains carrying troop reinforcements were likely to be rushed to counter the invasion. A single Tallboy dropped on the hill above penetrated through the solid stone overlay, entered the tunnel and detonated, and brought the entire hill down on top of the line. This meant another rail link was permanently closed to the German Army.

The most formidable targets on the Continent to confront the RAF were the immensely strong submarine pens which the German Navy had built in the Channel Ports to protect their U-Boats. These were massive concrete structures inside which

Razon Bomb (Range and AZimuth ONly)
In a standard bombing approach, once the bomb aimer released his bombs that was it. By fitting a radio receiver, movable rudders, and a gyro-stabilizer to a standard 1000-lb GP Bomb, US designers came up with a formidable unpowered guided missile

get out on the field and clear them away. In order to confound this activity, the other half of the fuze, which became sensitive only after landing, reacted to any movement of the bomb. Any attempt to pick it up or sweep it away detonated the charge to the detriment of whoever was trying to shift it. Numbers of these bombs were also included in normal air raids on factories and other targets in order to make life difficult for the fire-fighting parties.

An interesting American development in the bomb field was the attempt to produce a 'Slow Burning Explosive', called SBX for short. Experience had shown that the sharp blast of a conventional high explosive bomb frequently had little effect on a building other than blowing in all the windows, while records of industrial and mining explosions showed that the slow, heaving effect of coal-dust and similar explosions seemed to have a better effect in wrecking buildings and work began on trying to adapt this principle to a weapon.

Bombs filled with coal-dust and flour, stone-dust and similar finely divided substances were developed, and controlled experiments in old buildings showed that the theory was quite correct: SBX – a comparatively small bomb completely obliterating a large building in slow motion –

had a devastating effect. But the practical problems of controlling the operation so as to obtain the perfect proportions of dust and air eventually defeated the experimenters. Finally, of course, the development of the nuclear bomb removed any need for the SBX bomb.

In the large bomb field, most of the oddities came from Britain, the USA being solely interested in straightforward large bombs which would achieve their aim by blast effects alone. But in Britain was Barnes Wallis, a remarkable inventor who had some definite ideas on making bombs work in other ways. His most famous achievement was, of course, his cylindrical bomb used for the attack of the Möhne, Eder and Sorpe dams in Germany, but some of his other designs were probably more significant. His 22,000-lb 'Earthquake' or 'Grand Slam' bomb, for example, was a piercing bomb which went through the sound barrier on the way down, developing sufficient terminal velocity to plunge deep into the ground before detonating. Thus, when it went off, it sent shock waves through the earth to attack the foundations of nearby structures. Its most famous application was against the Bielefeld Viaduct, which carried a main railway line of vital importance to the German war eco-

the submarines could shelter while being repaired, serviced and restocked preparatory to a fresh sweep into the Atlantic. The roofs of these pens were initially some 3·5 metres thick, but they were generally added to with successive layers of concrete and brick until some of them reached 30 or 35 ft in thickness. Normal bombs simply landed on the roof, detonated, and did no damage at all, and it was not until the advent of the Tallboy and Grand Slam bombs that any impression was made.

But the full and final answer to the U-Boat

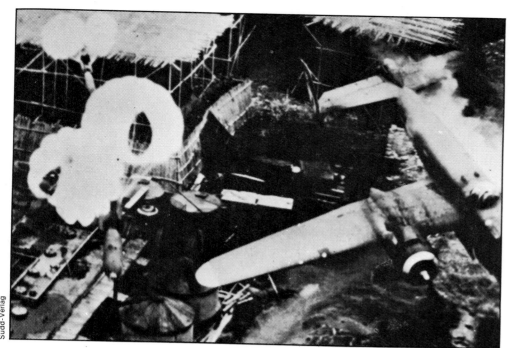

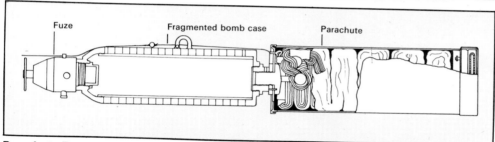

Parachute Fragmentation Bomb A small fragmentation bomb incorporating a parachute container: on being dropped from an aircraft, the parachute opened and the bomb floated down to explode in mid-air, showering shrapnel. *Top:* A B-25 Mitchell parachute bomb over a Japanese factory

pens turned out to be a bomb developed by, of all people, the Royal Navy. It may seem a little odd that the sailors were concerning themselves in what appeared to be Air Force business, and indeed the project ran into stiff opposition on no better grounds than that, but looked at from another direction it was quite logical. The Navy's business was to deal with the U-Boat, and if they could catch the U-Boat while it was unprepared in its pen, then this offered a considerable advantage in the battle. Hence their interest in aerial bombing of the pens.

The Navy's idea was born in September 1943 when Commander (later Captain) Terrel OBE, one of the staff of the Admiralty Miscellaneous Weapons Development Department, suggested using a rocket to drive a piercing bomb through the roof of the submarine pens so that the bomb could be detonated inside the pen. A design was drawn up for a 4500-pounder propelled by nineteen 3-in rocket motors. It was to be dropped from an aircraft at 20,000 ft and, after falling slowly, a barometric device would initiate an ignition system and fire the rockets 5000 ft above the ground. This would accelerate the bomb to a speed of 2400 ft per second to give it immense penetrative ability.

Indeed, it was this last portion of the flight which caused the greatest worries, since it meant that the bomb would pass through the sonic barrier, and at that stage of the war there was very little known about the performance of missiles at supersonic speed. The Barnes Wallis Tallboy and Earthquake bombs were also supersonic at the end of their drop, and had to be given canted fins to rotate them in order to overcome stability problems in the transsonic region, and the Air Force were not slow to point out the potential troubles ahead. But the Navy, very shrewdly, pointed out that they had been firing cannon shells at supersonic speeds since before the Air Force existed, and they were going to make their bomb the same shape as a cannon shell. The arguments were interminable and on a very high level indeed, but eventually the Admiralty were given authority to go on with their design, and in the spring of 1944 the first trial bombs were dropped. The design worked surprisingly well, and the Admiralty's faith in their design was vindicated. But now came problems in getting the necessary manufacturing capacity for the bombs, and it was not until February 1945 that the weapon was first used in action.

Due to its size the rocket bomb could only be carried beneath the wing of the American B-17 Flying Fortress, and the first attack with the bomb was mounted by the US 92nd Bombardment Group against the U-Boat pens at Ijmuiden in Holland. The bombers achieved direct hits on the difficult targets from 20,000 ft, and the bomb-aimers reported seeing flames and smoke coming out of the entrance to the pens, indicating that the bombs had, as planned, penetrated the concrete cover and detonated inside the pen, destroying the anchored U-Boats there. In the following month an attack was made on the heavily protected U-Boat assembly plant at Farge, on the Weser River 15 km north of Bremen. This was still uncompleted at the end of the war and was the hardest target of all, the roof being a solid prefabricated slab seven metres thick. Even this did not stop the rocket bombs. Unfortunately for the research scientists who were learning something new with each attack, the war ended without any further attacks with this weapon.

The rocket bomb turned out to be startlingly accurate, but the same could not be said for all bombs, since the mass-produced blast bombs were devoid of any sort of ballistic shaping and were little more than square-ended drums of explosive with fins on the end to give them some reasonable stability. Another factor militating against accuracy was the question of flying a bomber into a hail of anti-aircraft fire and expecting the bomb-aimer to keep cool, calm and collected while he aimed his bombs. As a result the Americans began to look at the prospect of developing bombs which could be released some distance away from the target and guided in their flight. The first to appear was 'Gargoyle', a winged bomb fitted with liquid-fuel rocket boosters. This had no guidance, but the rocket boost and wings gave it a degree of stability which allowed its flight to be accurately predicted. This went into production late in 1944 but was never used during the war.

More effective was the radar-guided bomb 'Bat'. Using rocket-boost, this had a range of 20 miles and could be controlled with remarkable accuracy. It was never used in the European Theatre but saw some striking successes in the Far East, where Japanese supply lines in Burma were cut by guiding the Bat on to river bridges. Among its achievements was the sinking of a Japanese warship in April 1945 at the maximum range of the bomb.

'Bat' Guided Bomb
The US 'SWOD Mk 9 "Bat" 1000-lb Bomb' was a radar guided air-to-surface missile with a 1000-lb warload. In April 1945 an air-launched Bat sank a Japanese destroyer 20 miles from its launch point, its maximum range

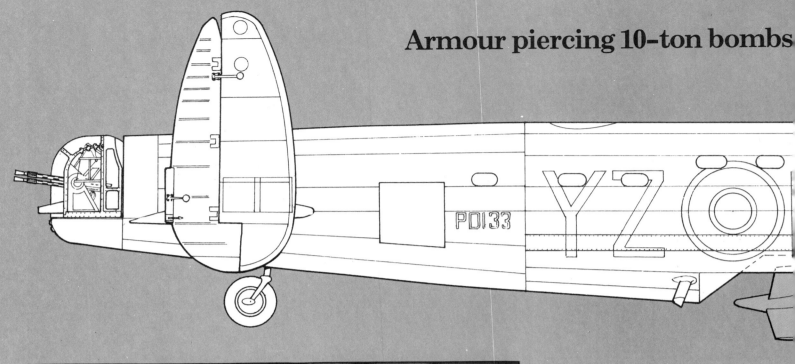

Primary target of the deep-penetration super-bomb offensive were the massive concrete U-Boat pens (above) stretching along the Atlantic Coast from Brest to Bergen. Barnes Wallis's bombs were both streamlined and armoured, capable of withstanding the shock of smashing into concrete at a velocity greater than the speed of sound to explode deep within the target. Left: What the 'Grand Slams' did to the U-Boat pens, 15 feet of reinforced ferro-concrete drilled straight through

falling at Mach 1: The way to crack the toughest nuts

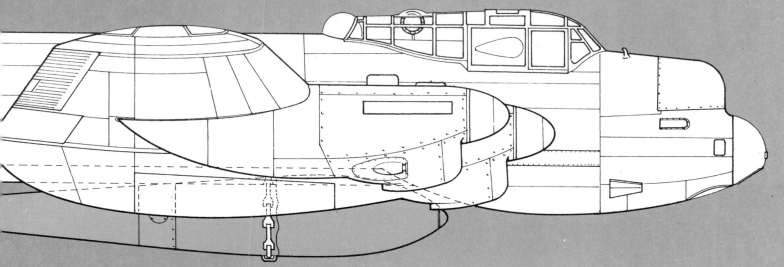

Avro Lancaster B Mk I Special ('Grand Slam')
A special version of the Lancaster to enable it to lift the 22,000-lb 'Earthquake' or 'Grand Slam' bomb
Span: 102 ft *Length:* 69 ft 6 in *Engine:* 4×1280 hp Rolls-Royce Merlin
Max speed: 280 mph *Armament:* 4 mg *Bombload:* 22,000 lb

Winching a 'Tallboy' up to a Lancaster BIII. With its cavernous bomb-bay, the Lancaster could carry the 12,000-lb bomb to almost any part of Germany

Imperial War Museum

What 'Tallboys' did to the Tirpitz. Thirty-two Lancasters bombed the battleship at its heavily guarded anchorage in Tromsöfiord (below). Two bombs penetrated its armour to explode deep inside the hull, capsizing the ship

Imperial War Museum

Lancaster Special B Mk III ('Dam Buster')
A Lancaster of the type that attacked the Ruhr Dams
Span: 102 ft *Length:* 69 ft 6 in *Engine:* 4 Packard Merlin 224 *Armament:* 6 mg *Speed:* 287 mph at 11,500 ft *Ceiling:* 24,500 ft *Range:* 1660 miles *Bombload:* 14,000 lb

Spinning the bomb backwards made it hurdle the torpedo nets, press itself against the inner face of the dam and sink to explode at its base – as was essential. It was the 'earthquake' effect of the shock waves which did the damage. Dropping height was determined by the alignment of pre-fixed lights, while distance was computed by sighting the dam towers in a simple frame pre set from reconnaissance to give the exact distance

The Dam Busters: The story of the Bouncing Bomb

The target: Möhne Dam and its torpedo nets

Ten minutes before attack, the cylindrical bomb was spun backwards at 500 rpm, and released by allowing the calipers to spring outwards

Imperial War Museum

The morning after the raid, with Möhne Lake rapidly emptying

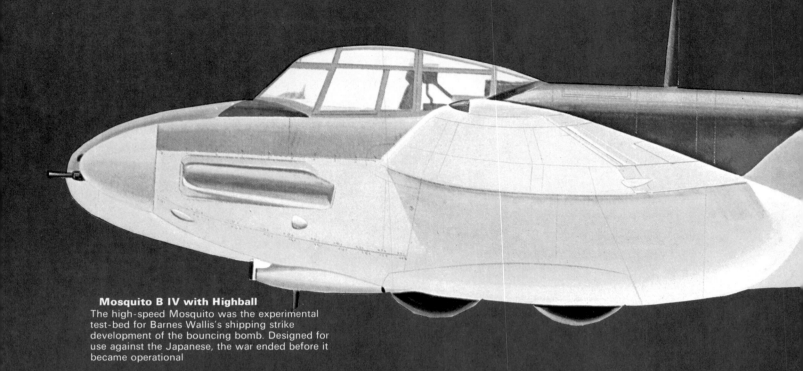

Mosquito B IV with Highball
The high-speed Mosquito was the experimental test-bed for Barnes Wallis's shipping strike development of the bouncing bomb. Designed for use against the Japanese, the war ended before it became operational

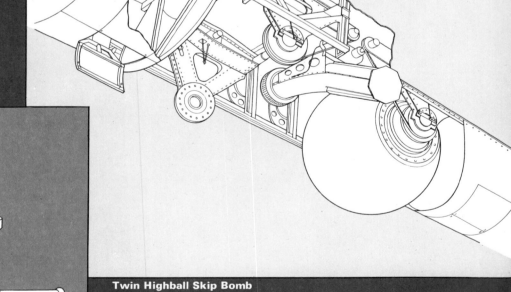

Twin Highball Skip Bomb
Highball was experimentally installed in tandem in a Mosquito B IV. A spherical case was devised with excellent 'bouncing' characteristics and strong enough to withstand impact with the water

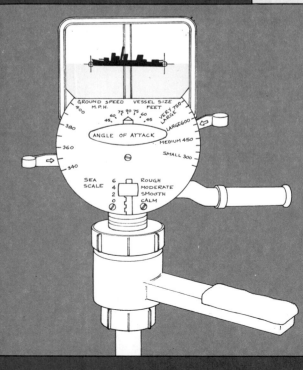

Highball Bomb Sight
All the relevant information on the attack — size and speed of target, angle of attack and condition of sea — was computed on the special bomb sight, which set the viewfinder and ensured that the bomb was aimed correctly

The Highball project: A potent new way of attacking a ship

Barnes Wallis – designer of the R100, the geodetic Wellington, the Dambuster bomb, the 'Grand Slam' and 'Tallboy', and the experimental Highball bouncing bomb

Imperial War Museum

Vickers Ltd

Mosquito launches a Highball (left) at a pre-set height. The bomb bounces towards its surface target carrying a far greater warhead than any standard air-launched torpedo. These stills are taken from a film of a test launch

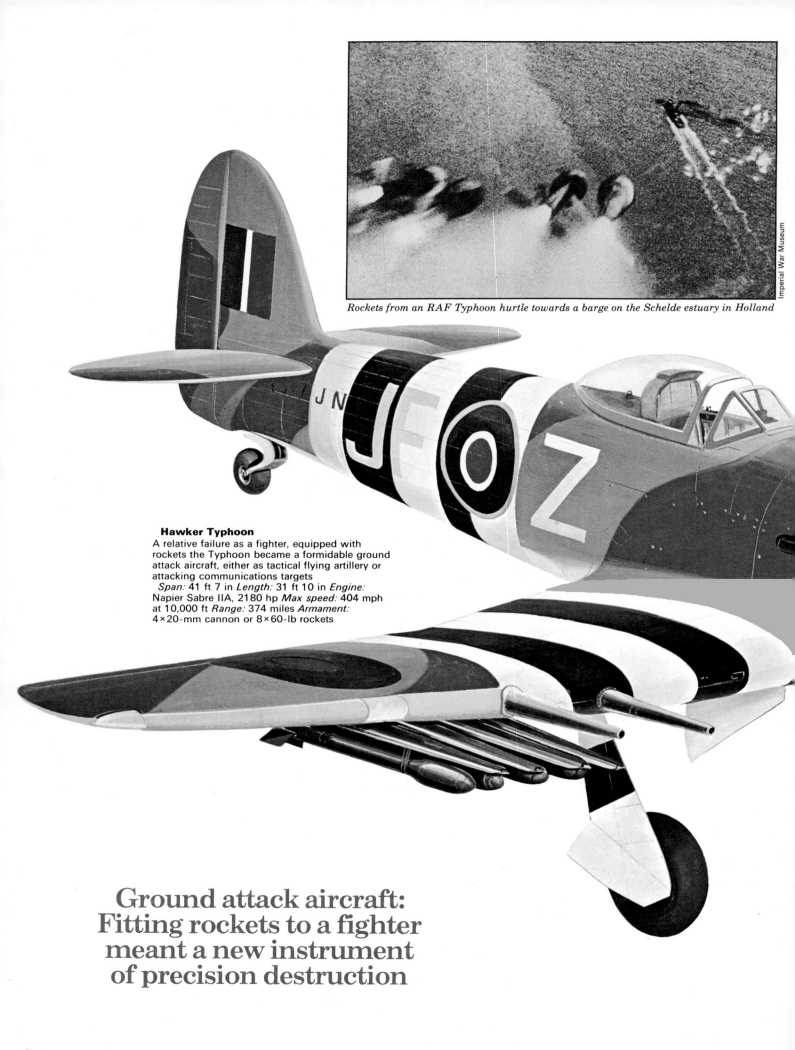

Rockets from an RAF Typhoon hurtle towards a barge on the Schelde estuary in Holland

Hawker Typhoon

A relative failure as a fighter, equipped with rockets the Typhoon became a formidable ground attack aircraft, either as tactical flying artillery or attacking communications targets
Span: 41 ft 7 in *Length:* 31 ft 10 in *Engine:* Napier Sabre IIA, 2180 hp *Max speed:* 404 mph at 10,000 ft *Range:* 374 miles *Armament:* 4×20-mm cannon or 8×60-lb rockets

Ground attack aircraft: Fitting rockets to a fighter meant a new instrument of precision destruction

Beaufighter-launched rockets streak in to destroy the German headquarters on the Aegean island of Calino in 1944 after the first salvo had missed (left)

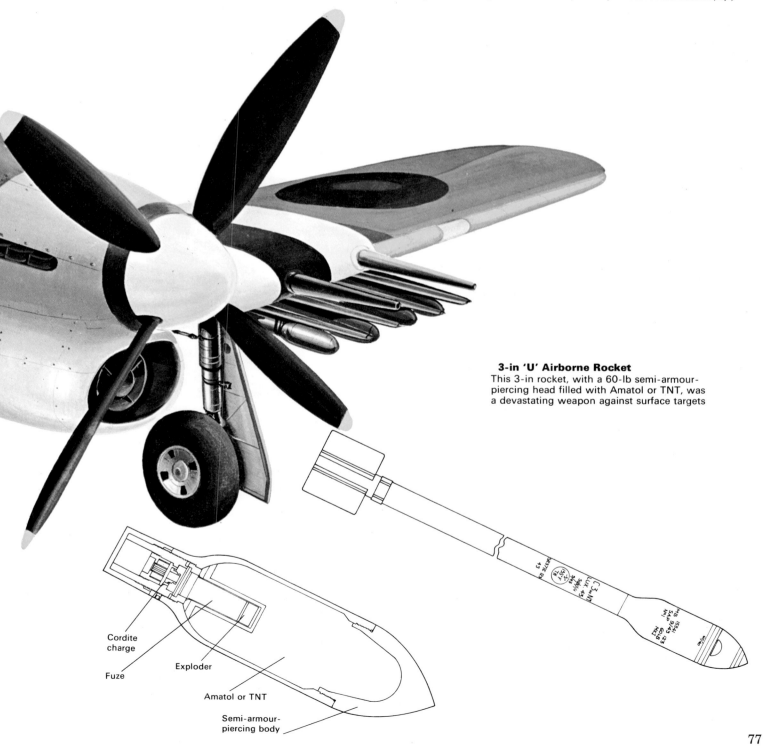

3-in 'U' Airborne Rocket
This 3-in rocket, with a 60-lb semi-armour-piercing head filled with Amatol or TNT, was a devastating weapon against surface targets

Cordite charge

Fuze

Exploder

Amatol or TNT

Semi-armour-piercing body

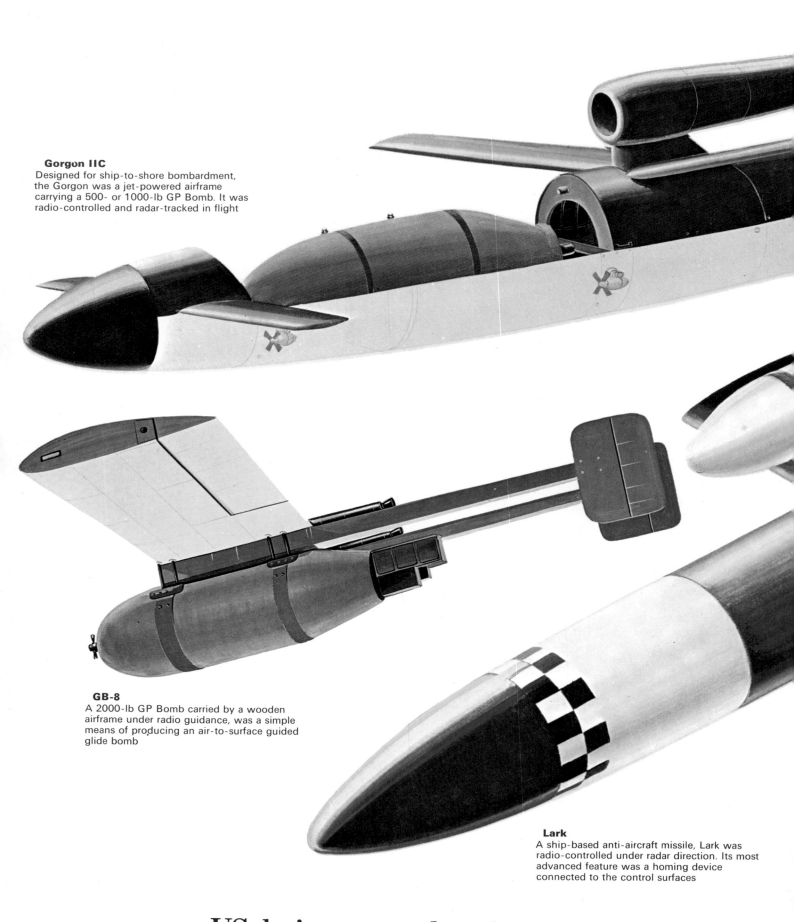

Gorgon IIC
Designed for ship-to-shore bombardment, the Gorgon was a jet-powered airframe carrying a 500- or 1000-lb GP Bomb. It was radio-controlled and radar-tracked in flight

GB-8
A 2000-lb GP Bomb carried by a wooden airframe under radio guidance, was a simple means of producing an air-to-surface guided glide bomb

Lark
A ship-based anti-aircraft missile, Lark was radio-controlled under radar direction. Its most advanced feature was a homing device connected to the control surfaces

US designers produced a range of bombardment and AA missiles with sophisticated guidance and fuze systems

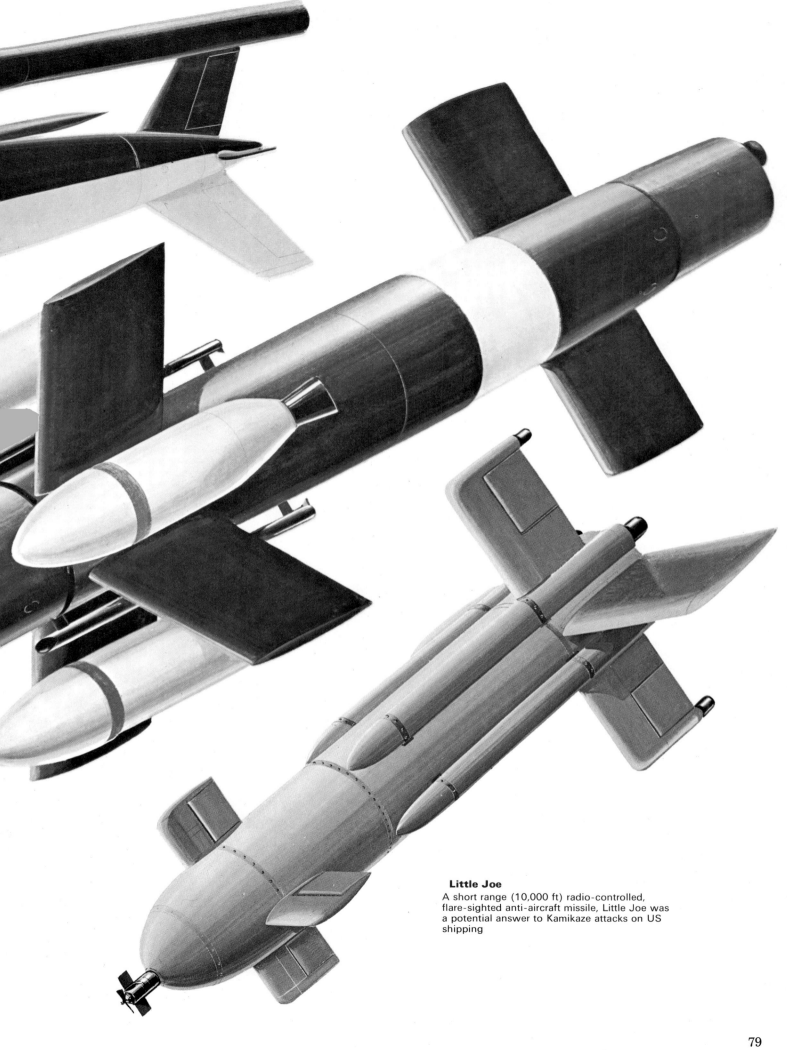

Little Joe
A short range (10,000 ft) radio-controlled, flare-sighted anti-aircraft missile, Little Joe was a potential answer to Kamikaze attacks on US shipping

THE ROCKET POWERED FIGHTER

Some of the German scientists' most bizarre and spectacular weapons were in the field of aircraft and the weapons to go into them — among them rocket powered fighters, and a recoilless gun so big it would have shaken to pieces the aircraft mounting it. But they did produce the world's first jet aircraft, and did much work in the field of guided missiles

The war in the air divides itself into two sectors, the offensive war and the defensive war. In the matter of offence, the prime requirement was firstly aircraft and, after that, weapons to go into them, and in both fields the German *Luftwaffe* had some unusual ideas.

The *Luftwaffe* was, in many respects, an extension of the Army's fighting ability, insofar as it was primarily intended as a supporting arm for the ground troops and less of a long-range strategic weapon. As a result, fighter aircraft had a high priority. One of the early ideas in this line was to produce a fighter propelled by a rocket motor, in order to get up to operational height very quickly after which it could cruise down, dealing with enemy aircraft on the way. The first practical rocket fighter was the Messerschmitt Me 163A, a stubby and awkward-looking single-seat machine powered by a liquid-fuel Walter rocket. After being towed around in order to prove that it could fly – for its appearance was against it on that score – the Me 163A was finally given its first powered flight in May 1941, when it was timed at speeds of over 600 mph. If one remembers that the average speed of a fighter aircraft at that time was about 350 mph, the Me 163A held out great promise. A second version, the Me 163B, was built, with a more powerful bi-fuel rocket motor and with disposable rockets to boost the take-off speed. Then another variant was developed by the Junkers company, the Ju 263, but the project remained firmly in Messerschmitt hands and this model was renamed the Me 263.

Too much time
However, there is a lot more to producing a viable fighter aircraft than simply making it fly. It has to be armed, it has to be controllable, and it has to be put into production, and all these things take time. Although the Me 163 flew in 1941, it was not perfected before the war ended. A handful were built and armed in the last months of the war and were sent to various experimental airfields around Germany in order to be tried against Allied air raiders. From accounts of RAF and USAF fliers who met these machines, they were highly impressive and very dangerous, moving so fast that the air gunners had little or no chance to deal with them. But their combat duration was very short – little more than 25 minutes, most of which was unpowered – and they were too

few in number to make much impression.

Another rocket-propelled project was the 'Natter' area defence fighter. This was conceived by the Bachem company in August 1944. Its official description was a 'rocket-propelled interceptor for the defence of vulnerable points against mass bomber formations' and it was a vertical take-off machine capable of flying one mission only. Armed with 24 73-mm rockets in its nose, the Natter sat on its tail to be launched,

more like a rocket than an aircraft, at 425 mph. The maximum height it reached was 39,000 ft, after which it turned into horizontal flight, moving at 620 mph, plunged down on the enemy formation, and shot up as many bombers as it could with the 24 rockets. Then the pilot baled out by parachute and the aircraft dived to the ground to be destroyed. The whole affair was over in three or four minutes. Needless to say, with this concept in mind, the construction was of the most elementary form; the body was built of wood, nailed and glued together as simply as possible, and consisted

Messerschmitt Me 163
The Me 163, the world's first successful rocket-propelled combat aircraft, first flew in May 1941

of not much more than a support for the rocket motor, the pilot's seat and the battery of rockets in the nose. The length was 18 ft 9 in, the wingspan 10 ft 6 in, and the weight about a ton and a half at take-off. The rocket motor was the same as that in use on the Messerschmitt designs, while two jet-assist rockets were attached to boost the speed on take-off.

That, at least, was the idea. What happened was somewhat different. The Bachem company put forth the idea, and in September 1944 it was accepted by (of all people) the SS, an organisation not generally thought to be in the anti-aircraft business. Experimental models were built, and in November testing began at Neuberg, near Sigmaringen, with the airframe being towed behind a Heinkel bomber to prove its flying ability. In February 1945 the SS demanded faster progress and a manned flight, and although the manufacturers were dubious about the wisdom of trying this so soon in the development programme, they preferred not to get on the wrong side of the SS and agreed to try it. The plane was duly prepared, the pilot climbed in, and the rockets were fired. At a height of about 350 ft the complete cockpit unit fell out and the pilot was killed. The plane continued to rise for a couple of hundred feet, then turned on its back, climbed again to 1600 ft, then rolled over and dived into the ground, exploding as it struck.

In all 30 'Natters' were built. Eighteen were used up on unmanned take-offs, one crashed during glide tests, one crashed on the manned flight, six were burned to prevent them falling into Allied hands, and the other four were captured by the US Army in Austria. There was also another project being discussed towards the end of the war for a piloted version which would survive for several flights, being landed after each

combat and refuelled; this was known as 'Julia', but never got off the drawing-board.

With the arrival over Germany of the RAF's four-engined bombers, the proposal to develop an equivalent German machine was put forward and the Heinkel company undertook the development. Their Heinkel He 111 was the standard German twin-engined bomber and a highly effective one at that. Numerous variations were developed as the war called for improvements, and taking this well-tried design as a starting point Heinkel designed the He 177 four-engined bomber. Known as the 'Greif' (Griffin), it had obvious affinities with the He 111 in the shape of its nose and fuselage and was capable of carrying almost eight tons of bombs. But in their enthusiasm the designers called for engines which were too powerful; while they pulled the machine through the air at a respectable speed, they overheated badly. This heat was conducted through the air-frame to the adjacent petrol tanks in the wings, where the fuel was brought rapidly to boiling point and vapourised. The vapour then seeped to the engines, met the flame from the exhaust, and in seconds the plane had exploded. This did its reputation no good at all and did much to set back the development programme. Eventually, with a change of engines, the problem was solved, but now the speed had gone down to the point where it became questionable whether the machine was worth it. More trouble arose over armament, the high command demanding a weight of guns and equipment which reduced the performance even further, and eventually the whole programme fell to pieces. Some reports say that almost a thousand of these machines were built to one specification or another, but except for one or two raids over England in late 1944 they were never used and finished up on the scrap heap.

Another bomber idea was the Focke-Wulf design somewhat grandiosely known as the 1000 × 1000 × 1000, because it was predicted that it would carry 1000 kilograms of bombs at 1000 kilometres an hour to a range of 1000 kilometres. It was a highly-streamlined, delta-winged machine, but since it never got out of the drawing office we have no idea of how close it might have got to the magic figures.

Equally blue-sky was another Focke-Wulf design called the Fw-03-10225. This doesn't seem to have any mysterious significance and is probably the drawing number. The 10225 was a design for a long-range bomber capable of flying 5000 miles to attack the USA with a bombload of 3000 kilograms. This was intended to fly at extreme altitudes – 35,000 feet and above – at 350 mph or more, but, again, never reached even the trial stage.

One way of extending range, which was explored by the British well before the war, was to have your long-range plane lifted into the air by a heavier aircraft, better equipped for lifting off the ground. Once airborne the 'piggy-back' rider could be turned loose; this overcame the problem of lifting vast weights of fuel into the air and allowed the Imperial Airways to run long-range airmail services with extremely light and fast aircraft with their 'Mercury-Maia' combination. The flying-boat 'Maia' took off carrying the float plane 'Mercury' on its back.

The Germans now took this idea and proceeded to turn it inside out. Instead of using the big aircraft to carry the little one up and turn it loose, the big aircraft would be controlled by the small one and flown by it; the idea was to use fighter aircraft as glider tugs, setting them on top of the gliders. There were a number of drawbacks to this idea, though, and little came of it as far as glider-

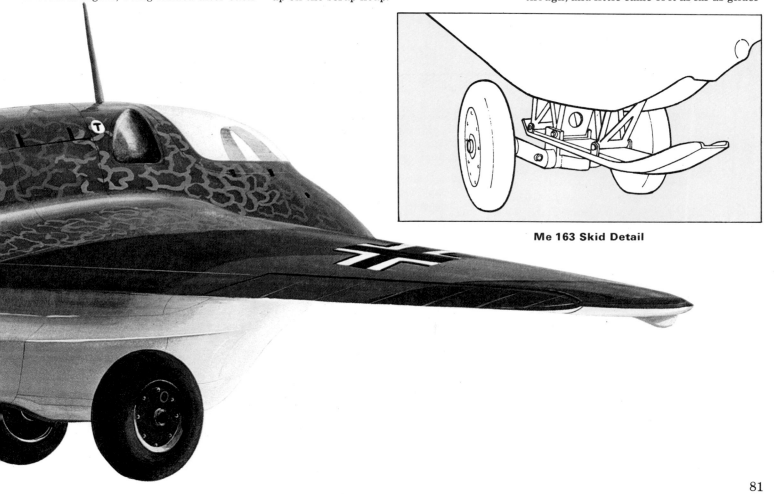

Me 163 Skid Detail

These cross-sections of the Natter are taken from the original training manual on the weapon

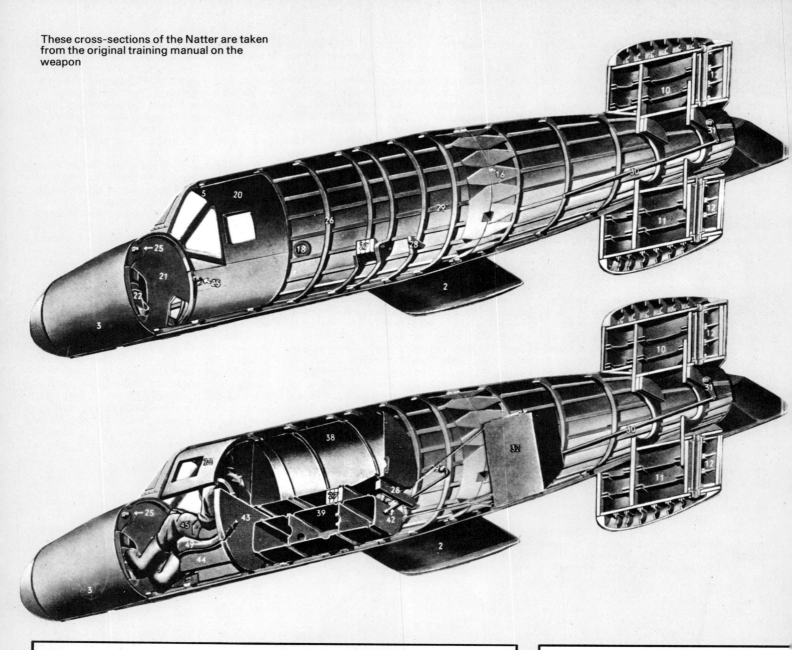

KEY

1	Elevators	37	Parachute opening cables
2	Wing	38	T-Stoff tank
3	Nose	39	C-Stoff tank
5	Forward hood	40	C-Stoff inlet
10	Upper tailfin		
11	Lower tailfin	41	Ventilation pipe
12	Rudder	42	C-Stoff overflow
16	Aft joint	43	Bulkhead
18	Hand-hole cover	44	Seat
20	Canopy	45	Protective suit
		46	Waist strap
21	Armour plating	47	Shoulder strap
22	Foot rudder	48	Rudder stick
25	Firing button	49	Seat parachute
26	Body strut	50	T-Stoff overflow
27	Main spar	51	T-Stoff inlet
28	Auxiliary spar	52	Access tube
29	Strut	53	C-Stoff outlet
30	Elevator control rod	54	T-Stoff outlet
31	Driving pulley	55	T-Stoff tank ventilator
32	Fuselage parachute container	56	Rocket motor
33	Fuselage parachute	58	Rudder cable
34	Ejecting springs	59	Lining
35	Catch	60	Emergency air-supply
36	Catch release cable		

Bachem Natter

The 'Natter' ('Viper') rocket-propelled interceptor was a 'one-shot' machine from which the pilot was intended to bale out after the completion of his mission

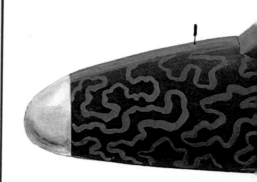

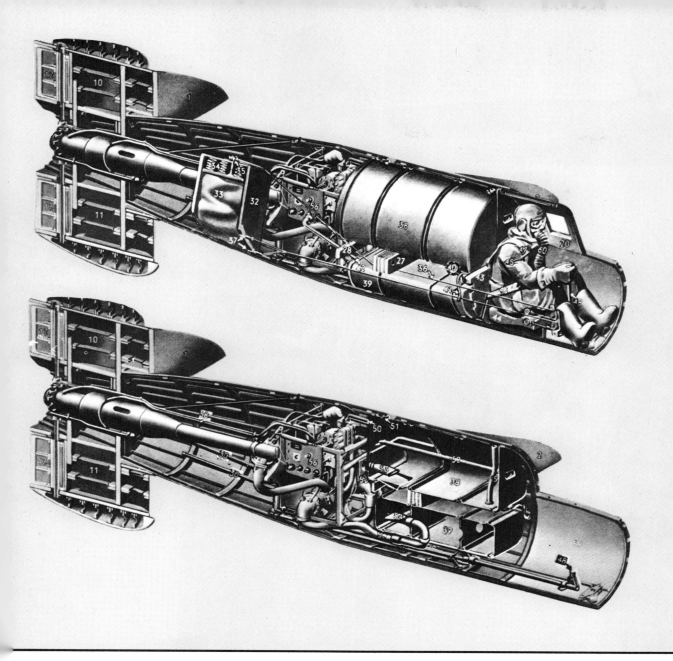

Messerschmitt Me 263

The Junkers-designed Me 263, the final version of the rocket fighter, failed to reach production before the war ended

Cockpit is a totally enclosed unit for pressurisation purposes, although no service machines were ever pressurised

Tank filler cap

Radio loop

Stabiliser adjusting motor

238-gallon tank

Flaps

132-gallon auxiliary tank

Radio

Master compass

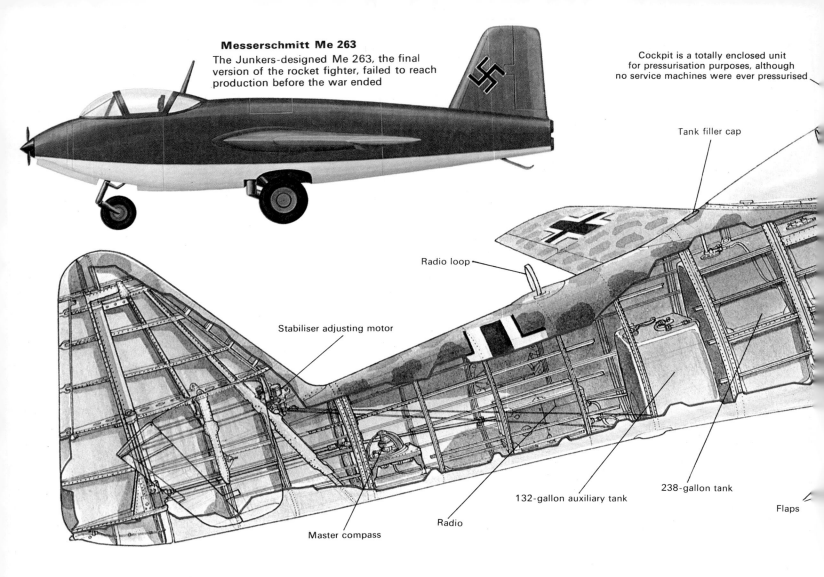

towing went, but during the work on the original idea, a second and much more effective one was born. Now the combination became one of bomber and fighter, a Heinkel or Junkers bomber carrying a Messerschmitt or Focke-Wulf fighter, and after playing with this for a while, the final design appeared. Take a Junkers Ju 88 bomber, rip out the insides, fill it with high explosive and fit a fighter plane on top. Connect the controls of the bomber to the fighter. Now start the bomber engines and allow the fighter pilot to fly the whole assembly off, using only the bomber engines until the target area is reached. Once there, the combination was pointed at the target in a dive and the bomber motors locked at full throttle, after which the fighter cast himself free, started his own engine and set off for home.

This became known as 'Mistel' (Mistletoe) and production of the combination began in 1943. The original intention was to fly some to Scapa Flow and dive them onto the British Fleet there. Some 200 were built, but when a reconnaissance plane was sent to check on the target, it was discovered that the British Fleet didn't live in Scapa Flow any more, and that the various ships were so scattered about that there were no worthwhile targets to be found. Eventually a use was found for them in destroying bridges on the Eastern Front in an attempt to hold up the advancing Russian armies, and they were also used in the same role once or twice on the Western Front. Otherwise, they only

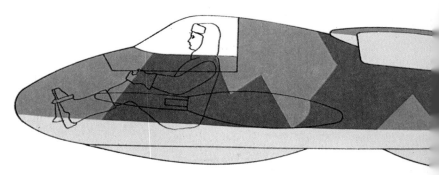

Julia

The Bachem 'Julia' was a derivation of 'Natter' intended to undertake a number of missions before being written off. There were two versions, 'Taipen' (above) in which the pilot sat normally, and 'Seite' (below) with the pilot prone. It never reached the hardware stage

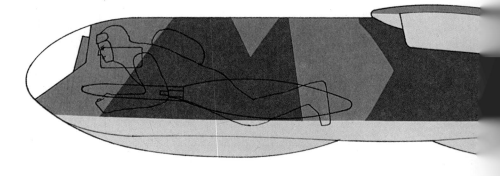

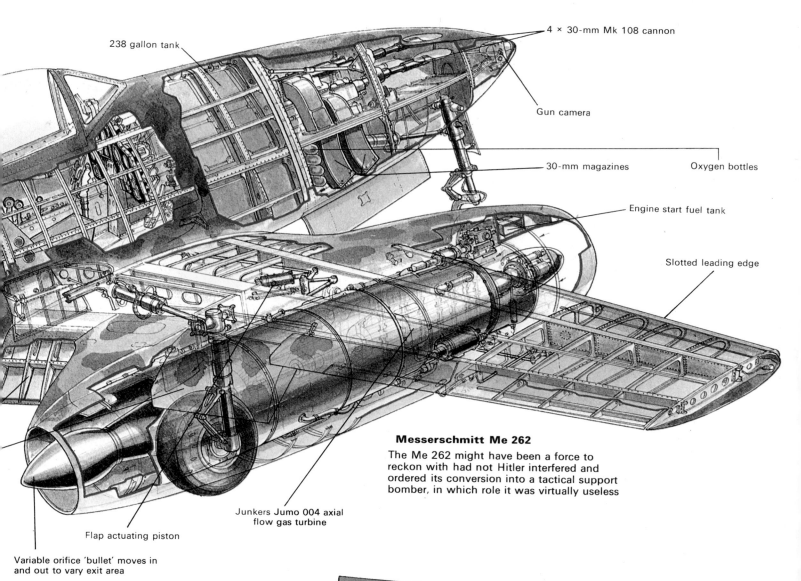

238 gallon tank

4 × 30-mm Mk 108 cannon

Gun camera

30-mm magazines

Oxygen bottles

Engine start fuel tank

Slotted leading edge

Messerschmitt Me 262

The Me 262 might have been a force to
reckon with had not Hitler interfered and
ordered its conversion into a tactical support
bomber, in which role it was virtually useless

Junkers Jumo 004 axial
flow gas turbine

Flap actuating piston

Variable orifice 'bullet' moves in
and out to vary exit area

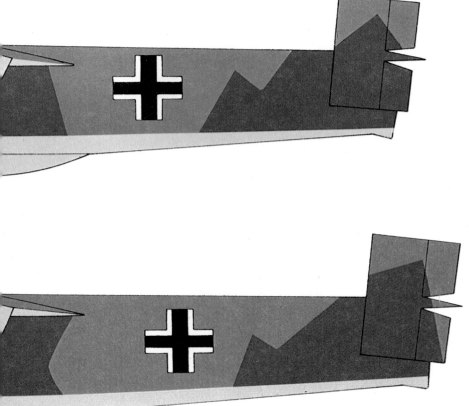

appeared against Allied shipping off the
French coast and in attempts to break up the
concentration of shipping off the invasion
beaches after D-Day, though in this latter
task the pilots appear not to have been very
well briefed as to what was what, since they
almost all landed on useless blockships.

Far more fundamental than all these
peculiar designs was the aircraft feature
which, of all those which were developed
during the war, has affected design in post-
war years the most: the jet engine. Like
radar, infrared, and a lot of other ideas,
warlike or peaceful, the jet engine appears
to have occurred to different people in
different places at more or less the same time,
and the subsequent development was solely
a matter of how much faith they had and
how well they could 'sell' their ideas to
higher authority. In Germany the bulk of
the work was done by the Heinkel company;
the idea had occurred to them in the early
1930s and in the following years they quietly
worked on the theory of it. A suitable aircraft
was designed, and, in order to prove it, was
flown using a rocket motor at the Peenemünde Research Establishment in the early
summer of 1939. After a successful flight, the
rocket motor was replaced by the first
Heinkel jet engine and the aircraft, known
as the He 178, flew under jet power at the end
of August 1939, the world's first jet-powered
flight.

Now came the 'selling' part, and here
Heinkel were unsuccessful; nobody was
interested. Not the *Luftministerium*, not

even Hitler himself. And then, to make matters worse, when the war broke out, the military staffs were so convinced that it would all be over quickly that they forbade the development of any project which could not be guaranteed to be brought into service within twelve months. The Heinkel company went home with their jet aircraft and, officially, put it to one side. In fact, they kept up their research work, though at a reduced priority.

But there was somebody else looking at the same idea. The Junkers company had also thought of jet propulsion, but instead of trying for an aircraft straight away, they contented themselves with perfecting an engine. In the latter part of 1941 they finally

Focke-Wulf Fw 1000 x 1000 x 1000

The Fw 1000 x 1000 x 1000 was intended to carry 1000 Kg of bombs at 1000 kph to 1000 km range, which would have given it a formidable bombing ability against England

fitted one into a converted Messerschmitt Me 110 for flying tests, and as a result of these managed to stimulate some interest in the *Luftwaffe* – who by now had realised that the 'one-year ban' was a dead number and were casting around for new ideas. Unfortunately the *Luftwaffe* had the disastrous habit of asking for too much; whenever a designer went before them with a proposition, the *Luftwaffe* chiefs would invariably agree, but would ask for twice the speed, treble the ceiling, double the fire-power, five times the muzzle velocity, or some equally unlikely figures.

A nasty shock

In the case of jet fighters they demanded a production rate of a thousand machines a month, and with this made clear they authorised production of the Messerschmitt Me 262B fitted with Junkers engines in the autumn of 1943. By late 1944 production had reached one hundred a month, whereupon the *Luftwaffe* demanded 2500 a month. But in spite of this slight disagreement, the jet fighter managed to get into production in respectable figures, and the few which got into the hands of service pilots before the war ended gave the Allied air forces a nasty shock.

Another company which went into the jet engine business was the well-known motor company of BMW. They had begun their development in 1934 in conditions of extreme secrecy, and their first engine ran in the summer of 1940. When the Junkers engine was approved by the *Luftwaffe*, BMW were brought in as contractors to Junkers, but they later managed to interest the *Luftwaffe* in their own designs and eventually the BMW engine was used in the four-engined Arado 234 bomber, a machine which could travel at over 550 mph at an altitude of 33,000 ft.

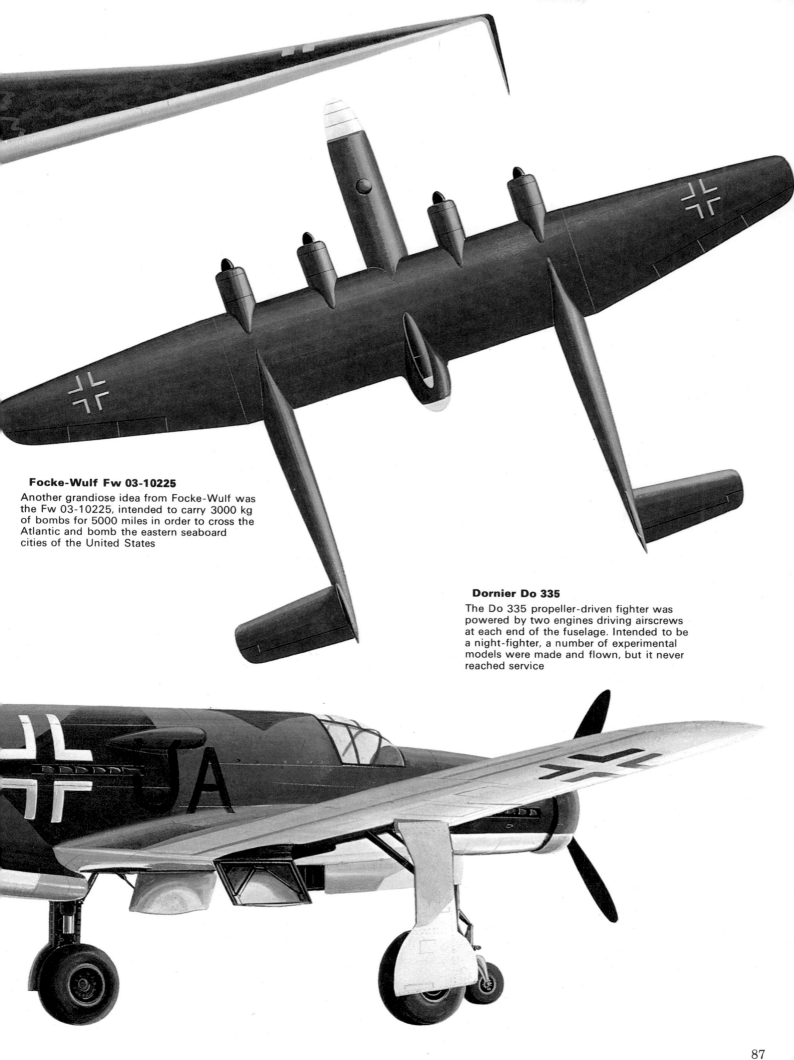

Focke-Wulf Fw 03-10225

Another grandiose idea from Focke-Wulf was the Fw 03-10225, intended to carry 3000 kg of bombs for 5000 miles in order to cross the Atlantic and bomb the eastern seaboard cities of the United States

Dornier Do 335

The Do 335 propeller-driven fighter was powered by two engines driving airscrews at each end of the fuselage. Intended to be a night-fighter, a number of experimental models were made and flown, but it never reached service

Mistel

'Mistel' ('Mistletoe') was the pick-a-back combination first envisaged as a method of attacking warships by launching an airframe full of explosives at them. Numbers of these were actually built and used, though their effectiveness was marginal. This particular model consisted of an Fw 190 A-8 fighter and a Ju 88 G-1 bomber

Mistletoe Attack Diagram

3000 ft —

2000 ft —

1000 ft —

Low level approach under radar cover

Up to 2500 ft
2½ miles from target

Pilot starts approach dive (15°)
1½ miles from target

Pilot pulls away from combination

Auto pilot takes over to fly bomb to target

4 miles   3 miles   2 miles   1 mile

Arado Ar 234B Blitz
The Ar 234 twin-engined reconnaissance version of the world's first jet bomber, of which a few were completed before the end of the war, was never built in sufficient numbers to make any impression

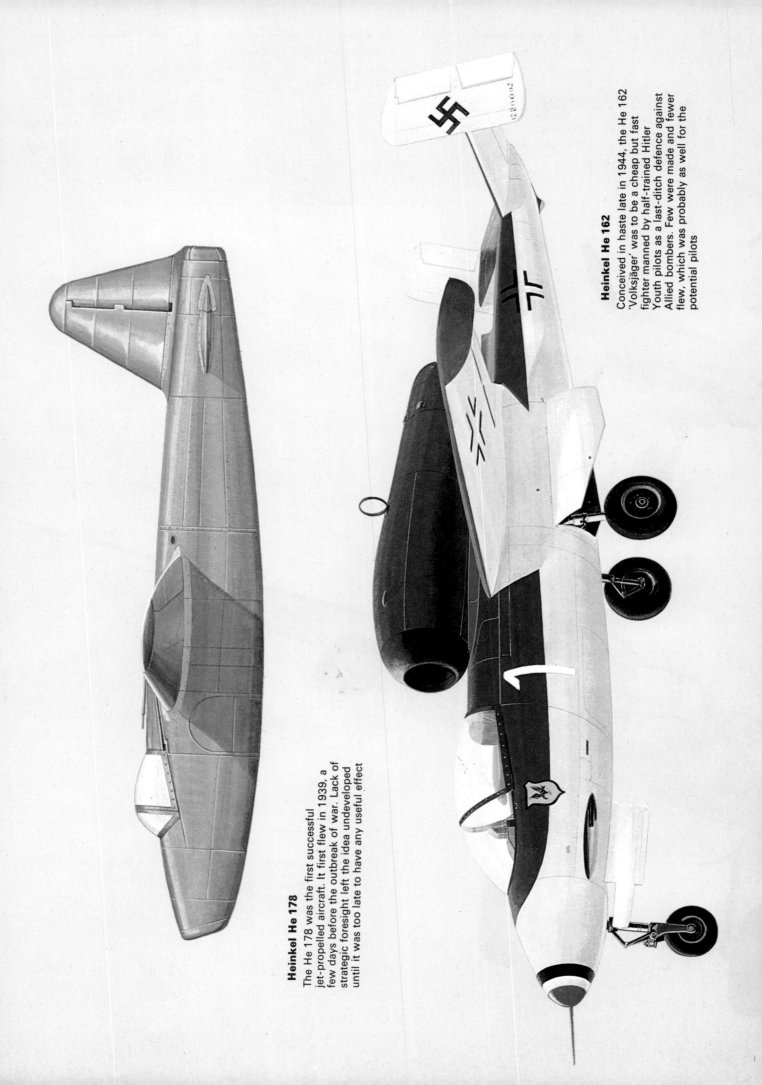

Heinkel He 178

The He 178 was the first successful jet-propelled aircraft. It first flew in 1939, a few days before the outbreak of war. Lack of strategic foresight left the idea undeveloped until it was too late to have any useful effect

Heinkel He 162

Conceived in haste late in 1944, the He 162 'Volksjäger' was to be a cheap but fast fighter manned by half-trained Hitler Youth pilots as a last-ditch defence against Allied bombers. Few were made and fewer flew, which was probably as well for the potential pilots

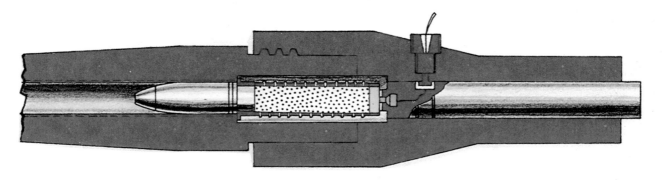

30-mm Recoilless Gun
The Rheinmetall 30-mm recoilless aircraft gun posed some difficult technical problems which were never totally overcome

AIRCRAFT ARMAMENT

Getting an aircraft into the air is only part of the problem in war. Once it is there it has to have some form of offensive armament to do some damage, and possibly some defensive armament as well. And the armament ideas of the *Luftwaffe* ranged from the brilliant to the absolutely crazy, though it must be admitted there was a bias to the former.

In the 1920s the American aviator 'Billy' Mitchell gave some startling demonstrations of the ability of aircraft to bomb, disable and even sink a battleship – so convincing, indeed, that he got himself court-martialled for his pains. The German Air Force, with their modern outlook and absolute conviction of the worth of airpower in a future war, were intensely interested in this problem of attacking heavy ships from the air, but they were realists enough to appreciate that dropping a bomb on a tethered and unmanned hulk was a different matter to trying to drop one onto a real live battleship which was trying to shoot back. They therefore looked for solutions which would allow a heavy weight of explosive to be delivered from a distance with some degree of accuracy and some chance of success, and Rheinmettal-Borsig believed they had the answer in the recoilless gun.

The recoilless gun had first seen the light of day as an aircraft weapon during the First World War. Known then as the 'Davis Gun' after its inventor, a Commander Davis of the US Navy, it had been adopted in small numbers by the Royal Naval Air Service for shooting at ships and submarines, though since it did not get into service until the latter weeks of the war its efficiency was never really tested. The problem facing the RNAS was to be able to fire a heavyweight shell from a stick-and-string aeroplane without the recoil shaking it to pieces. The Davis Gun was, in its essentials, two guns joined back-to-back; a shell went into the gun pointing forward and a 'counter-shot' of grease and buckshot into the gun pointing backwards. Between the two projectiles went a cartridge. When the cartridge was fired, the shell went out of the front to hit the target while the counter-shot went out of the back to disperse harmlessly in the air.

Since each gun recoiled the same amount, the two cancelled each other out and the result was a recoilless gun. Obviously, the gunner had to be careful how he pointed it, or the counter-shot could blow his own tail off, but as long as he bore this slight drawback in mind, he had a formidable weapon.

Trouble in the air
Using the Davis Gun as their starting point, the Rheinmettal company began developing their ideas in about 1937, starting with a 30-mm gun. Once they had proved that they could make it recoilless on the ground, it was fitted to an aircraft, whereupon their troubles really started. The system adopted was not to use a counter-shot, but to allow some of the gas from the cartridge to be exhausted from a jet at the back of the gun at high speed. Provided the mass of gas multiplied by its speed was the same as the mass of the gun's shell multiplied by its speed, then the two effects balanced each other and the gun stayed still. But the high-speed jet did some unfortunate things to the underside of the aircraft beneath which it was fitted, even after the floor was reinforced by 3-mm thick steel plates.

Work began on modifying the design to use a jet pipe which directed the blast away from the fuselage, but simply turning the pipe upset the gun due to the angle of the back-blast. The next solution tried was to split the jet between two pipes, leading one downwards and the other up, through the aircraft body, to exhaust above. This balanced matters and the gun was considered successful. Now came the question of reloading it; obviously, a single-shot weapon in such a small calibre was useless. After more trials a rotary magazine feed was developed which allowed ten rounds to be carried. In order to get the release of gas needed for the jets, the cartridges had their forward section made of plastic. When fired, the plastic disintegrated and allowed some of the gas to pass into the jets while the rest was pushing the shell forward through the barrel.

The gun was subsequently developed to the point of installing it into a Junkers Ju 88, but the priority of the demand had almost vanished by the time it was ready and it

never went into service. There is some doubt as to whether, in fact, it was as good as the designers claimed. One of the design team claimed in 1943 that trials in aircraft had shown no damage, but the pilot of one of the test machines, interviewed in 1945, said that every ten-round burst sprang rivets out of the fuselage.

Once the basic recoilless principle had been proved, work also began on a monster gun in response to a request from the *Luftministerium* for an anti-ship weapon capable of firing a 1400-lb armour-piercing shell and penetrating battleship deck armour. The result of this was *Gerät 104* (Equipment 104), a 35-cm calibre gun slung beneath an aircraft and retracted hydraulically during flight. With a weapon of this size, a jet efflux would doubtless have wrecked the carrying aircraft completely, so the Rheinmettal engineers went back to Davis's idea and produced a counter-shot weapon. Instead of using a second barrel and special counter-shot, the same result was achieved by making the cartridge case of a special heavy steel casing which weighed 1400 lb, the same as the armour-piercing shell. As the cartridge fired the shell forwards, so it fired the cartridge case backwards, achieving the necessary balance and recoillessness. Obviously, reloading a 1400-lb shell plus a cartridge of equal weight while in flight was out of the question, so the *Gerät 104* was strictly a one-shot weapon.

But before flight trials could take place, war broke out, and since it was thought that other things were more important, further development of the *Gerät 104* was stopped. A similar weapon, code-named *Munchausen*, was a 54-cm calibre gun on the same lines to be slung beneath the Ju 87 dive-bomber, but this proved to be too much of a good thing. The strain, even of a recoilless gun, was too much for the smaller aircraft, and the blast which came out of the breech end as the heavy cartridge case was ejected was sufficient to disturb the aircraft; as a result, the whole project was abandoned.

However, other recoilless gun ideas, slightly less ambitious, were more successful. One of the best was *Sondergerät 113A* (Special Equipment 113A), more popularly called the *Jägerfaust*. This was also based on the Davis gun principle of using a counter-shot. A single tube was mounted behind the pilot of a fighter aircraft, and in this was loaded a 5-cm anti-tank armour-piercing shell together with a cartridge and a counter-shot. The tube was open at top and bottom and the round was retained in place by a shear pin. The technique was very simple: the pilot simply flew close beneath the bomber and then fired the cartridge electrically. The explosion launched the armour-piercing shell upwards into the bomber and fired the counter-shot downwards to balance the recoil. The effect of a shell, originally designed to wreck a heavily-armoured tank, striking an aircraft can be imagined.

After proving that the idea worked, it was improved by being mounted beneath the wings of the aircraft, in order to attack from directly ahead of the bomber. The Me 163 carried six barrels, three beneath each wing, while the Me 262 was scheduled to carry thirty. The tubes were set at a slight angle so that the shells diverged to give a spread of about 20 yards at 100 yard range. At the end of the war there were twelve Me 163s equipped with *Jägerfaust* at Brandeis Airfield near Leipzig, and according to some reports at least one bomber was brought down by this weapon.

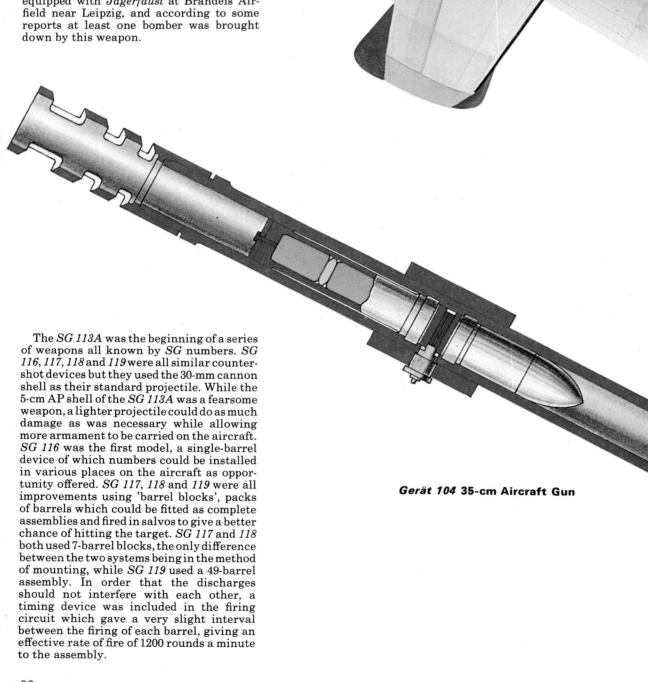

The *SG 113A* was the beginning of a series of weapons all known by *SG* numbers. *SG 116, 117, 118* and *119* were all similar counter-shot devices but they used the 30-mm cannon shell as their standard projectile. While the 5-cm AP shell of the *SG 113A* was a fearsome weapon, a lighter projectile could do as much damage as was necessary while allowing more armament to be carried on the aircraft. *SG 116* was the first model, a single-barrel device of which numbers could be installed in various places on the aircraft as opportunity offered. *SG 117, 118* and *119* were all improvements using 'barrel blocks', packs of barrels which could be fitted as complete assemblies and fired in salvos to give a better chance of hitting the target. *SG 117* and *118* both used 7-barrel blocks, the only difference between the two systems being in the method of mounting, while *SG 119* used a 49-barrel assembly. In order that the discharges should not interfere with each other, a timing device was included in the firing circuit which gave a very slight interval between the firing of each barrel, giving an effective rate of fire of 1200 rounds a minute to the assembly.

Gerät 104 35-cm Aircraft Gun

Gerät 104

Gerät 104, the enormous 35-cm (13·75-in) recoilless gun mounted beneath a Dornier 217. The firing of the 1400-lb shell was balanced by the ejection of a similar weight of cartridge case from the back end of the gun. It was proposed as a weapon for attacking warships, but the initial development was never followed up

Having got all this into the aircraft the only problem remaining was to make sure the pilot pushed the button at the right moment, and that wasn't as easy as it looked. With the Me 163 passing under the bomber at 500 mph and the bomber passing over the attacker at 300 mph, the margin of error was incredibly small, and if the pilot was a tenth of a second wrong in his assessment, he would miss. To solve this problem a photo-electric aiming device called *Zossen* was developed by a Doktor Orthuber of the AEG company at Neustadt. This contained a light source and a photocell arranged so that the light reflected from the target above would enter the photocell and automatically fire the weapon at the right moment. This was first tested at Werneichen Airfield near Berlin in mid-1944, using an aircraft fitted with an ordinary 20-mm cannon and flying it beneath a cloth target suspended between two balloons. It worked quite well and production began, but very few were ever finished and it is believed that only two were ever installed in aircraft for service.

Other variations on the same idea were *Bombersäge*, a 60-barrel 30-mm upward-firing gun mounted behind the pilot of a Fw 190, and *Harfe*, a similar battery of 20-mm barrels.

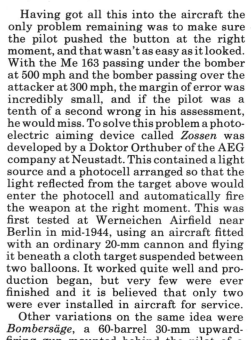

Henschel Hs 129
This version of the Hs 129 attack bomber mounting a 75-mm anti-tank gun, fitted with a 12-shot automatic magazine, was a devastating anti-tank weapon which gave a good account of itself on the Russian Front, but it was too late to have much effect

Another field of research which all the combatants entered was the question of mounting ever-larger orthodox guns into aircraft. The most well-known of these were the British and American 75-mm guns, but they were small beer compared to some of the armament proposed by the *Luftwaffe*. However, it must be pointed out that the prize in this field goes to the British who managed to mount a 32-pounder (94-mm) anti-tank gun in a Mosquito aircraft and fire it successfully, though this was not actually achieved until after the war had ended. In Germany the trend came about gradu-

ally as a logical progession from the rifle-calibre machine-guns to 20-mm cannon, then to 30-mm and larger calibres. The root of the problem was the combination of increased speed of the aircraft in combat, which led to shorter engagement times, and stronger construction of aircraft which meant that something more powerful than a rifle-type bullet was needed to do any worthwhile damage. Moreover, when the two were put together the whole problem resolved itself into doing as much damage as possible in the shortest possible time. There were two ways of solving it; either by exceptionally fast-firing guns of the normal small calibre or by slower-firing weapons from which one shot would do all the damage needed. Each point of view has its adherents. The Americans, for example, chose the first method and after the war produced the General Electric Vulcan Cannon firing the

normal 20-mm cannon shell but at the phenomenal rate of 6000 rounds per minute.

The Germans were not averse to this solution either, and did quite a lot of research into aircraft cannon design. Just one example was the Mauser MK213C 20-mm cannon which reached a rate of fire of 1400 rounds per minute. But far more work went into heavier weapons, the so-called *Bordwaffen* of calibres from 37-mm to 55-mm. The first requirement was, of course, to make sure that one shot from such weapons would be sufficient to wreck an aircraft, and much research went into designing *Minengeschoss* (mine shells) which had a much thinner wall of high-quality steel in order to carry the maximum amount of high explosive inside. At the same time, new types of high explosive were tried which gave much more violent detonation and consequently caused much more damage than was possible with the conventional TNT fillings. With these matters settled, work could then go ahead on producing the guns to fire them and the more difficult task of fitting them into aircraft.

The first model was the 5-cm *Bordkanone*, which was constructed by taking the now-obsolete 5-cm tank gun Model 39, fitting it to a suitable recoil-absorbing mounting and putting it into an aircraft. This was satisfactory, the recoil being well within the while the *115* tapped off gas from the barrel to drive the magazine mechanism. Both achieved a rate of fire of over 300 rounds a minute. Krupp of Essen also produced a design which combined the features of both the Rheinmettal models by using both gas and recoil to drive the mechanism, giving 300 rounds a minute, but the recoil strain on the aircraft was too much. But like the anti-aircraft gun, the 5·5-cm *Bordkanone* never got close to production, since development began too late and the war ended before it was completed.

Finally came the 75-mm aircraft cannon. This was no more than the standard 75-mm anti-tank gun model 40 with a new recoil system and highly efficient muzzle brake, mounted into a Henschel Hs 129 attack bomber. A 12-shot automatic magazine and loading mechanism was provided. Development began in the summer of 1944 and went so smoothly that by the end of that year 30 guns were contracted for. Early in 1945 the first equipments were issued and were flown into action against Soviet tanks, and it has

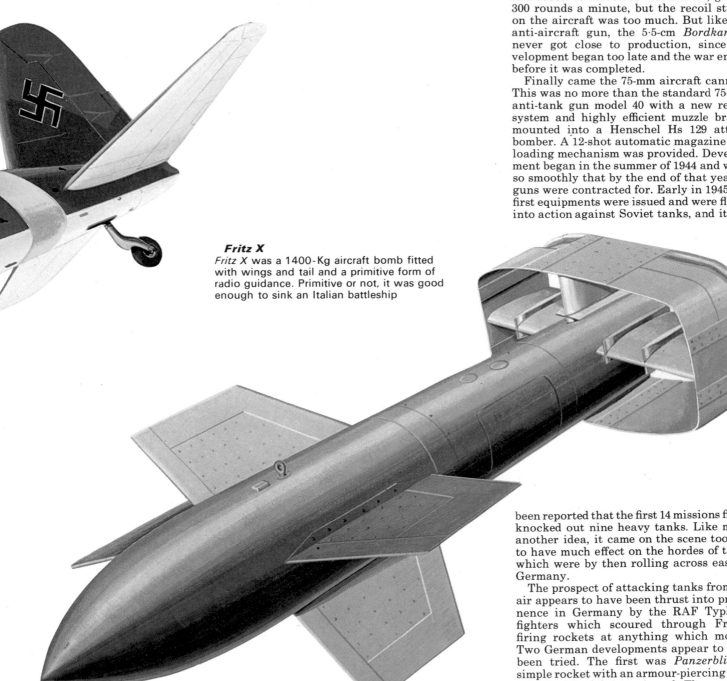

Fritz X

Fritz X was a 1400-Kg aircraft bomb fitted with wings and tail and a primitive form of radio guidance. Primitive or not, it was good enough to sink an Italian battleship

been reported that the first 14 missions flown knocked out nine heavy tanks. Like many another idea, it came on the scene too late to have much effect on the hordes of tanks which were by then rolling across eastern Germany.

The prospect of attacking tanks from the air appears to have been thrust into prominence in Germany by the RAF Typhoon fighters which scoured through France firing rockets at anything which moved. Two German developments appear to have been tried. The first was *Panzerblitz*, a simple rocket with an armour-piercing head to be fired from fighter aircraft. The warhead was the same 88-mm hollow charge head as used with the *Panzerschreck* infantry rocket launcher, fitted with a more powerful rocket motor. *Panzerblitz I* had a velocity of 300 metres per second and was soon replaced with *Panzerblitz II*, which used a more powerful motor from the R4M rocket and reached 370 metres a second. Both these were developed by the Waffenwerke Brünn in Czechoslovakia, and the *Panzerblitz I* was accepted for service with the intention of mounting it in the Hs 132 jet fighter, but since the Hs 132 never got into the air, the *Panzerblitz* never had a chance to show its paces. Two more models, the *III* and *IV*, were being worked on by the German Weapons and Munitions Company as the war ended. These were the same warhead with

Junkers Ju 88's ability to resist, and the next stage in the development was to produce a method of loading while in flight. Hand-loading by a crew member was scarcely feasible, and eventually a 22-round rotary magazine and automatic loader was produced. This allowed a rate of fire of 45 rounds a minute, and by the end of the war no less than 300 of these guns had been produced and fitted. They were almost all sent to the Eastern Front where, with armour-piercing ammunition in the magazines, they were a formidable tank-busting instrument.

The Mauser company now took a hand and developed their 5-cm *Maschinen Kanone 214* which was the same 5-cm tank gun

with a magazine of their own devising, capable of producing a rate of 140 rounds a minute. But development was only completed in the early days of 1945 and before series production of this model could get under way the war was over.

One of the major anti-aircraft developments attempted by the Germans was a 55-mm automatic gun, the story of which will be told later. While the weapon was being developed, it occurred to several people that it might make a very powerful aircraft cannon, and steps were taken to modify it to suit. Rheinmetall-Borsig designed two models, the *MK 112* and *MK 115*; the *112* used recoil to operate the magazine and reload, more powerful rocket motors which gave velocities up to 600 metres a second.

Another anti-tank weapon in the design stage when the war ended was *Förstersonde* which was quite normal as far as the rocket went, but somewhat unusual in its method of firing. Like the recoilless anti-bomber armament, *Förstersonde* was mounted vertically behind the pilot, and in order to simplify the problem of aiming it, a complicated fire control system was evolved which detected the magnetic field of the tank as the plane passed over and fired the rocket at the correct moment, without the pilot having to do anything more than keep a course straight over the top of the tank. Very little is known of this project except that trials were made in early 1945 on the fire control system which proved that it was feasible if not immediately perfect, but the weapon never got into service.

The other system of attacking ground targets which attracted the *Luftwaffe* was the possibility of controlling a bomb after it had been released. The most successful was *Fritz X*, which was basically a 1400-kilogram standard bomb filled with amatol and modified by the addition of four wings and a tail unit. Radio equipment carried in the tail picked up signals from an observer in the parent aircraft and pushed 'spoilers' out into the airstream to increase the drag on one side of the bomb or the other and thus steer it through the air with some fair degree of accuracy. The bomb was gyroscopically stabilised, and development was begun by a Doktor Kramer in 1939. Final acceptance tests were done near Foggia in Italy in the summer of 1942 and early in 1943 *Fritz X* was issued for operational service. Its most spectacular success was east of Sardinia on 9 September 1943 when one was used to bomb the Italian battleship *Roma* so effectively as to sink it. This led to more research, and eventually 2500-kilogram models, *Fritz X-5* and *Fritz X-6* were perfected, the *X-5* being an armour-piercing design and the *X-6* a high explosive blast bomb. One hundred of each were ordered, but the changing war situation led to a reassessment, and the order was cancelled late in 1944.

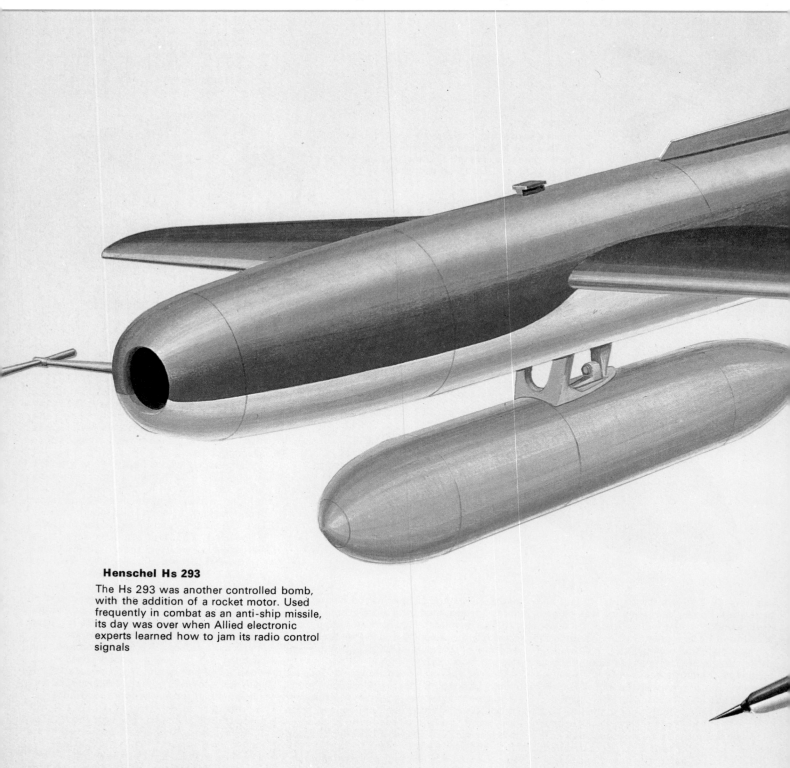

Henschel Hs 293

The Hs 293 was another controlled bomb, with the addition of a rocket motor. Used frequently in combat as an anti-ship missile, its day was over when Allied electronic experts learned how to jam its radio control signals

Another successful controlled bomb was the Hs 293 rocket-boosted bomb. This looked more like some sort of missile than a bomb, and indeed it was very close to being a missile. The warhead carried 550 kilograms of high explosive and was helped along by a Walter rocket motor which burned for ten seconds during flight. Once launched, and after the rocket was burned out, the remaining glide could be radio-controlled to the target. There were innumerable variations of the basic model, since it was a useful trial vehicle for different types of guidance, different control systems, new rocket motors and all sorts of other experimental devices, but even so some 12,000 of the service bombs were built, at least according to one source.

Dropped from Do 217s, they were used fairly often in 1942–43 against shipping in the Bay of Biscay and the Mediterranean, but, like most of their class, the weak link lay in the radio guidance which was easily jammed. Once this was appreciated, and once jamming devices were provided, it was quite useless and was withdrawn from operational use in 1944.

Similar to the Hs 293 was the Hs 294, which had a head of special shape to allow it to enter the sea and then carry on, following a predictable underwater trajectory to hit the ship like a torpedo. Development began in 1940 on this model, and although trials were successful, it appears not to have been used in operations, probably because of the jam-

ming problem. It is known that a number were converted to wire-control in an attempt to defeat jamming, and also that a few were fitted with television cameras in the head to allow the controller to see exactly where the weapon was going.

Long-range glide-bombs
One of the Allied devices which the Germans were keen to counter was the long-range radio navigation system which allowed Allied bombers to roam over Germany with uncanny accuracy. The *Luftwaffe* soon discovered where the 'Loran' transmitters were in the south of England, but several attempts to attack them ran into severe trouble, as the RAF were equally well aware

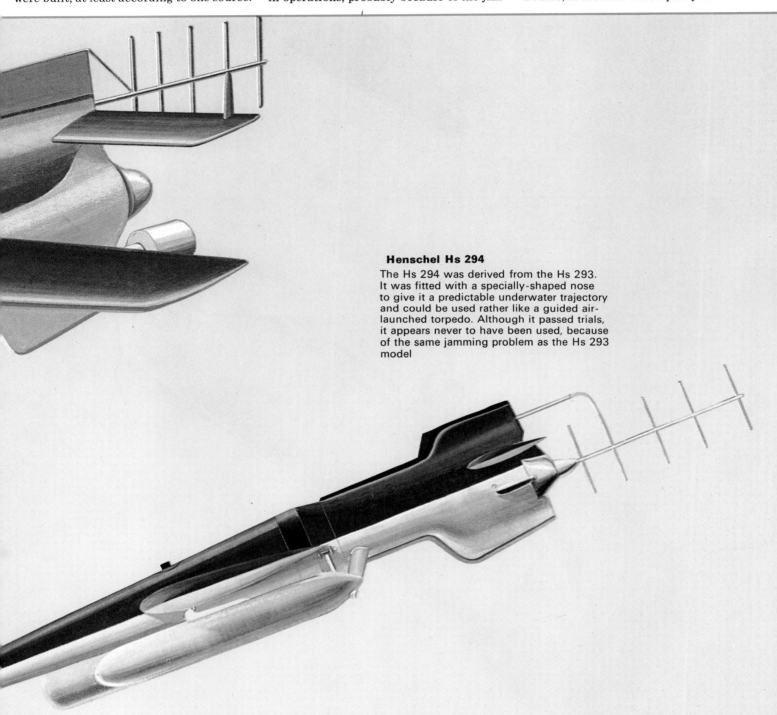

Henschel Hs 294

The Hs 294 was derived from the Hs 293. It was fitted with a specially-shaped nose to give it a predictable underwater trajectory and could be used rather like a guided air-launched torpedo. Although it passed trials, it appears never to have been used, because of the same jamming problem as the Hs 293 model

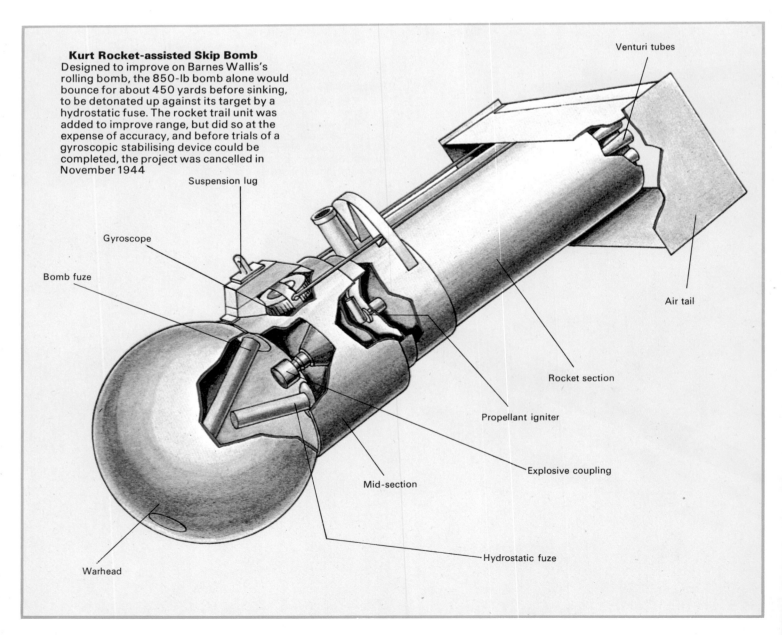

Kurt Rocket-assisted Skip Bomb
Designed to improve on Barnes Wallis's
rolling bomb, the 850-lb bomb alone would
bounce for about 450 yards before sinking,
to be detonated up against its target by a
hydrostatic fuse. The rocket trail unit was
added to improve range, but did so at the
expense of accuracy, and before trials of a
gyroscopic stabilising device could be
completed, the project was cancelled in
November 1944

Venturi tubes

Suspension lug

Gyroscope

Bomb fuze

Air tail

Rocket section

Propellant igniter

Explosive coupling

Mid-section

Hydrostatic fuze

Warhead

Blohm und Voss Bv-246

Known also as 'Radieschen', this was a guided bomb intended to fly down the beam of Allied navigational radio transmitters. Four hundred were ordered, but after the success of the V-1 missile, the project was cancelled

R4M

The R4M air-to-air rocket was used by the He 162 jet fighter. It was fitted with either a high explosive or anti-tank shaped charge warhead

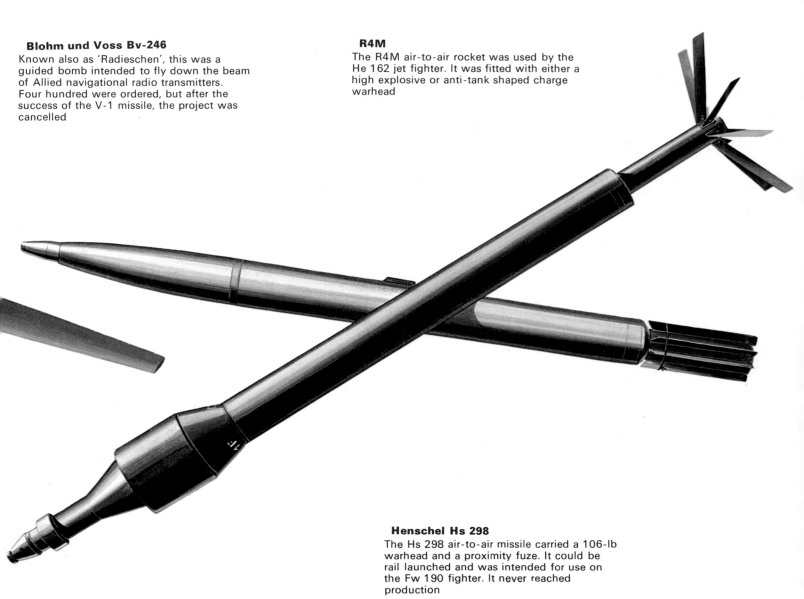

Henschel Hs 298

The Hs 298 air-to-air missile carried a 106-lb warhead and a proximity fuze. It could be rail launched and was intended for use on the Fw 190 fighter. It never reached production

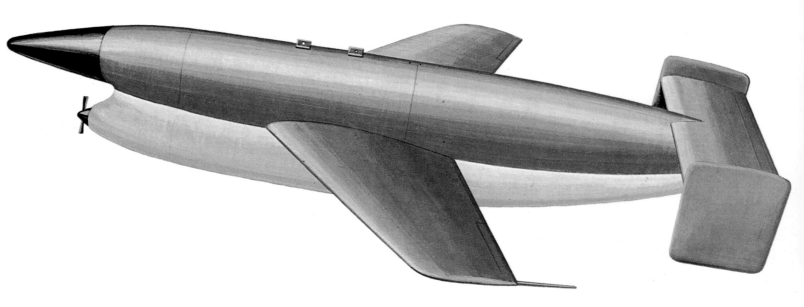

of their value and were quick to swamp the area with fighters when any German aircraft appeared. A Doktor Vogt of the Blohm und Voss shipbuilding firm produced a solution which seemed to hold promise: a gliding bomb with a radio controlling system actuated by the transmissions of the stations.

All the pilot of the bomber needed to do was get within 200 kilometres of the target and let the bomb go; its aerodynamic shape was exceptionally good, allowing a glide of 200 kilometres, and the homing system built in would keep it pointed at the Loran station until it finally landed dead on target. This idea was so attractive that 400 were ordered immediately, without waiting to see whether the bomb worked. Flight tests which took place at the Unterlüss Proving Ground late in 1944 were not particularly successful, since the gyroscopic stabilisation gave trouble and only two out of ten flew properly. At the same time the A-4 rocket (more usually known as the V-2) and the FZG-76 (or V-1) were both operating with considerable success, and it was thought that with a little care in setting these up they could probably be induced to land on the offending Loran stations. As a result, the Bv-246 or *Hagelkorn* project was dropped.

Blohm und Voss had also made an earlier attempt at an air-launched bomb, called the Bv-143, but this somehow got changed during its development and emerged as a guided missile. Using a liquid rocket motor, it was provided with gyro stabilisation, radio-controlled steering, and automatic altitude control by a radio device produced by Zeiss. The Bv-143 was tried out at Peenemünde in March 1941 and again in September 1942, but from the remaining accounts it seems that the altitude control was unreliable and as a result the weapon was uncontrollable.

When it came to attacking other aircraft, there seemed to be less interest in the rocket field than there was in the gun field. The only air-to-air rocket which reached any production was the R4M, a straightforward solid fuel rocket with a high-explosive head fired from the He 162 jet fighter. The rocket, weighing 7½ lb with its high explosive warhead, was a simple steel tube with spring-out fins.

More ambitious was the Henschel Hs 298, a rail-launched missile carried on Dornier Do 217 or Focke-Wulf Fw 190 machines. Weighing 265 lb, 6 ft 9 in long and with a wingspan of 4 ft, it carried a potent 106-lb warhead fitted with a proximity fuze which would ensure detonation of the warhead even with a near miss. Guidance was by

radio command from the parent aircraft, and the observer steered it onto his line of sight and kept it there until it struck. Propulsion was by a two-stage solid rocket, which gave a flight time of 25 to 30 seconds. Test firings were made in December 1944, but the results were not encouraging, and production was stopped in February 1945 as it seemed unlikely to reach a satisfactory stage of development in time to have any effect on the war.

The third potential air-to-air missile was the X-4, developed by the Ruhrstahl AG. This circumvented the jamming problem and did away with the involved development of radio devices, by a simple wire-control system. The wings of the missile carried bobbins which each held about 3¾ miles of wire, down which guidance signals could be sent from the parent aircraft. With a 44-lb warhead, it was fitted with a proximity fuze and reached a speed of 560 mph in flight to the target. Intended for mounting on Messerschmitt Me 262 and Focke-Wulf Fw 190 fighters, development began in June 1943 under Doktor Kramer. The first test flights were made in September 1944 and were very successful, but like several other projects it was cancelled in February 1945 as being unlikely to reach successful production in time to influence events.

X-4
Doktor Kramer's X-4 wire-guided missile was propelled by a liquid-fuel rocket motor. Designed for use by Me 262 and Fw-190 fighters, it passed its trials successfully but never managed to get into production

The war in the air also involved the question of ground defences against aircraft. In the case of the anti-aircraft gun, the first move was simply to make it bigger, but every time the gun designers got down to their drawing boards to solve the latest problem, the *Luftministerium* arrived with a fresh set of demands for higher velocity, higher ceiling, higher rates of fire, heavier shells and increased lethality, and the designers had to start all over again. The heaviest anti-aircraft guns in service were 12·8-cm (5·03-in), which fired a 57-lb shell to 48,500 feet at a rate of 25 rounds a minute. At the same time in 1936 as this gun was first requested, a demand was also made for a 15-cm gun.

Eventually, in the early part of 1938, the prototype of the 15-cm was ready, but trials showed that in the first place its performance was no better than the 12·8-cm model, and in the second place it had to be carried around in pieces and put together before it could be fired, which was something of a drawback for an anti-aircraft gun. More work was done in an attempt to improve things, but eventually in 1940 the project was given up and a fresh set of figures were produced for the designers to try for. This time the *Luftwaffe* wanted a gun which would fire a 92-lb shell to 60,000 ft and which would move in one load. But before much sense was brought out of this demand, the *Luftwaffe* changed their minds once more and decided that mobile guns over 12·8-cm calibre were not needed, and that was that. Then they relented and asked for designs for static-mounted guns, but after another year there was a change of policy again and these were cancelled so that design could be concentrated on missiles.

However, in 1941 the *Luftwaffe* had called for even bigger weapons, 21-cm and 24-cm in calibre. These, it was hoped, would fire 270-lb shells to 60,000 ft in the case of the 21-cm

and 435-lb shells to 60,000 ft in the case of the 24-cm. This project merged into a German Navy project for similar weapons, but in the long run neither of them got anywhere, having been cancelled by the 1943 decision to concentrate on missiles.

As a result of all this, the only useful work to be done on conventional guns was in the matter of improving the shells. As was discussed earlier, when dealing with anti-tank guns, the Germans amassed a wealth of experience and information on the design of guns having tapered barrels, a technique which allowed the velocity to be considerably improved. With an anti-aircraft gun this was important since it reduced the time taken for the shell to reach the area of the target, and thus reduced the liability to error. Several different designs of taper-bore gun were produced, but due to

development difficulties none of them ever reached service as an AA weapon.

One important project which was close to completion when the war ended was the production of an 'Intermediate' anti-aircraft gun. The light anti-aircraft guns such as the 20-mm and 37-mm were quite satisfactory against low-flying raiders, and the medium (88-mm) and heavy (105 and 128-mm) guns were effective against high flyers, but in between was a difficult zone. Planes flying at

A rare photograph, taken by Krupp's, showing the Gerät 50 anti-aircraft gun on their own proving grounds

about 7000 feet were too high to be effectively engaged by the light guns, and too low for engagement by the heavier weapons. This latter defect was not due to any weakness in the guns but to the simple mechanical difficulties of swinging the guns fast enough to keep up with targets at that altitude. As a result of this, work began before the war on a 50-mm anti-aircraft gun, an automatic weapon which was more or less an enlarged cannon. It was produced in moderate numbers and tried out, and while the *Luftwaffe* agreed that there was a need for the gun, they were less happy about the actual equipment. Among other things it had a distressing habit of turning over on corners when towed too fast, and when fired it vibrated so violently that the gunlayer could hardly see his sights.

By 1942 enough experience of air raids had been assembled to indicate that in some

ANTI-AIRCRAFT WEAPONS

John Batchelor

cases even one bomber getting through the defences was enough to do all the damage necessary; the Möhne and Eder Dams raid showed that. Therefore it was considered that if an anti-aircraft weapon system could be developed which absolutely guaranteed knocking down 100 per cent of the attack, then no matter what it cost in terms of development, effort or money, it would be worth it. From this came a very advanced plan for a complete anti-aircraft system, comprising six automatic guns, radar, computer, height-finder and tracker, all coupled together to give absolute certainty of finding and hitting any attacker in the medium

Gerät 50

The Krupp 15-cm super-heavy anti-aircraft gun, *Gerät 50*, had a ten-round magazine which allowed firing a semi-automatic burst at high speed. It was not accepted for service since it did little which the existing 12·8-cm gun could not do as well

height zone. The gun was to be an improved version of the 5-cm model, but by this time there had been some improvements in the design of shells, and it was particularly demanded that the shell should carry sufficient explosive to guarantee downing a four-engined bomber with one hit. There was no problem in making a shell to carry this charge of explosive, but there was a good deal of trouble when it came to making it fly straight to the target; due to various ballistic defects, every shell design tried turned out to be inaccurate.

After over a year of failure the designers gave up and decided that the only solution was to change calibre, and after some discussion a 55-mm gun was proposed. There was little problem in designing an accurate and lethal shell in this calibre, and in the early months of 1944 the 5·5-cm *Gerät 58* project finally got under way. But too much time had been wasted, and although some guns were assembled and fired before the war ended, the power-operated mountings, radar, computer and all the other gadgetry were nowhere near completion. There is some evidence to show that a good deal of the development equipment was spirited off to Russia after the end of the war, where work was continued and the German design eventually reached service as a Soviet 57-mm gun in the 1950s.

Two more photographs from the Krupp manual, showing the mobile assembly of the Gerät 50 and, top right, the method of loading the gun onto its transporter

John Batchelor

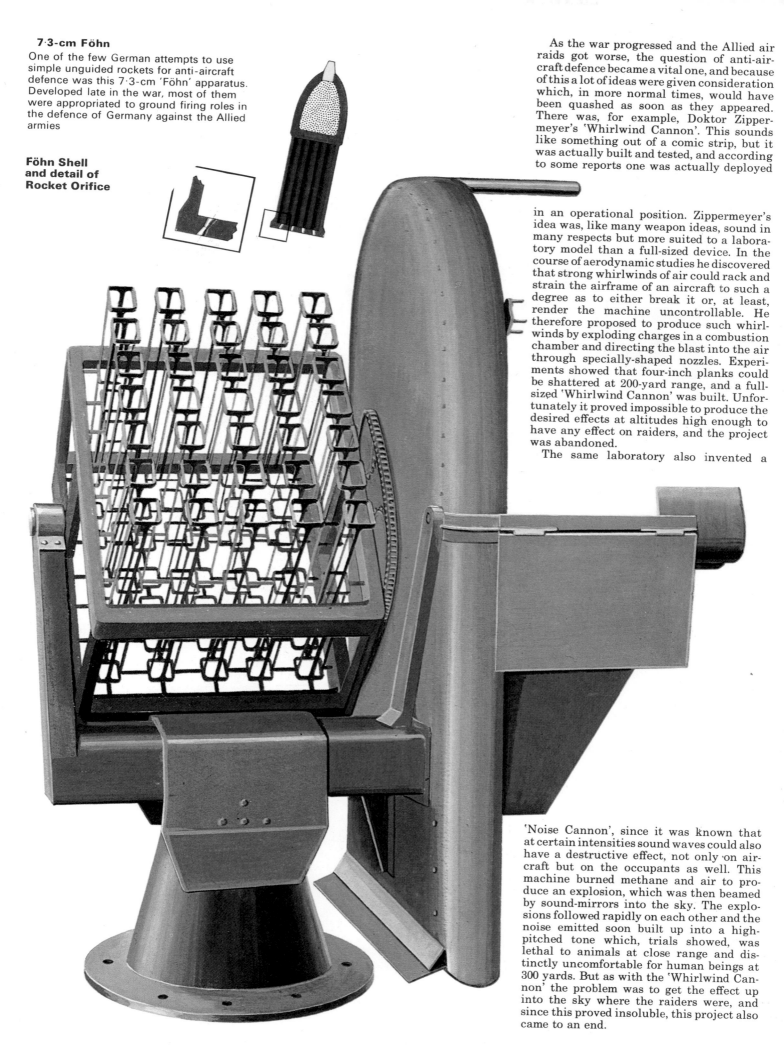

7·3-cm Föhn

One of the few German attempts to use simple unguided rockets for anti-aircraft defence was this 7·3-cm 'Föhn' apparatus. Developed late in the war, most of them were appropriated to ground firing roles in the defence of Germany against the Allied armies

Föhn Shell and detail of Rocket Orifice

As the war progressed and the Allied air raids got worse, the question of anti-aircraft defence became a vital one, and because of this a lot of ideas were given consideration which, in more normal times, would have been quashed as soon as they appeared. There was, for example, Doktor Zippermeyer's 'Whirlwind Cannon'. This sounds like something out of a comic strip, but it was actually built and tested, and according to some reports one was actually deployed in an operational position. Zippermeyer's idea was, like many weapon ideas, sound in many respects but more suited to a laboratory model than a full-sized device. In the course of aerodynamic studies he discovered that strong whirlwinds of air could rack and strain the airframe of an aircraft to such a degree as to either break it or, at least, render the machine uncontrollable. He therefore proposed to produce such whirlwinds by exploding charges in a combustion chamber and directing the blast into the air through specially-shaped nozzles. Experiments showed that four-inch planks could be shattered at 200-yard range, and a full-sized 'Whirlwind Cannon' was built. Unfortunately it proved impossible to produce the desired effects at altitudes high enough to have any effect on raiders, and the project was abandoned.

The same laboratory also invented a 'Noise Cannon', since it was known that at certain intensities sound waves could also have a destructive effect, not only on aircraft but on the occupants as well. This machine burned methane and air to produce an explosion, which was then beamed by sound-mirrors into the sky. The explosions followed rapidly on each other and the noise emitted soon built up into a high-pitched tone which, trials showed, was lethal to animals at close range and distinctly uncomfortable for human beings at 300 yards. But as with the 'Whirlwind Cannon' the problem was to get the effect up into the sky where the raiders were, and since this proved insoluble, this project also came to an end.

Fliegerfaust

Fliegerfaust was a nine-barrel hand-held rocket launcher that fired a small projectile based on the standard 20-mm cannon shell with a rocket motor attached. Travelling at over 1000 ft per second, the rocket could reach out to 2000 yards with reasonable accuracy. Like so many other ideas, it arrived too late to be of any use

J. B. King

This photograph shows *Fliegerfaust* in the firing position. The pouch over the operator's shoulder is an ammunition container

Inset: Fliegerfaust's complete ammunition load of nine rockets

Just as unorthodox, though slightly less ridiculous, was the project for an electric gun. As every schoolboy knows, if a coil of wire is wrapped around a soft iron core and an electric current is passed through it, the core will jump out of the coil. This is the solenoid, a well-known electrical control mechanism. In the 19th century it occurred to various experimenters that if the coil were made big enough and the current strong enough, then the core could be made to leave at high speed and might thus become a projectile. But try as they might, nobody ever managed to develop enough electric current to get a worthwhile speed out of the core.

During the First World War a French experimenter came up with a new idea using a winged arrow connected across two conducting bars; this worked quite well but before he could do much with it, the war ended and nobody was interested any longer. His idea was later developed into what is today known as the 'linear motor'. During 1944 a German company looked once again at this proposition and came to the conclusion that since there had been considerable advances in electricity since 1918, the idea might now be workable. In October 1944 a preliminary specification was agreed with the *Luftwaffe* for a 40-mm electric anti-aircraft gun, with a velocity of 6500 ft per second and a rate of fire of 6000 rounds per minute. Each shell was to carry one pound of explosive, and six 'barrels' were to be connected to a single power supply.

The work went ahead, although nothing but small laboratory experiments were achieved before the war ended. It is doubtful if anything would ever have come of it, as the gun demanded 1,590,000 amperes of power at 1345 volts in order to get the velocity and range predicted. Even today it would demand formidable engineering to produce a machine which could withstand that sort of power, as well as requiring a complete power station for each gun.

Anti-aircraft rockets

As the need to produce anti-aircraft defences grew quickly, Britain began experimenting in 1937 with unguided rockets, and eventually produced a wide variety of such weapons for anti-aircraft defence. Germany was better off for anti-aircraft guns and took very little interest in such things until about 1943, when it became apparent that extra defences were needed and needed fast. This reluctance to look at rockets earlier is all the more strange when one remembers that the Germans were the first to see the military possibilities of rockets and had some of the finest research facilities in the world at their service. It seems that simple 'firework' rockets were beneath their dignity, and all the work that went on was aimed at more sophisticated pieces of equipment. However, the advantages of the simple rocket were too great to be denied, and after some initial argument designs for air defence were put in hand.

The first to make an appearance was the 7·3-cm 'Föhn', a 35-barrel launcher mounted either on a trailer or set in a concrete bed for static sites. The rocket was a short and stubby article which, at first glance, resembled an ordinary gun shell. The nose carried 250 grams of high explosive and a percussion fuze, while the rest of the body contained a solid fuel motor burning for nine-tenths of a second to boost the speed to 850 mph. As it fired in salvos, the Föhn was a useful weapon but its chief liability was an

impact fuze that demanded a near-impossible direct hit on the target. Numbers of these launchers were deployed in Germany and, towards the end of the war, several were used as field artillery weapons, but so far as can be determined they were never successful in downing aircraft.

More ambitious was a 46-lb rocket driven by a liquid-fuel motor, 'Typhoon', which travelled at over 3000 feet a second to reach an altitude of nine miles or more. Work on this began at the latter end of 1944, and the design was accepted for production in October. Production began in January 1945, but only 600 rockets had been made before the war ended. One of the more remarkable things about it was that in spite of being liquid-fuelled, with all the apparent complexity which that arrangement brought with it, the cost was estimated at being 25 marks – about 80 pence in today's prices. A parallel design was 'Tornado', basically the same rocket but one which used a solid-fuel motor. The performance was almost the same, but due to the shortage of propellant materials affecting Germany by the beginning of 1945 there was some reluctance to approve Tornado for production. While the arguments were still going on the war came to an end.

All these weapons, of course, were crew-served and quite large, but with the introduction into service of one-man anti-tank weapons it seems to have occurred to somebody to try and produce an equivalent one-man anti-aircraft weapon. The result of this was *Fliegerfaust*, a little-known development which, had it come earlier in the war, would have made life very unhealthy indeed for low-flying aviators. It consisted of nine 20-mm tubes in a simple frame, with a shoulder rest and a pistol grip. Into the end went a clip carrying nine small rockets, and squeezing the trigger generated an electric current to ignite them. Five rockets were immediately fired from alternate tubes and the other four a tenth of a second later. This delay allowed the rockets to launch without disturbing each other by their blast and also gave a dispersion to the salvo which improved the chance of hitting.

The rockets were adaptations of the standard 20-mm aircraft cannon shell which had a steel tube crimped to the base of the shell and carried a stick of smokeless propellant. In the bottom of the tube were four angled vents and an electric ignition squib. When the squib fired and lit the propellant, the blast came through the angled vents and caused the rocket to spin in flight, stabilising the whole affair in the same fashion as a bullet fired from a rifled gun. Fitted with a simple optical sight, *Fliegerfaust* was a highly effective and dangerous weapon out to a range of about 2000 metres. But like so many ideas, time was against it: it was approved early in January 1945 and arrangements were made to manufacture 10,000 for immediate issue. Very few were, in fact, made, and as far as is known they never got into the hands of the soldiers who so desperately needed them. Indeed, it seems that only one or two specimens ever survived to be found by the Allies.

Another low-altitude device was the 'Short Time Barrage', more properly known as 'RSK 1000', intended for the defence of airfields. Developed by Rheinmettal-Borsig, this consisted of a number of 21-cm rocket motors buried in short mortar-like launching tubes around the perimeter of the airfield. Attached to the rocket was a parachute

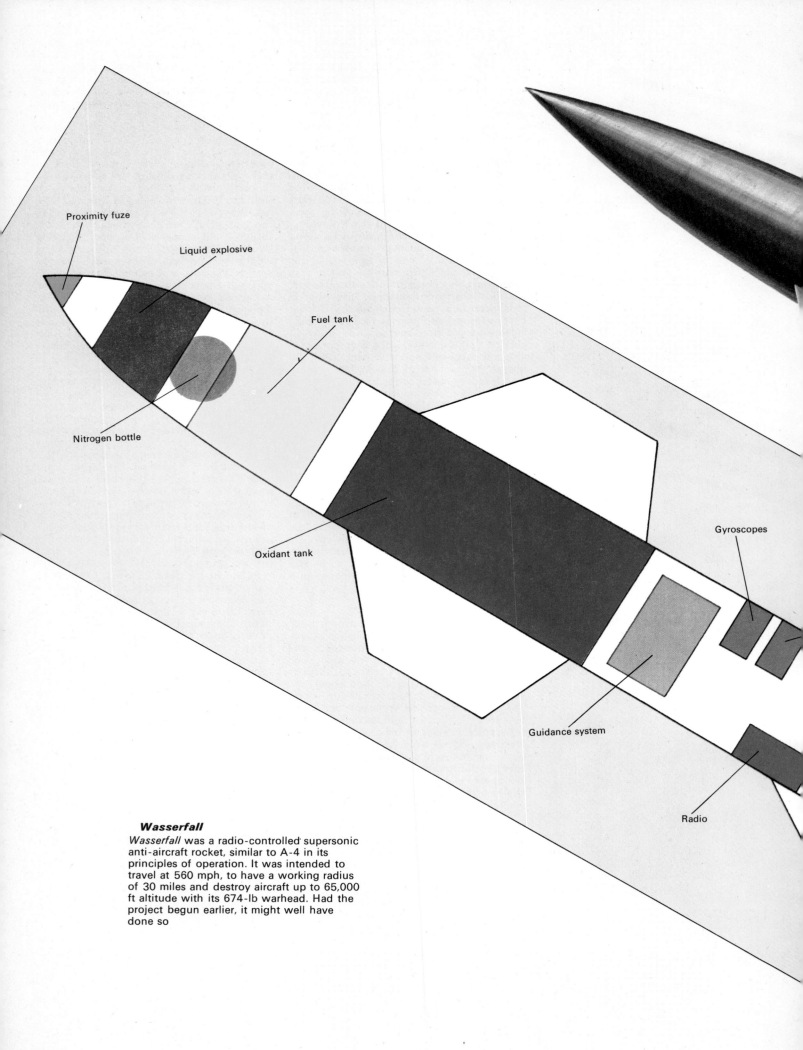

Proximity fuze

Liquid explosive

Fuel tank

Nitrogen bottle

Oxidant tank

Gyroscopes

Guidance system

Radio

Wasserfall

Wasserfall was a radio-controlled supersonic anti-aircraft rocket, similar to A-4 in its principles of operation. It was intended to travel at 560 mph, to have a working radius of 30 miles and destroy aircraft up to 65,000 ft altitude with its 674-lb warhead. Had the project begun earlier, it might well have done so

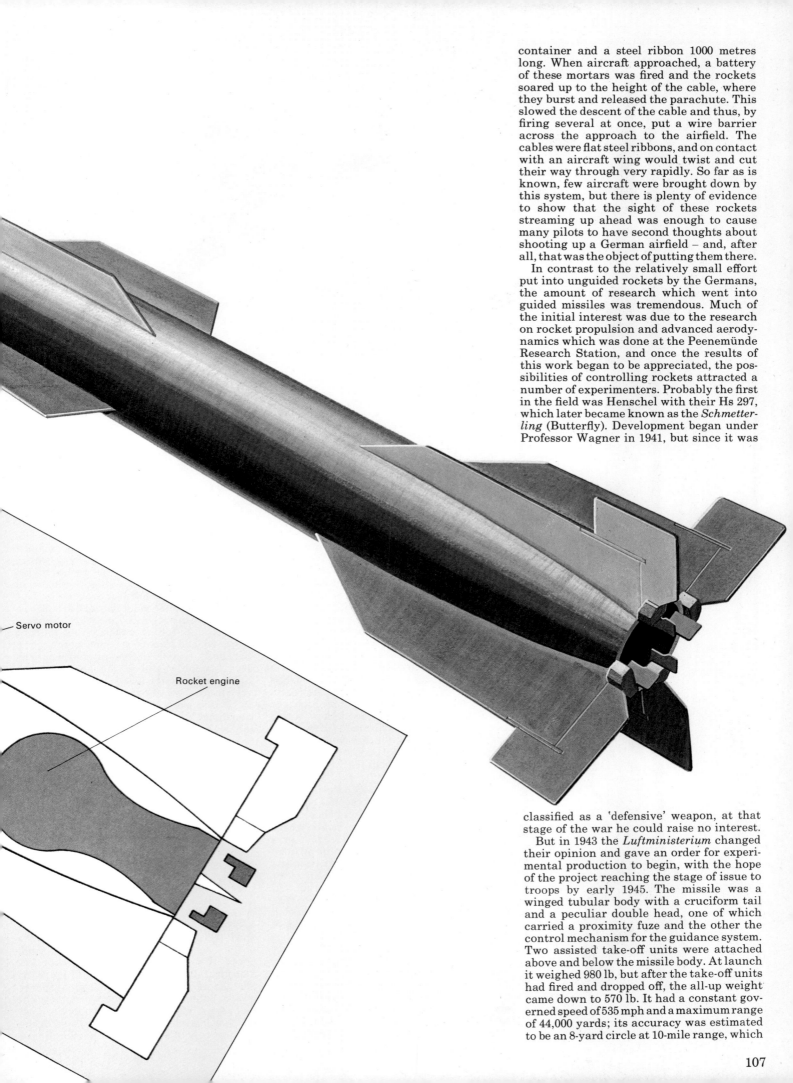

Servo motor

Rocket engine

container and a steel ribbon 1000 metres long. When aircraft approached, a battery of these mortars was fired and the rockets soared up to the height of the cable, where they burst and released the parachute. This slowed the descent of the cable and thus, by firing several at once, put a wire barrier across the approach to the airfield. The cables were flat steel ribbons, and on contact with an aircraft wing would twist and cut their way through very rapidly. So far as is known, few aircraft were brought down by this system, but there is plenty of evidence to show that the sight of these rockets streaming up ahead was enough to cause many pilots to have second thoughts about shooting up a German airfield – and, after all, that was the object of putting them there.

In contrast to the relatively small effort put into unguided rockets by the Germans, the amount of research which went into guided missiles was tremendous. Much of the initial interest was due to the research on rocket propulsion and advanced aerodynamics which was done at the Peenemünde Research Station, and once the results of this work began to be appreciated, the possibilities of controlling rockets attracted a number of experimenters. Probably the first in the field was Henschel with their Hs 297, which later became known as the *Schmetterling* (Butterfly). Development began under Professor Wagner in 1941, but since it was classified as a 'defensive' weapon, at that stage of the war he could raise no interest.

But in 1943 the *Luftministerium* changed their opinion and gave an order for experimental production to begin, with the hope of the project reaching the stage of issue to troops by early 1945. The missile was a winged tubular body with a cruciform tail and a peculiar double head, one of which carried a proximity fuze and the other the control mechanism for the guidance system. Two assisted take-off units were attached above and below the missile body. At launch it weighed 980 lb, but after the take-off units had fired and dropped off, the all-up weight came down to 570 lb. It had a constant governed speed of 535 mph and a maximum range of 44,000 yards; its accuracy was estimated to be an 8-yard circle at 10-mile range, which

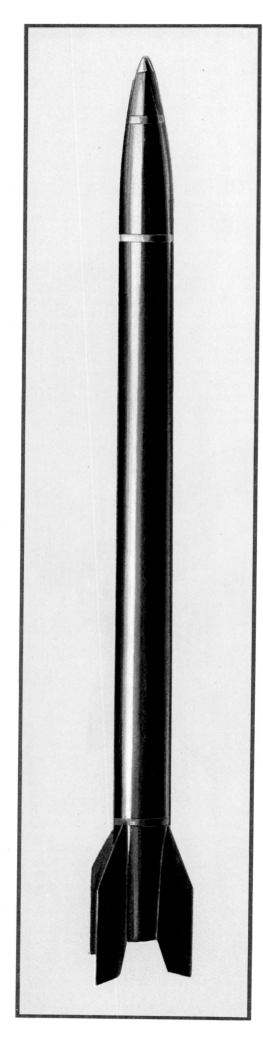

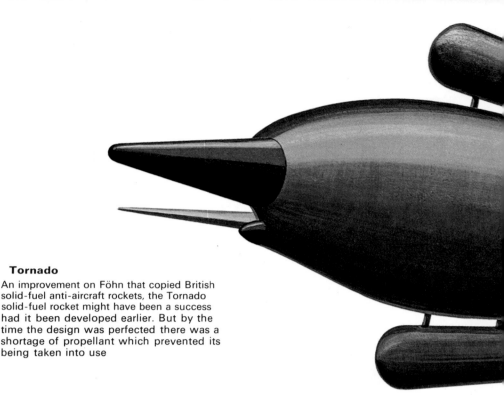

Tornado

An improvement on Föhn that copied British solid-fuel anti-aircraft rockets, the Tornado solid-fuel rocket might have been a success had it been developed earlier. But by the time the design was perfected there was a shortage of propellant which prevented its being taken into use

sounds a little optimistic. Control was by radio command from an operator who had the missile and target in view all the time.

Due to Allied bombing of the factory and also of the works of various subcontractors, the planned production schedule went wrong and the weapon never got into service. Moreover, the problems associated with controlling rockets at high speed were entirely new and took a lot of solving. Out of 59 test missiles launched, only 25 flew successfully and responded to guidance.

Next came *Wasserfall* (Waterfall), a 26-ft long liquid-fuelled rocket which bore a lot of resemblance to the A-4 bombardment rocket – not surprisingly since it was developed at Peenemünde. It was proposed in 1942 as a weapon for the defence of large cities, and the plans envisaged 200 batteries in three zones, fifty miles apart, which would virtually seal off Germany from the North Sea. A later revision of this idea proposed 300 batteries, which it was claimed would completely defend all Germany if suitably spaced out. To back up this deployment, a production of 5000 rockets per month would have to be achieved. Technically, *Wasserfall* was very advanced for its day. Vertically launched, it was gathered into the beam of a radar within the first 5 or 6 seconds of flight, and then controlled by radio in accordance with the indications of the radar which tracked both it and its target. At 3 or 4 kilometres from the target, an infrared homing system would detect the heat from the enemy bomber's engines and take over guidance of the missile to the target. To ensure success even should a near-miss occur, a proximity fuze was fitted, working on infrared principles and firing the warhead when within 10 metres of the target.

Work began in late 1942, and the first firing tests took place on the Griefswalder Oie, an island in the Baltic near Peenemünde, on 28 February 1944. The missile reached an altitude of 23,000 feet – a third of what had been hoped for. Eventually some fifty rockets were made and fired, but about a third were failures for one reason or another.

Development was eventually stopped in February 1945, though it is believed that one or two experimenters continued to work on the project until the last days of the war.

Next came *Enzian* (Gentian), a design which came very close to success. This was developed by a Doktor Wurster of Holzbach-Kissing AG in its early stages but in late 1943 the project was given to Messerschmitt to produce. It was an extremely powerful device, fuelled by a Walter liquid rocket and carrying half a ton of high explosive in the warhead. Take-off was assisted by four solid-fuel rockets, and it flew at 650 mph to a maximum range of 25,000 metres. There were at least 15 different models either built or proposed, and some 60 specimens were actually built to one design or another. The development was slow, but showed every sign of eventually being successful. However, in January 1945 the project was stopped by the *Luftwaffe* on the grounds of production difficulties which threatened to hold up the project indefinitely. Production of control systems and so forth actually continued for some time while Messerschmitt tried to argue with the *Luftwaffe*, but work finally stopped in March 1945. According to some reports, had the *Luftwaffe* been more co-operative in the early stages of development there is every chance that *Enzian* would have been in operation before the end of 1944. It seems that the aircraft production side of the *Luftwaffe* were adamant that Messerschmitt's job was making aeroplanes and not fooling around with missiles, and they lost no opportunity of making things difficult when it came to the supply of materials and allocation of sub-contractors.

The last anti-aircraft missiles to be developed were the *Rheintochter* series. This project began in 1942 when the *Luftwaffe* asked Rheinmettal-Borsig to develop an anti-aircraft rocket which would go to an altitude of 12,000 metres. What developed was an enormous 20-ft long two-stage solid-fuel rocket which carried a 300-lb warhead and was launched from a frame fitted to the gun-carriage of an 88-mm anti-aircraft gun.

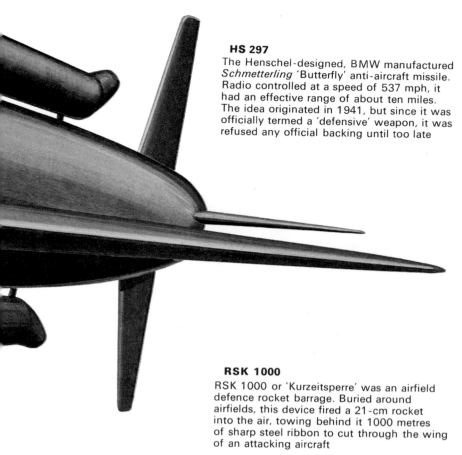

HS 297

The Henschel-designed, BMW manufactured
Schmetterling 'Butterfly' anti-aircraft missile.
Radio controlled at a speed of 537 mph, it
had an effective range of about ten miles.
The idea originated in 1941, but since it was
officially termed a 'defensive' weapon, it was
refused any official backing until too late

RSK 1000

RSK 1000 or 'Kurzeitsperre' was an airfield
defence rocket barrage. Buried around
airfields, this device fired a 21-cm rocket
into the air, towing behind it 1000 metres
of sharp steel ribbon to cut through the wing
of an attacking aircraft

Flight testing began in the late summer of
1943 near Leba on the Baltic, and by the
beginning of 1945 some 80-odd had been
fired with only a handful of failures. However, in mid-1944 the *Luftwaffe* had decided
that their target ceiling of 12,000 metres was
too small, and requested a more powerful
model. *Rheintochter I* then became simply a
test vehicle, and a new design, called
Rheintochter III (nobody knows where *II*
went to) was developed as the future service
missile. This was a much more efficient
design, 4 ft shorter, capable of using either
solid- or liquid-fuel rocket motors, with boost
motors to assist launching. Control was by
radio command, with the operator keeping
the missile in sight by watching red flares
attached to the tips of the tail unit. Once
arrived at the target, the warhead could be
detonated either by command from the
operator or by a proximity fuze which detected the noise of the bomber motors.

More ambitious still was the manned
Rheintochter project. This envisaged a pilot,
prone in the nose of the weapon, guiding it
towards its target on instructions from the
ground. Once set on a target interception
course, the pilot took to his parachute and
left the missile to go on and hit the target.
This project never got off the drawing board,
but *Rheintochter III* at least got to the test-
firing stage by early 1945. This rocket
worked well enough, but the radio control
system was never completed in time to be
tested before the whole project was stopped
in February.

A *Rheintochter* rocket photographed by John Batchelor at Aberdeen Proving Grounds in the United States

Rheintochter

Rheinmettal's attempt at a guided anti-aircraft rocket was *Rheintochter*, which carried a 330-lb warhead. Just as the company were beginning to get it to work, the *Luftministerium* demanded more range, so a fresh design was begun. This change of policy effectively prevented either model from reaching production

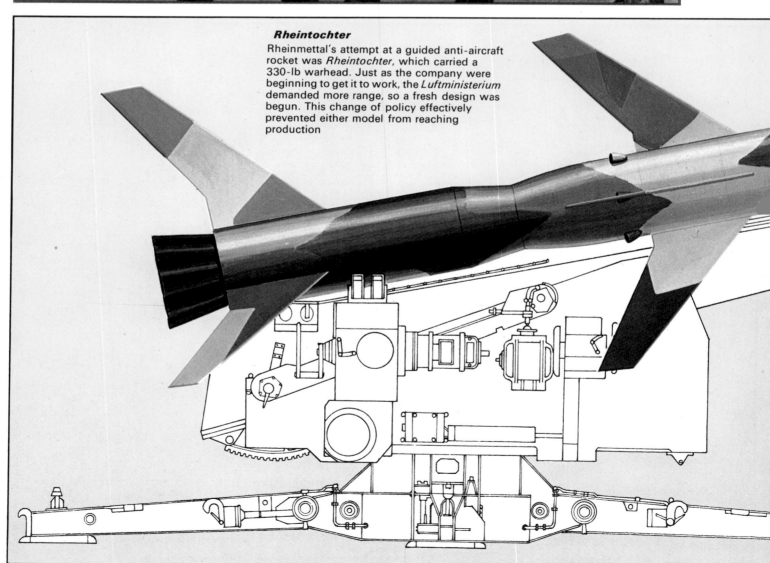

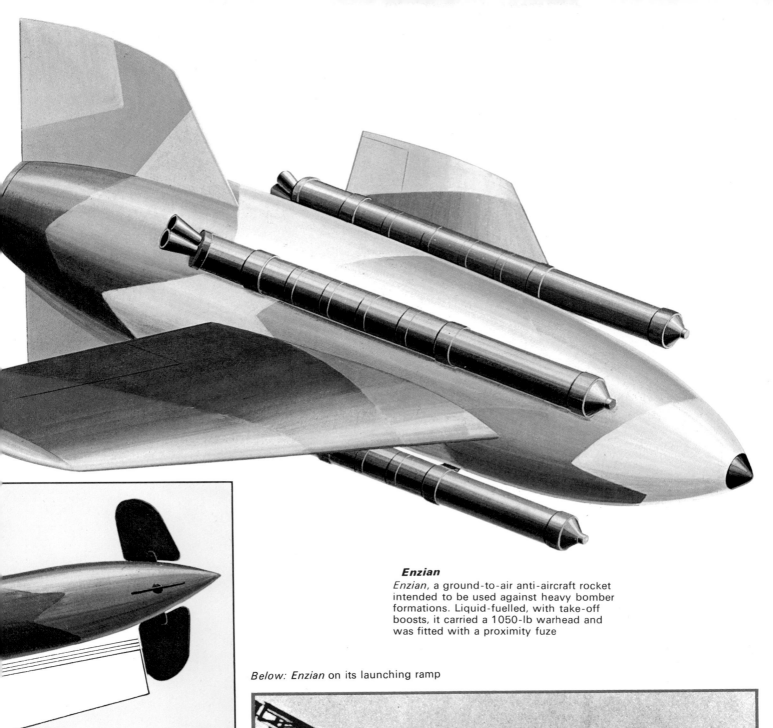

Enzian

Enzian, a ground-to-air anti-aircraft rocket intended to be used against heavy bomber formations. Liquid-fuelled, with take-off boosts, it carried a 1050-lb warhead and was fitted with a proximity fuze

Below: Enzian on its launching ramp

Perhaps the most vital secret weapon of the war, a screen of radar masts covered Britain during the German air offensive of 1940. Information was fed by high frequency radio-telephone to the Hurricane and Spitfire squadrons which were vectored onto the incoming enemy bomber streams

CASTING A NET TO THE SKY

In the middle 1930s the threat of the bomber loomed large over Europe; it seemed to be an insuperable threat, and when Mr. Baldwin made his famous observation that 'the bomber would always get through' he was only reflecting the official military opinion of the time. There seemed to be no way of stopping it short of filling the sky with fighter aircraft 24 hours a day. The man in the street was warned daily that war would bring hordes of bombers to swamp his city with poison gas, and when this warning began to wear thin, fuel was added to the fire by highly coloured accounts coming from Spain, notably the greatly exaggerated destruction of Guernica. But fortunately, by that time, Britain had begun to get the measure of the bomber threat.

As with submarines, the first problem was to locate the bomber, the second to deal with it. The standard method of location was by sound, and in order to get the best possible advance notice of an enemy bomber fleet crossing the North Sea, large curved 'sound mirrors' of concrete were built in southeastern England. These reflected the faint sound to sensitive microphones to give a few minutes warning of the approach of aircraft – sufficient, it was hoped, to allow guns to be manned and fighter aircraft to become airborne. But the margin of time was slim, and every time a faster bomber was announced, the margin grew slimmer.

Backing up the fighters
As is well known, the answer to this problem came with the development of Radar, with its beginnings in 1935. The story of this particular secret weapon has been so well documented and discussed that we need not go into it closely here. The point which concerns us is that with the question of detection and warning solved – or at least on the way to being solved – the question of attacking the bomber could now be explored. Fighter aircraft were on the drawing board, but the prime problem was the production of anti-aircraft guns in sufficient numbers to back up the fighters.

At the end of the First World War the anti-aircraft strength of the army had been slashed so rapidly that by 1924 there were virtually no anti-aircraft guns left in service except for an experimental handful. This was due to the opinion that the proper enemy of the aircraft was another aircraft, and it took some years before the error of this view became apparent. During the 1920s the Army were busy working on designs of a new anti-aircraft gun, but due to the shortage of funds very little could be done until re-armament began. Then, with

the threat stark before them, the Government finally authorised funds for anti-aircraft guns, and the 3·7-in gun was rapidly put through the final phases of its development and placed in production. This was an excellent gun, the best of its class in the world at the time. Originally mooted in 1920, designs were put forward in 1934, the pilot tested in 1936, production approved in April 1937 and the first gun supplied to the Army in January 1938. With such a long procedure to get the weapon into service, it was obvious that some other solution had to be looked for in order to find the necessary gun strength to defend the approaches to London against bombing attacks.

A Heinkel He 111 caught by a British fighter. Radar gave the defences an absolute advantage

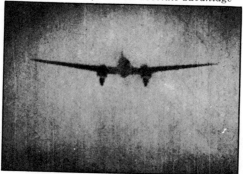

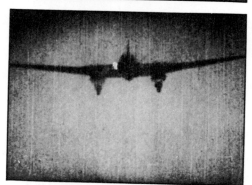

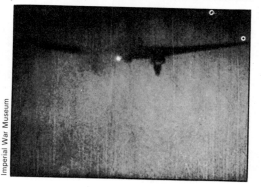

Imperial War Museum

As a result of this problem, the Research Department at Woolwich Arsenal were asked, in 1935, to develop some sort of rocket device which would replace the missing anti-aircraft guns. Their terms of reference were startlingly simple; they could make what they liked, but whatever they made, it had to get up to 15,000 ft altitude as fast as a gun shell.

The experimenters were very much on their own. While numbers of people had been playing with rockets for years, very little of what they had found out – or at least, had publicly announced – bore much significance to this line of research, and the Woolwich team had to start at square one. Fortunately there was, in British service, a suitable solid propellant – a variety of cordite – which could be extruded in thick sticks to make rocket motors, and it was this material which decided the sizes of rockets designed. The smallest stick which would produce an efficient rocket was two inches in diameter, while the largest which could be extruded on the existing machinery was three inches.

By the autumn of 1936 successful rocket motors in both sizes had been designed and fired, and work began on producing warheads and fuzes. Existing gun fuzes could not be used, since they were designed to be armed by the violent acceleration in the gun and the centrifugal force developed by the spinning of the shell, and neither of these forces was available in a rocket environment. Lethality trials showed that the 3-in rocket carrying a 20-lb head gave the best results against aircraft, and from mid-1937 onwards the perfection of this became the principal task. The 2-in model was kept, however, as an experimental vehicle and it was later to prove its worth in a number of weapon applications. A fuze which relied on air pressure on launch to ignite a pyrotechnic timing delay was developed, and in the spring of 1939, 2500 rockets were shipped to Jamaica, in utmost secrecy, for extensive firing trials.

The design of a suitable launcher was, however, causing problems. The Army wanted a closed tube launcher resembling a gun, and this gave rise to great technical difficulties, the net result of which was poor accuracy. And as an inaccurate anti-aircraft gun was felt to be worse than no anti-aircraft gun at all, in the middle of 1939 the whole project was abandoned as being insoluble at the current level of knowledge.

A few weeks after this decision, war broke out, and before the end of September the Royal Navy were asking for some sort of device to deter dive-bombers from attacking coastal vessels. The first solution was

Parachute and Cable in action

a 'Parachute and Cable' (PAC) device propelled by a 2-in rocket, officially called the 'Apparatus Air Defence Type L'. A 2-in rocket motor towed a canister up to 1000 ft altitude and there ejected a 600-ft cable carrying a parachute at each end, one of which also supported a small explosive mine with a contact fuze. If an aircraft struck the cable, the drag of the larger parachute drew the cable across the wing until the mine came into contact, whereupon it detonated with sufficient force to blow off the wing.

Another model, the 'Type J', had the cable coiled in a drum on the ship's deck. This allowed the rocket to soar to 2000 ft, uncoiling the cable as it went and then lifting it into the air. At the top of the trajectory the cable was cast free and the action was the same as that of the Type L.

Parachute and Cable Apparatus

The 'Apparatus Air Defence Type L' involved a 2-in rocket towing 600 ft of parachute-supported cable up to 1000 ft. An aircraft catching the cable would drag a mine on one end against its wing

While these were effective, they were involved weapons. Each required three parachutes, cable, mine, fuzes, explosive ejection devices and timing devices, and a complicated assembly job. The Royal Navy felt that it might be simpler just to fling a salvo of plain, high-explosive, impact-fuzed rockets into the air. Fill the sky with metal and something was bound to happen. The result of this line of thought was 'Pig Trough', a simple gimballed rack carrying 14 2-in rockets, fired electrically. This rack was fitted on the ship's foredeck; being gimballed, it was independent of the ship's motion and would always fire straight up into the air. Since the course of the dive-bomber invariably took it across the ship, a salvo of rockets fired skywards was a highly efficient deterrent even if it did not actually hit the aircraft. And the inherent inaccuracy of the short 2-in rocket gave a useful random pattern to the salvo which, if anything, increased the chances of hitting.

Pig Trough was moderately successful, even considering that it was impossible to

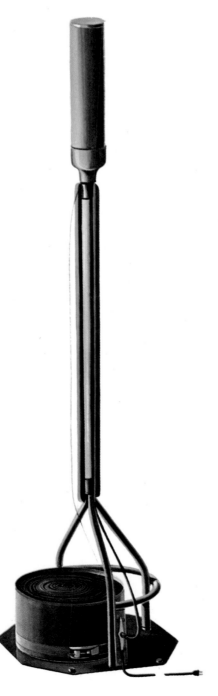

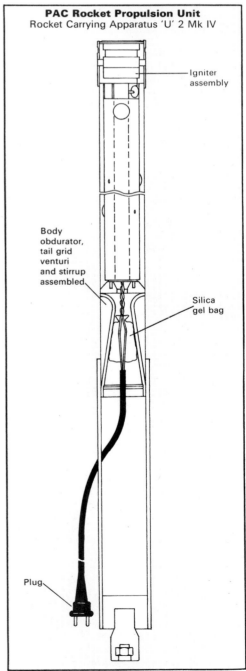

PAC Rocket Propulsion Unit
Rocket Carrying Apparatus 'U' 2 Mk IV

Igniter assembly

Body obdurator, tail grid venturi and stirrup assembled

Silica gel bag

Plug

aim it. There followed a spate of improvements, adding the ability to aim and point and thus repel the aircraft sooner in the action. The first attempt, an ambitious remote-controlled device, was a failure: the hydraulic control system never worked as it was supposed to, and the rockets rarely went where they were intended. The next, known as 'Pillar Box', was rather more successful. It was a circular metal box in which the gunner sat, with a rack of ten rockets on each side of him. From his central position he could elevate and traverse the whole unit, select the number of rockets needed, and fire the salvos while being protected from the back-flash of the rockets.

An offshoot of Pig Trough was known as 'Radiator', probably because the plan drawings rather resembled a domestic hot-water radiator. This was a ten-rocket launcher, very similar to Pig Trough, but fixed rigidly on a shore-based installation and used to discourage dive-bombers from attacking harbours and dockyards.

Rough but ready
So far all the rocket weapons had been built with the dive-bomber in mind, but now thought turned to the conventional level-flight bomber, which was proving just as big a nuisance. In the spring of 1940, with the military situation rapidly getting worse and with the prospect of massive air attacks in the near future, the British Army took another look at the rocket weapons, and in conjunction with the Royal Navy designed a simple launcher to fire a 3-in rocket. The overriding consideration in its design was its manufacture from cheap and easily available materials. This weapon became known as the 'Harvey' projector, since the early models were all made by the G A Harvey Company of Greenwich, although its official name was the 'Projector 3-in No 1 Mk 1'.

It is worth noting here that the names of all the devices so far mentioned give no clue as to their system of operation; rockets were a closely guarded secret at this time. They were not even referred to as rockets, but were known as 'Unrotated Projectiles' – 'UPs' – and the use of the word 'rocket' was strictly forbidden.

One of the things which sparked off the sudden revival of military interest in the 3-in rocket was the promise of something really revolutionary – a proximity fuze for the warhead. The biggest problem in anti-aircraft fire was the difficulty of bursting the shell at the correct moment in its flight. It was accepted that a direct hit was highly unlikely, and therefore time fuzes were used. The fire control process involved calculating the time of flight of the shell from gun to target, and the fuze was set accordingly.

With the best will in the world, the result could only be an approximation. The initial prediction of the target's position could be in error; the time between working out the setting, applying it to the fuze, and then firing the shell from the gun was variable from shot to shot; the shell's velocity might not be exactly what the calculators thought; and finally the operation of the fuze itself was far from precise since it relied on the burning of a length of gunpowder, something which was affected by a number of variables in the atmosphere. The upshot of all these possible errors was the existence of a zone of error in the bursting of the shell which could extend to two or three hundred

RN ratings load 2-in rockets into 'Pig Trough'. The device was impossible to aim, but could fill the sky with impact-fuzed high explosive, an excellent deterrent against attacking dive-bombers

'Strength through Joy', a development of Pig Trough, involved two sets of rocket launchers, one on each side of the operator who could aim them from his box. Unfortunately, the hydraulics gave constant trouble

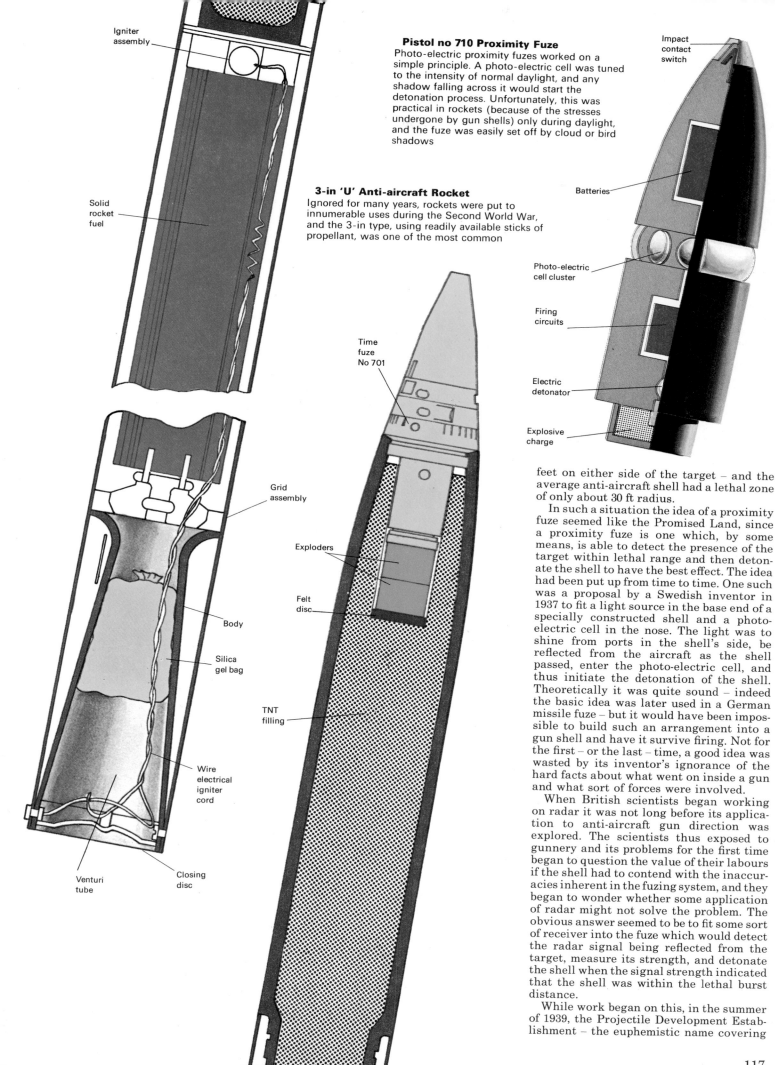

Igniter assembly

Solid rocket fuel

Grid assembly

Body

Silica gel bag

Wire electrical igniter cord

Venturi tube

Closing disc

Time fuze No 701

Exploders

Felt disc

TNT filling

Impact contact switch

Batteries

Photo-electric cell cluster

Firing circuits

Electric detonator

Explosive charge

Pistol no 710 Proximity Fuze
Photo-electric proximity fuzes worked on a simple principle. A photo-electric cell was tuned to the intensity of normal daylight, and any shadow falling across it would start the detonation process. Unfortunately, this was practical in rockets (because of the stresses undergone by gun shells) only during daylight, and the fuze was easily set off by cloud or bird shadows

3-in 'U' Anti-aircraft Rocket
Ignored for many years, rockets were put to innumerable uses during the Second World War, and the 3-in type, using readily available sticks of propellant, was one of the most common

feet on either side of the target – and the average anti-aircraft shell had a lethal zone of only about 30 ft radius.

In such a situation the idea of a proximity fuze seemed like the Promised Land, since a proximity fuze is one which, by some means, is able to detect the presence of the target within lethal range and then detonate the shell to have the best effect. The idea had been put up from time to time. One such was a proposal by a Swedish inventor in 1937 to fit a light source in the base end of a specially constructed shell and a photo-electric cell in the nose. The light was to shine from ports in the shell's side, be reflected from the aircraft as the shell passed, enter the photo-electric cell, and thus initiate the detonation of the shell. Theoretically it was quite sound – indeed the basic idea was later used in a German missile fuze – but it would have been impossible to build such an arrangement into a gun shell and have it survive firing. Not for the first – or the last – time, a good idea was wasted by its inventor's ignorance of the hard facts about what went on inside a gun and what sort of forces were involved.

When British scientists began working on radar it was not long before its application to anti-aircraft gun direction was explored. The scientists thus exposed to gunnery and its problems for the first time began to question the value of their labours if the shell had to contend with the inaccuracies inherent in the fuzing system, and they began to wonder whether some application of radar might not solve the problem. The obvious answer seemed to be to fit some sort of receiver into the fuze which would detect the radar signal being reflected from the target, measure its strength, and detonate the shell when the signal strength indicated that the shell was within the lethal burst distance.

While work began on this, in the summer of 1939, the Projectile Development Establishment – the euphemistic name covering

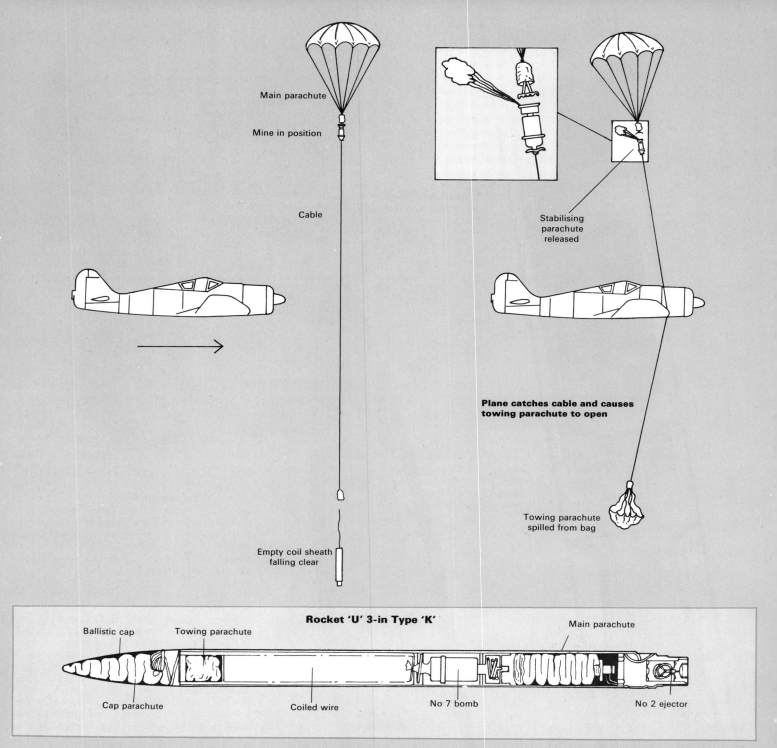

Main parachute

Mine in position

Cable

Stabilising
parachute
released

**Plane catches cable and causes
towing parachute to open**

Empty coil sheath
falling clear

Towing parachute
spilled from bag

Rocket 'U' 3-in Type 'K'

Ballistic cap

Towing parachute

Main parachute

Cap parachute

Coiled wire

No 7 bomb

No 2 ejector

the rocket research station at Aberporth in Wales – looked again at the idea of using a photo-electric cell. Since the acceleration of a rocket was much less violent than that of a gun shell it seemed likely that even such a delicate device might survive launching to function in the sky. The refinement of a self-contained light source was discarded, reliance being placed on a more powerful and more easily available one – the sun. The proposition, as it eventually took shape, was very simple: the photo-electric cell would be 'tuned' to the intensity of normal daylight, and if the shadow of an aircraft fell across the fuze, reducing the light level, the cell would trigger a circuit to detonate the shell.

It was the promise of this fuze – officially called the Pistol No 710 – which now revived interest in the dormant 3-in rocket. A thousand Harvey projectors were built and distributed, fuzes went into production, and by the spring of 1941 the new anti-aircraft defences, known as 'Z' batteries, were ready

for anti-aircraft operation both on land and on Royal Navy ships.

Unfortunately things didn't go quite as well as had been hoped. The Pistol 710 performed erratically – sometimes the varying strength of daylight caused it to act prematurely, sometimes the shadow of clouds or passing birds was enough to set it off. Its failings were underlined by the attempt to use the rocket projector as if it were a gun, predicting the target and attempting to aim the rocket so as to get the warhead close to the target. This system fell down because of the rocket's inaccuracy in comparison with a gun, even though the Harvey projector, using open rails to hold the rocket, was more accurate than the original closed-tube model the Army had demanded. But the rocket had advantages which could not be denied: cheapness, simplicity and robustness of the launcher. An analysis of anti-aircraft firings in the southeastern part of England during 1940/41 indicated that firing the rockets in pre-

calculated barrages might well prove effective; it could certainly be no worse than the existing method of fire control.

By this time a new design of projector, firing two rockets at once, had been developed and was in production. But the Pistol 710 had reached the end of its usefulness. While it had been tolerable against daylight raiders, it was totally useless when the Luftwaffe switched to night bombing methods. It was therefore phased out and a conventional time fuze took its place. Since the system of fire control no longer worried about getting the rocket particularly close to the target, the fuze error was not significant any more.

Batteries of 64 launchers, firing 128-rocket salvos, were now installed, principally in coastal sites or in locations where there was a fair acreage of open space. The 'Z' Batteries had one slight drawback: 128 rockets and warheads went up – and shortly afterwards, 128 spent rocket motors fell back to the earth beneath. In those days,

3-in 'U' Type K AA Rocket

This device was fired up to 19,000 ft, where it ejected 100 ft of wire, with a small stabilising parachute on one end, and a parachute container on the other. When the cable was snagged by the wing of a plane, the towing parachute opened, dragging the mine against the wing. Fired in barrages of 128, this device could create havoc among a bomber formation

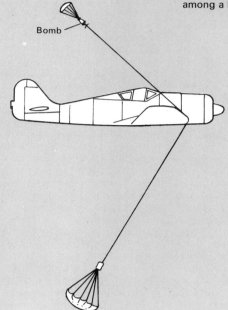

Bomb

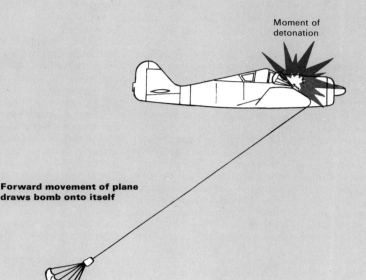

Moment of detonation

Forward movement of plane draws bomb onto itself

an acquaintance of mine was stationed on a coast gun site on Flatholm Island, in the Bristol Channel, and whenever the 'Z' Batteries near Cardiff opened fire, the entire strength of the garrison of Flatholm Island immediately took cover, anticipating the shower of rocket motor tubes – each almost five feet long and weighing 18 lb – which would shortly descend upon them.

Devastating effect

These batteries turned out to be highly effective, and before long a more lethal type of barrage was evolved. This was the 'K' rocket, nine feet long with a head carrying 1000 ft of wire, parachutes and a contact mine. This soared to 19,000 ft and there released the parachute and cable assembly to float down at 15 ft a second. It worked in the same fashion as the 2-in PAC models had done – the mine being dragged into contact by the parachute when an aircraft struck the cable – and the effect of 128 of these devices fired into the path of a bomber formation, particularly at night, was, as can be imagined, devastating.

When the bomber threat was considered, in pre-war days, it seemed to divide itself conveniently into two distinct and separate sections: there was, on the one hand, the high-altitude bomber, and on the other the dive-bomber and low-altitude attacker – or 'strafer' as it was still known, a hang-over from a First World War phrase. To deal with the first threat, the Army developed their 3·7-in gun, firing a 28-lb shell to 32,000 ft.

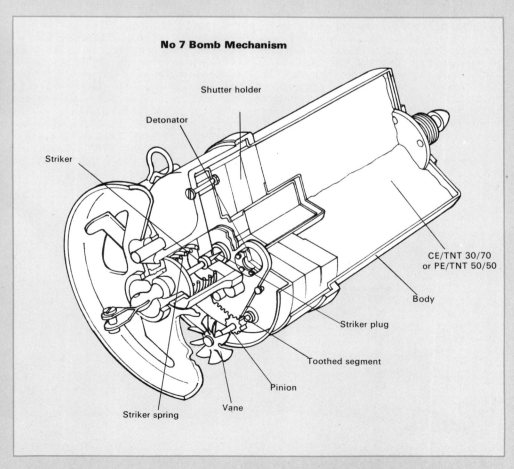

No 7 Bomb Mechanism

Shutter holder

Detonator

Striker

CE/TNT 30/70 or PE/TNT 50/50

Body

Striker plug

Toothed segment

Pinion

Vane

Striker spring

To deal with the second, after looking at various alternatives and weighing up the production problems, the Swedish 40-mm Bofors gun was selected. In April 1937 the decision was taken to buy 100 guns and half-a-million rounds from Sweden and set up production in Britain.

Subsequent thought on the problem showed that between them, these two guns left a hole in the sky. The Bofors gun could deal with anything up to about 5000 ft, but the 3·7 was not at its best until about 12,000 ft, due to the angular speed of a low-flying aircraft being more than the traversing mechanism of the gun could follow. It seemed that there was room for a third gun – an 'intermediate' anti-aircraft gun. It might be said here that the same sort of sums were being done elsewhere, and at about the same time – 1938 – the German Army were beginning studies into an intermediate gun as well.

But in 1938 there was so much pressure on the munitions factories to turn out the more immediately required guns – both anti-aircraft and field – that there was little hope of introducing yet another design into the service, so the question had to be shelved. From time to time it was reconsidered, largely to see if there was any existing gun which could be made to fill the bill, but it was not until April 1941 that a decision was taken to develop a new weapon.

A series of conferences had been held from January onwards at which various suggestions were put up and examined in detail. It was not simply a matter of designing a gun – there had to be a radar and predictor and other fire control instruments to suit. Eventually in April the call went forth for a 6-pounder 57-mm gun, firing an impact-fuzed shell at 3000 ft per second, to a height of 15,000 ft, and at a rate of 100 to 120 rounds a minute. Broadly speaking, the weapon was to be based on a twin 57-mm gun design from Bofors of Sweden.

To understand what follows, it is necessary to know that there were already two designs of 6-pounder guns in British service: the 6-pounder of seven hundredweight, an anti-tank and tank gun; and the 6-pounder of ten hundredweight, a coast defence gun. Since these existed, it obviously occurred to someone that if one of them could be used

as the basis of the new gun, then production would be simplified. The choice fell on the coast defence gun, and a number of elderly Hotchkiss 6-pounder equipments which had in years gone by been relegated as training guns were taken for conversion. But the Hotchkiss design dated back to 1885 and had been designed with a muzzle velocity of no more than 1800 ft per second in mind, so it was obviously incapable of producing the sort of fire-power demanded for modern conditions.

Nevertheless, these guns formed a useful basis on which to start designing a mounting, and a twin-gun mount riding on a three-wheeled transporter was put in hand. By December 1941 the design of this had taken shape and it was refined by giving the equipment an anti-tank capability as well as an anti-aircraft one. Work then began on developing a suitable automatic loading gear, but this was easier said than done since the guns used hand-operated breech mechanisms, and coupling these to an automatic loading system was straining things. In May 1942 the Molins Company, who had made quite a reputation for their auto-loading designs for other guns, were introduced to the twin 6-pounder and invited to do their best, while at the same time a completely new gun was designed. When this eventually arrived it incorporated all the latest refinements in rifling and construction and weighed slightly over six hundredweight, so that now there was a third class of 6-pounder in service.

While all this had been going on, a single-gun equipment had also been in the design and development system, while other establishments had worked on new shells, fuzes and cartridge cases. The electronics people were also working on the radar and computer, but it soon became obvious that the original estimate of having the equipment in service by mid-1942 was never going to be achieved. The picture then became even worse and was complicated by certain

suggestions which had been made to modify the coast artillery 6-pounder. This was also a twin-gun unit, mounted in a turret, and it was proposed that these should be modified to make them capable of shooting upwards and thus doubling as anti-aircraft guns. And so by 1944 there was a single-gun AA 6-pounder with automatic loading; a twin-gun AA 6-pounder capable of firing at low angles and with semi-automatic loading; and a twin-gun coastal 6-pounder capable of firing AA, with hand loading. At this point the development of these three weapons gets so intermingled that it is almost impossible to explain simply. There is, however, little point in pursuing the process to its end, for the fact of the matter is that the war ended without the 6-pounder AA gun ever getting into service.

The principal drawback had been the automatic loading. By the time it was licked into shape the performance of aircraft had so surpassed the 1941 specification that there was no point in continuing to develop the gun. The single-barrel weapon was kept in existence for a few more years, principally as a test-bed for a variety of automatic loading systems which were produced for trial, but once that function was complete, the whole design was scrapped. The only consolation about the whole affair was that the Germans also had troubles and never got their design into production either.

Radar in miniature

From a secret weapon which failed, we can now happily turn to one which was one of the most potent developments of the war. We have already mentioned the development of a proximity fuze for rockets

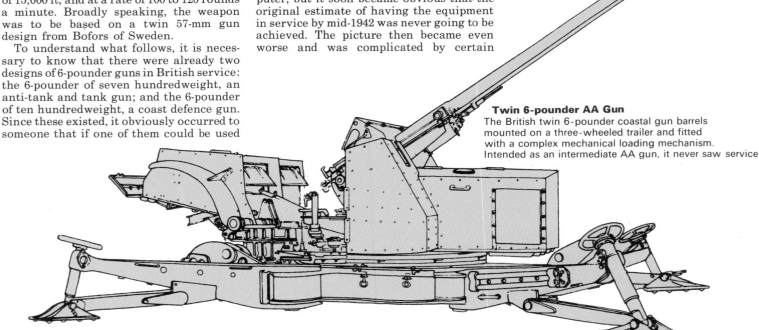

Twin 6-pounder AA Gun
The British twin 6-pounder coastal gun barrels mounted on a three-wheeled trailer and fitted with a complex mechanical loading mechanism. Intended as an intermediate AA gun, it never saw service

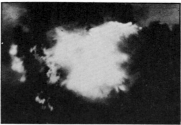

The end of a flying bomb as recorded by a gun camera fitted to an RAF fighter. Secret developments in the anti-aircraft field backed up the efforts of the fighters, and soon most of the V-1s were being stopped before reaching their target

US Navy Mk 45 Proximity Fuze
A masterpiece of electronic engineering, and one of the most useful developments of the war, this fuze contained a miniature radar transmitter and receiver powerful enough to detonate the shell when a target was detected

Condensors

Condensors

Surrounding capsule

Brass tip

Red translucent plastic

Detonator

Steel

Charge

that worked on photo-electric principles, and it will be remembered that the original concept called for some form of radar receiver in the fuze which would detect the radar reflections from the aircraft due to its being 'illuminated' by the gun control radar. Work had gone on with this idea during 1938/39, but it soon became obvious that it was impossible. The radar reflections were so weak that large and complex assemblies of receivers and amplifiers were required to produce any sort of signal which could be made to operate a triggering circuit. The tiny space available inside a shell fuze could not permit such a receiver to be built. So the scientists turned to the idea of constructing the whole unit – transmitter and receiver – in the fuze. This would ensure that the signal would be strong enough to go out, strike the target and be reflected with still sufficient power to operate a circuit.

By the spring of 1940 the theoretical studies were completed and showed that the idea was feasible, provided one or two small items which had not yet been invented could be produced – such as electronic valves 10 mm long, a tiny battery capable of delivering over 100 volts and similar ingenious components. The wireless and electrical industry in Britain was by this time fully employed in producing radios for the Armed Forces and radar for the new Royal Air Force bombing devices and Navy and Army gun control, and there was no research facility which was not fully engaged. Moreover, even had the problem components been designed, there was no factory available to manufacture them.

In the autumn of 1940 a scientific mission led by Sir Henry Tizard went to the United States in order to exchange information

with American scientists and enlist their help in solving some of the scientific problems facing Britain. Among the many projects revealed by the mission were the first British researches on the atomic bomb, the cavity magnetron which led to the development of microwave radar – and the plans for the proximity fuze. The United States Navy decided to take on the development of the fuze, and they enlisted the aid of a variety of commercial companies: Eastman Kodak for the general design, Exide for the special batteries, Sylvania for the tiny valves. Vast resources were poured into the programme, and by early 1943 working fuzes were fired and proved effective and production began. In June 1943 the USS *Helena* fired at Japanese aircraft in the Pacific the first gun proximity fuze to be used in combat.

The proximity fuze (or 'Pozit' fuze, or 'Peter' fuze or 'VT' fuze – it laboured under a variety of names in its early days for

Sir Henry Tizard, famous as head of the celebrated Committee for the Scientific Survey of Air Defence

security reasons) was essentially a self-contained radio transmitter and receiver built into an oversized fuze. The head section carried the radio components and aerial, the body of the shell also forming part of the aerial array. The shank of the fuze, concealed inside the shell body when the two were assembled together, contained a powerful battery and a multiplicity of safety devices to ensure that the fuze could not possibly operate in or near the gun. The battery was an ingenious design, a number of doughnut-shaped plates surrounding a glass ampoule of electrolyte.

Until the fuze was fired from a gun, the battery was quite inert, but firing the fuze broke the ampoule and allowed the acid to run into the cavity of the plates. The spinning of the fuze in flight caused the acid to spread over the plates by centrifugal force, and within three seconds the battery was delivering 140 volts, which was tapped off in suitable amounts to drive the receiver, the transmitter, and charge up a firing condenser. With the battery alive, the transmitter began radiating signals from the aerial, and the polar diagram of the signal was matched to the lethal burst area of the shell's fragments. This made sure that any item which reflected the signal was in the best place to receive the subsequent benefit. When the shell approached a target, the signal from the aerial was reflected back and picked up by the receiver, and when the strength of this signal indicated that the shell was within lethal distance of the target, the receiver triggered a firing circuit which allowed the firing condenser to discharge into an electric detonator and thus detonate the shell.

Not unnaturally, since the US Navy were the developers of the fuze, they had first priority on it, and it was not until 1944 that models suitable for use in British guns were in production and were shipped across to Britain. They were just in time: on 13 June the Germans began their long-awaited flying bomb campaign with the first of the FZG-76 'Doodlebug' missiles.

Preparations had been made for this eventuality, and three days later the 'DIVER' plans went into action; 192 heavy and 246 light anti-aircraft guns were spread across Kent and Sussex, backed up by 480 barrage balloons to catch anything which got past. The Royal Air Force fighters had the rest of Kent and the English Channel in which to do their part. By the end of the month about 100 flying bombs were coming across each day, of which the fighters would get 30 and the guns and balloons eight or ten. Considering that the guns were being presented with a target which flew straight, at a constant height and at a constant speed, it was felt that they should do better than that, and more guns were poured into the defences until by the end of the month there were 376 heavy and 1275 light guns and a total of 1700 balloons.

One of the first moves in the battle of the flying bomb had been by General Sir

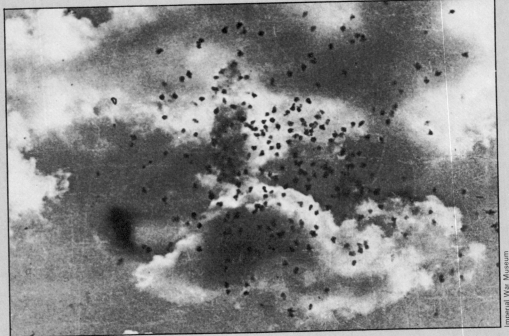

'Tonsil' anti-V-1 barrage rockets being fired (above) and exploding (top), July 1944. A battery of 20 projectors each fired two bursts of ten 2-in rockets with HE heads and time and impact fuzes which exploded the shells at 1500 yards. The shadow of a blown-up V-1 can be seen in the top picture

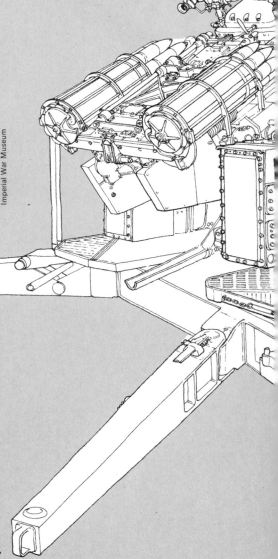

US 75-mm Skysweeper AA Gun
Designed to take advantage of the proximity fuze, and one of the most advanced anti-aircraft guns ever built, the Skysweeper's mounting contained its own radar and fire control equipment.
It did not reach service until the early 1950s

Frederick Pile, commanding Anti-Aircraft Command. He sent an emissary to the United States with a flying bomb; in Washington General George C Marshall, US Chief of Staff, heard of this visitor and called him in. Having digested the nature of the threat, General Marshall asked what was needed. '300 radar sets and 3000 proximity fuzes' was the reply, to which General Marshall answered 'The first lot will be on board ship tomorrow . . . . but see Eisenhower when you get back and see if he agrees.' Eisenhower not only agreed, he sent three regiments of American guns along to help.

The final solution
But having the proximity fuzes wasn't the whole battle. In those early days of development there was a constant danger that a fuze might not function properly and might fall back to earth without having detonated the shell, and the subsequent damage could well be serious. Therefore proximity fuzes could only be used where there was no danger of their falling on friendly ground. As it happened, this difficulty was removed just as the fuzes arrived. On 10 July it was decided that the guns were

unable to produce their best performance since they were hampered by the fighters. Often guns could not engage a target because RAF fighters were in the area or because fighters had priority in that zone. So in order to remove these restrictions, a final re-shuffle was organised. All the guns went to the South Coast; this left the Channel and the inland zones free for the fighters. By 19 July, 412 heavy guns (including 16 American), 1184 light guns and 200 rocket projectors were in position along the coast, the proximity fuzes were issued, and new American radar sets with automatic following capability were in position.

The results were spectacular: in the following seven weeks the guns got 1198 missiles out of a total of 3800 launched, the proportion of missiles downed by the guns being increased from 43% to 83% of those destroyed. The best day was 28 August: of 97 missiles launched against England, the guns got 65, fighters 23, and balloons 2. Only four reached London, the other three falling harmlessly in open country. Without any

Skysweeper Loading Gear
Twin revolving magazines carried 10 rounds each
and fed alternately on to a swinging tray.
The round was loaded automatically, and as the
tray returned for the next round, the gun fired
and ejected the empty cartridge case

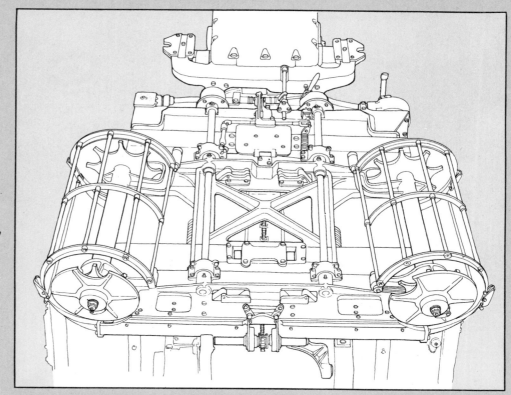

doubt, the proximity fuze saved London from a fearsome battering at the hands of the Doodlebug.

While all this was going on, designers in America were looking at one of the fundamental facts of the proximity fuze – that it did not need any form of setting before firing – and they began working on a specification for a gun to take advantage of this. The need to set fuzes before loading them had always been a hampering factor in anti-aircraft gunnery, and some weird and wonderful machinery had been devised to try and automate the process. If the gun could be designed around the proximity fuze in order to do away with the time-consuming business of fuze-setting, the rate of fire would increase spectacularly.

On 10 August 1944, a specification was drawn up for a gun of about 75-mm calibre, firing proximity-fuzed ammunition at 2000 ft per second at 35 rounds a minute. It was also to be provided with anti-tank ammunition, and was to be power-operated to be able to track and engage an aircraft flying at 550 mph at only 250 yards range. In this way it was hoped to produce a weapon which would function as an intermediate anti-aircraft gun and also replace the Bofors 40-mm for close-range work.

Last minute re-think
In less than five months the gun was ready, though the mounting took rather longer since it included all the fire-control equipment, radar and predictor actually on the mounting, but by June 1945 the design was clear. By then the specification had been looked at once again and it was realised that a velocity of 2000 ft per second was distinctly second-class. A re-design was put in hand in order to produce 3000

ft per second. This change of specification effectively ruled out any chance of getting the gun into service before the war ended, and as an insurance policy, work began on designing a new 3-in gun which, it was hoped, would do all the same things but still get 3000 ft per second rather easier. A contract was let for one million dollars in August 1945, but before the designers could do much more than sharpen their pencils the war ended and the project was cancelled. Work continued at slightly lower pressure on the 75-mm project, and this eventually reached service in the early 1950s as the 75-mm 'Skysweeper' gun, doing everything its designers had predicted but settling for a velocity of 2800 ft per second.

In the heavy anti-aircraft field there was very little in the way of new weapons developed for artillery, but a great deal of fundamental research was carried out. Both Britain and the USA entered the war with good heavy anti-aircraft guns, the British with the 3·7-in and the US with the 90-mm and 120-mm guns, and the only work which went on was simply to refine them. The British 3·7 was improved by what amounted to putting the 3·7-in barrel into a 4·5-in mounting and arranging things so that the 4·5-in gun-cartridge was used to push the 3·7-in shell. This enormous punch sent the shell out of the muzzle at 3425 ft a second to a maximum height of 59,300 ft, a performance which outclassed any other anti-aircraft gun in service during the war.

The only drawback to this sort of performance was the wear of the gun barrel; the 3·7-in high-velocity barrel could be worn beyond further use after about 450 shots, and this was not beyond the bounds of a single night's hard firing. As a result of this sort of problem a great amount of work in the USA went into trying to develop high velocity anti-aircraft guns with different systems of rifling and various other modifications in an attempt to discover the secret of making longer-lasting guns. All this work was invaluable in later years, but little of it showed any results which could be taken into use in wartime.

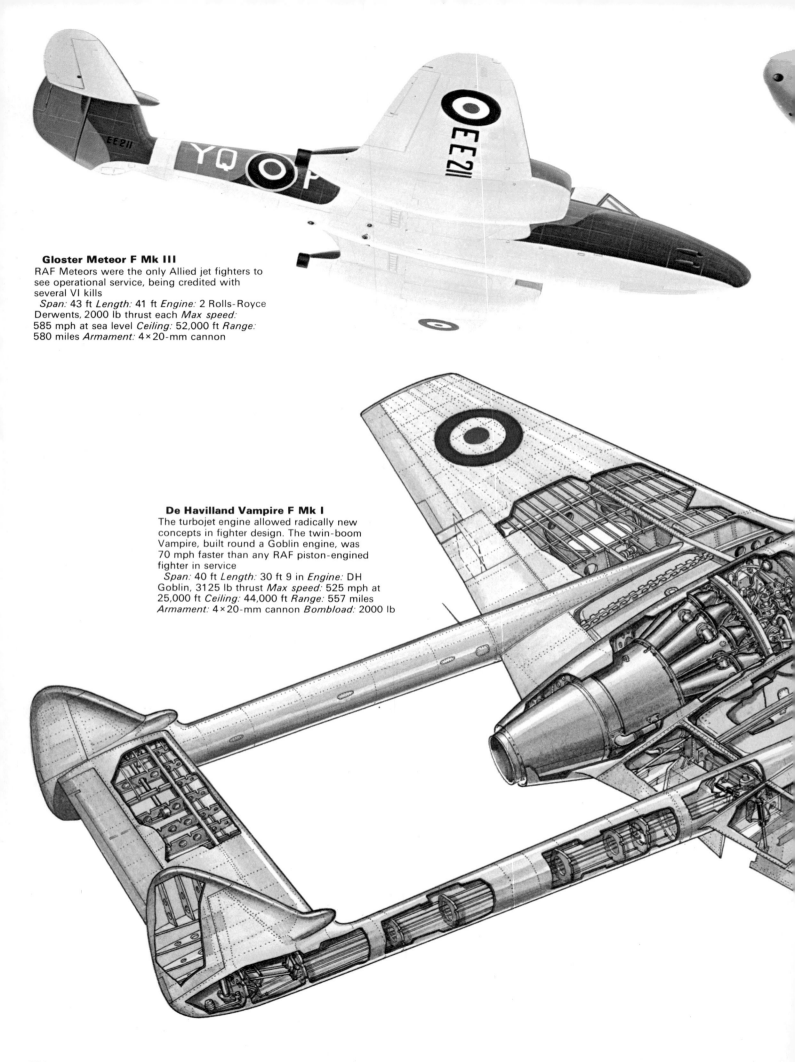

Gloster Meteor F Mk III
RAF Meteors were the only Allied jet fighters to
see operational service, being credited with
several VI kills
  Span: 43 ft *Length:* 41 ft *Engine:* 2 Rolls-Royce
Derwents, 2000 lb thrust each *Max speed:*
585 mph at sea level *Ceiling:* 52,000 ft *Range:*
580 miles *Armament:* 4×20-mm cannon

De Havilland Vampire F Mk I
The turbojet engine allowed radically new
concepts in fighter design. The twin-boom
Vampire, built round a Goblin engine, was
70 mph faster than any RAF piston-engined
fighter in service
  Span: 40 ft *Length:* 30 ft 9 in *Engine:* DH
Goblin, 3125 lb thrust *Max speed:* 525 mph at
25,000 ft *Ceiling:* 44,000 ft *Range:* 557 miles
Armament: 4×20-mm cannon *Bombload:* 2000 lb

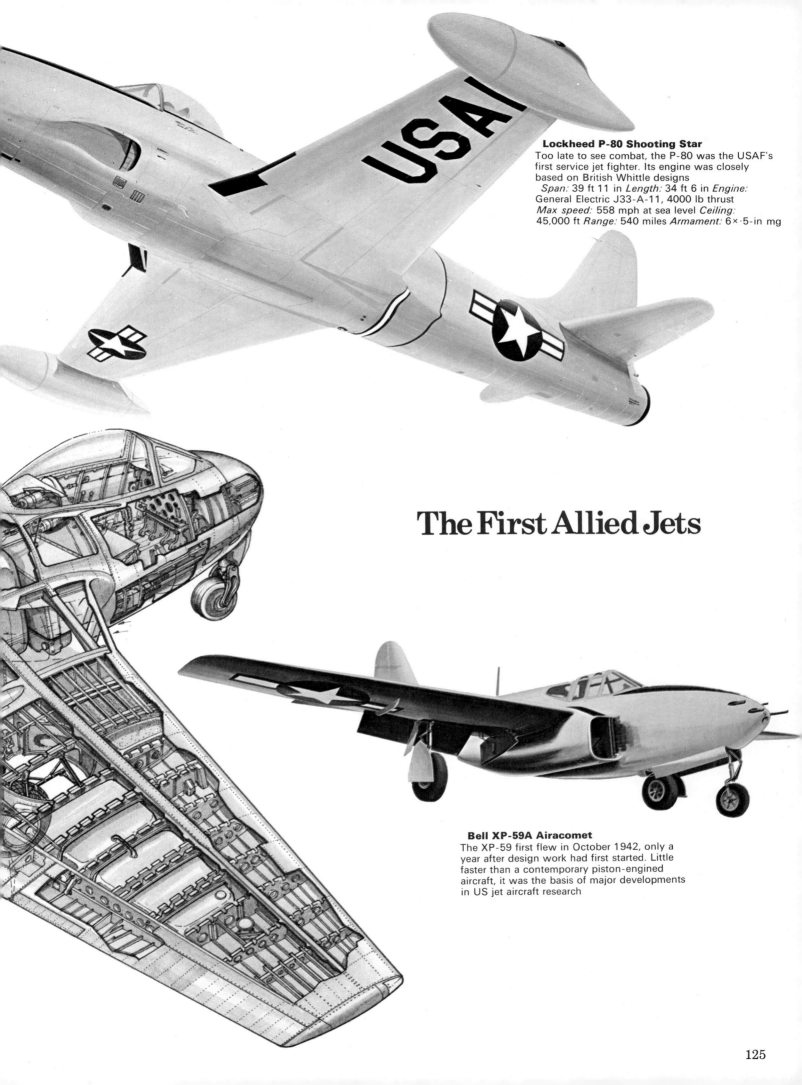

Lockheed P-80 Shooting Star
Too late to see combat, the P-80 was the USAF's first service jet fighter. Its engine was closely based on British Whittle designs
Span: 39 ft 11 in *Length:* 34 ft 6 in *Engine:* General Electric J33-A-11, 4000 lb thrust
Max speed: 558 mph at sea level *Ceiling:* 45,000 ft *Range:* 540 miles *Armament:* 6 × ·5-in mg

The First Allied Jets

Bell XP-59A Airacomet
The XP-59 first flew in October 1942, only a year after design work had first started. Little faster than a contemporary piston-engined aircraft, it was the basis of major developments in US jet aircraft research

'Little Boy'
the Hiroshima bomb

'Fat Man'
the Nagasaki bomb

THE ULTIMATE SECRET

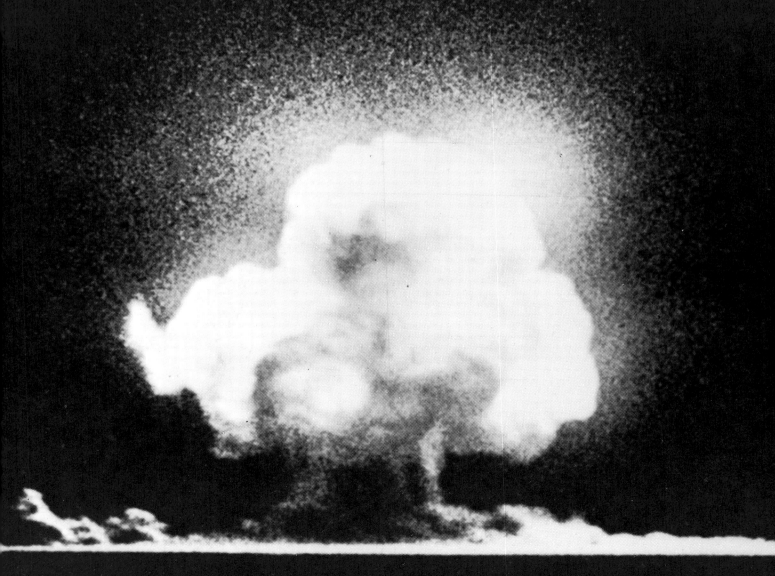

Hiroshima. What once was a Japanese industrial city became a charred, atomic desert in an instant, seared by the flash, crushed by the blast

The explosion of two nuclear bombs over Japan was the climax of the Second World War. It was the climax too, in blast and fire, of the secret war waged in the laboratories and testing grounds.

The most rapid scientific revolution of all times had increased man's destructive power a thousandfold.

It was to be in anger that the ultimate secret was revealed.

28 cm Kanone auf "Raupenlafette

Tarnbezeichnung R2"

Gewicht - 136 t

Gesamtrohränge = 54 5 Kaliber

Mündungs-

bremse

Fahrstand

Plattform auf Drehk

Unt